Justice and the
Politics of Memory

Editor

Gabriel R. Ricci

Justice and the Politics of Memory

Religion & Public Life

Volume
33

Routledge
Taylor & Francis Group

LONDON AND NEW YORK

First published 2003 by Transaction Publishers

Published 2017 by Routledge
2 Park Square, Milton Park, Abingdon, Oxon OX14 4RN
711 Third Avenue, New York, NY 10017, USA

Routledge is an imprint of the Taylor & Francis Group, an informa business

ISSN: 1083-2270
ISBN 13: 978-0-7658-0999-5 (pbk)

Volumes 1 through 28 were originally published under the title *This World: An Annual of Religion and Public Life.*

Contents

Introduction

Gabriel Ricci

"Let the past be the past." With this exhortation in the final prison scene, Faust is unable to quell Gretchen's delirium. Her reluctant relationship with Faust, who has persuaded her to ignore her intuitive dislike for his dark companion, has ended in the death of her mother, her brother, and her child. While the past terrorizes Gretchen, it has no hold on Faust. His pact with the ultimate negator has eliminated his history; he is content to live in a present disconnected from the past and the future. His temporal diremption has produced an amoral character who can easily ignore the pangs of Gretchen's tortured conscience. On the other hand, Gretchen is immobilized by the past and cannot summon the will to go on. In each case, these characters demonstrate a temporal discontinuity that undermines moral responsibility. We might sympathize with Gretchen whose personal losses have diminished her, but Faust's behavior demands our condemnation. Their mutual problem with the underlying historical structure of human existence guarantees that the future will be equally susceptible to the moral failings of the past.

This scene provides a literary model for the contemporary preoccupation with resolving problematic pasts that have the kind of toxic legacies both Faust and Gretchen, in their own ways, wish to ignore. Faust's denial welcomes an eradication of the past and Gretchen's condition invites the elimination of the future. Frozen between these two aspects of history, consciousness becomes unfocused and bereft of real incentive. Without memory identity is denied; without plans for the future the will is moribund. Consequently, human existence is suspended. Faust is questionably redeemed at the end of Part 2, but Mephistopheles has triumphed in the first round. Mephistopheles' earlier wish that all things be negated is realized in Faust's and Gretchen's predicament. Imprisoned in the present means that they have relinquished their historical status; nothing is produced from an isolated present. To efficiently realize the negation of everything, Mephistopheles need only seduce us into living in a present detached from the past and the future.

The moral and political dimensions of facing up to problematic pasts is the subject of this issue of *Religion & Public Life*. Though Faust's and Gretchen's difficulties with recalling the past and imagining a future pales in comparison to the real-life concerns faced by nations and states confronting monstrous pasts, their final exchange can serve as a model for the kind of temporal fissure that destroys the historical duration that sustains moral conceptualization. The integral link between the past and morality is mediated by what Avishai Margalit categorizes as care in his new work, *The Ethics of Memory*. For example, to remember an anniversary is to care about a past occasion that is packed with feeling and is recalled and reconstituted in the present. Margalit's focus is on the past, so it does not encompass the political concerns of memory set forth in this issue. Margalit's intentions, however, are to enunciate an ethics of responsibility. Had he offered a more full-bodied ethics of memory, he surely would have appropriated Heidegger's temporal analytic to which he refers. While Margalit's emphasis is on recollection of the past, Heidegger outlined the manner in which recollection (*Wiederholung*) entails the reflexivity of all the facets of time, with an emphasis on the future. This temporal condition is summed up in the word *Sorge* or care, and it is complemented by yet another solicitous condition when the focus is on humanity, rather than on mere instruments that may help us negotiate a particular environment. Heidegger reserved the word *Fürsorge*, characteristic of modes of help for those in special need, for this special form of attention. Heidegger's emphasis on the future makes his reading of the temporal dialectic mediating the care structure more applicable to a politics of memory. At the heart of the distinction between Margalit and Heidegger is a consideration of the nature of history. Margalit, with an emphasis on revealing and acknowledging the events of the past, conceives history and the past as a repository in which material might be stored. The proper science, as Leopold von Ranke, the master of nineteenth-century historiography, would have argued, is all that we require to unveil historical truth. Heidegger, who challenged Ranke's reconstructive methods, clarified that history cannot be limited to the mere past, nor should time be conceived as a sequence of nows. History and time must understood on the basis of that entity concerned with history, human existence or *Dasein* in Heidegger's vocabulary. And the totality of *Dasein* can only be understood as a stretching along in which all the facets of time are caught up in their mutual articulation.

If we posses an intuitive sense of the passage of time, we would have to agree that we feel as if we are moving forward, into the future. This projection does not function independently, but requires a momentary present to initiate plans and considerations of the past, voluntary or involuntary. The common road sign "Pass With Care" represents the internal cooperation of the facets of time: When in a position to pass on the road this sign should trigger a dynamic that will include a glance into the rear-view mirror to see if the back is clear, an appraisal of oncoming traffic in front of you, and all things clear, a determined movement from behind a vehicle (in the present) to a position forward the vehicle you have just passed. This operation represents Heidegger's conceptualization of the temporal condition of human existence. Care, as the temporal structural totality of human existence, always involves a consideration of where you want to be in some future time and where you have come from, a *Woher* and a *Wohin.* Thus in any future time, the past and present are never left behind, likewise in any present or past time the future is never detached. Ontologically speaking, human existence can never detach from any of the facets of time. To do so is to invite ontological denial.

A condition in which the truth (about the past) is sufficient for an ethics of memory denies the incentives that result from historical analysis. Consequently, a politics of memory cannot be realized, since truth is never sufficient in the reconfiguration of political and communal orders, as in the paradigmatic German case, the South African Truth and Reconciliation movement to name only two. Truth is not sufficient, as Wole Soyinka argues in *The Burden of Memory, the Muse of Forgiveness.* Against the backdrop of the colonialization and degradation of Africa and more recent internecine threats of genocide, truth alone cannot "minister to the wrongs of dispossession on the one hand, and chasten those who deviate from the humane communal order on the other." Such societal reconfigurations must devise procedures that instruct *future* conduct, while they serve to mitigate distress and even heal. To neglect whatever these imaginative steps demand is to sanction "the culture of impunity" (pp. 81-82, Soyinka). The memory of slavery, following Soyinka's argument, is not adequately expressed by a memorial to the past. Moreover, such a large part of the history of the West, particularly its economic history, must be ignored if the story of the degradation of the Africa is suppressed. Before the Jewish Holocaust, the African slave trade called into question the legacy of European humanism. For the values of European humanism to remain intact, reparations ought to be part of the "structure of memory and critique." Without critique we sanction the historical attitude expressed in Scarlet O'Hara's refrain: "I can't think about that now, I'll go crazy if I do—I'll think about that tomorrow."

Putting off memory and the commemorative gestures for troubling pasts, however, can have positive outcomes. In the case of the Berlin Memorial, James Young, who served on the *Findungskommission,* recognizes the value inherent in the misgivings people have about memorializing horrific pasts. Unable to come to a decision on the appropriate form of commemoration satisfies the "academic bystander" intent on keeping the conversation alive. Though, in the end, a project was selected and carried out, it cannot enshrine the need for each generation to perpetuate the process of recollecting. Peter Eisenmann's field of stone pillars serves as a kind of traditional memorial cairn, but it has not satisfied the debate and controversy over providing a site in the very city that gave birth to the Final Solution. How can any memorial satisfy this goal?

Young's primary insight in "Germany's Holocaust Memorial Problem—and Mine" is that memorials cannot substitute for action. A permanent reminder of Germany's monstrous past is now ensconced in Berlin, but coming to grips with the memory of crimes perpetrated in its name can only be measured in social policy that displaces blood-based citizen laws with residency-based codes; foreign policy that joins initiatives against new genocides. How Germany deals with its past can only be judged by how it moves into the future. The troubled waters stirred in selecting a fitting Berlin memorial offers a lesson to those grappling with a suitable memorial for the World Trade Center catastrophe. Following Young, we should not shy away from conversation; it should not be an opportunity to wallow in hackneyed political rivalries. Some public intellectuals became vulnerable when they dared to speak out against the backdrop of administratively sanctioned appeals that evildoers must be eradicated. This inflammatory and simplistic rhetoric was satisfying for the self-appointed righteous, but it quashed the historical perspective that may have provided an explanatory framework for the geopolitical arrangements behind the events of 9/11. Those who warned against the tradeoffs we would suffer at the hands of heightened security measures missed an opportunity when ex cathedra voices began to spread the Manichean gospel of us good guys vs. those bad guys. While an appropriate memorial may always be out of reach, we ought not be asked to sacrifice our intellectual drive to uncover what caused something to happen. Palliative measures should not be proffered at the expense of understanding. Explanation is the twin sister of prediction, and the ability to predict helps us invent the future.

The problems associated with Germany's vision of its future are addressed in Jeffrey Olick's review of the varied history of post-World War II German administrations in regard to its collective memory. In "The Value of Regret? Lessons from and for Germany" Olick uses the German case to explore how juggling a monstrous past had a spotted history after World War II. At the same time the Adenauer administration negotiated an unprecedented reparations agreement with Israel, Germans who experienced the denazification procedures also drew attention to the suffering of Germans. Martin Heidegger, who did not recant the anti-American attitudes and his enthusiasm for National Socialism expressed in his writings, was typical of the Germans who indulged themselves at the same time the Nuremberg trials made the Third Reich's systematic atrocities public. To this day, you can still hear stories of the atrocities perpetrated by the Russians in 1945 Berlin, echoes of equating German suffering with the Jewish Holocaust. Olick's review of the various approaches to Germany's collective past makes it clear that conventional ethical guidelines elide the complexity of the problem. Olick finds a more adaptable framework in Max Weber's distinction between an "ethic of conviction" and an "ethic of responsibility." The Truth and Reconciliation Movement in South Africa is an argument in favor of "an ethic of responsibility," since it avoids punishment for punishment's sake and combines knowledge of the past with acknowledgment of wrongdoing. This latter function eluded the first post-World War II German administration, since it was burdened by keeping a tattered and disillusioned people together, and could not adequately lay the foundation for reconciliation. Not simply reconciliation between victim and perpetrator, but for their children, since, as Olick argues, this "is the only way to meet our responsibility to the future where memory and power become interchangeable."

The problems presented in searching for an appropriate memorial for an historical epoch in which violence exceeds all rational limits is also the subject of James Hatley's essay, "Nameless Memory: Levinas, Witness and Politics." How can one remember the unjustifiable? Can the restoration of political equity meaningfully put an end to suffering? These are the sorts of questions Hatley uncovers in his treatment of Emmanuel Levinas's philosophical attempt to come to grips with the impossibility of engaging a past that could not have been mine, what Levinas called the immemorial. Hatley's approach to the memory of unprecedented violence is that it is not just a problem to be resolved but an enigma to be returned to incessantly. It is, then, a challenge to all future generations, since, as Levinas emphasized, awareness of unprecedented evil demands unprecedented good. Remembering the immemorial, then, means that reparation and reconciliation are not satisfied without restoration. That is, restoration of the moral and political order that once seemed arbitrary in the midst of the chaos of violence, as well as the reclamation of an inner life in which the other is simultaneous with one's own being.

The philosophical note embodied in the use of Levinas's work is complemented by the concrete work performed by Truth Commissions as outlined in Heribert Adam's lead article. Given the two broad categories that apply to collective memory, historical injustice and contemporary abuses, the recent case of South Africa illuminates the need to pursue justice through legal recourse as well as the need to develop new institutions that facilitate reconciliation. Once again, the general aim is not just to keep the memory of injustice alive, but to pursue political education that can foster a collective legacy. Such efforts, Adam notes, must not exclude the obvious aggressors who will remain as part of the institutional structure. In the case of South Africa, there was some initial surprise that the Afrikaners would so easily release political controls if their economic control remained intact. This compromise, however, is an element in the sort of truth that can be expected when there are divided memories and the tendency for survivors to be greedy and conquerors deniers, particularly when the atrocities are so great. Metaphysical truth, even as an ideal, is ruled out since memory can never be the same as history. For those in a position to translate thought into action, for those who must craft a new state, the pursuit of an ideal will suppress the kind of compromises that must be tolerated. If memory amounts to a social construction, as Adam argues, then we must have the same expectation of truth and the law of which Benjamin Cardozo outlines in the eloquent treatise *The Growth of Law*.

When an exact description of events will necessarily be muddled by conflicting memories, then we must, as Santayana recommended, "find some minor symbol of reconciliation with reality on our own part, bringing comfort, safety and assurance." Thus truth will always lie in compromise. Truth, under the conditions of reconciliation, can only be partial truth to oneself since it must serve the ends of social conventions. Since there can be no general rules through which a collective memory can be established, responsibility to past injustice ought to be defined in terms of keeping the debate about it alive. Victims are best remembered by educating new generations against future injustice. Honoring past victims, Adam concludes, must embody the responsibility of progressive memory, while at the same time avoiding the counterproductive forces of victimology.

Derick Wilson's article offers a practical guide for reconciliation in which distance and separation are the social norm. Within the context of Northern Ireland Wilson explores the dynamics of what can be called "an ethnic frontier," where citizenship is displaced by communal loyalties, and the dichotomy between us and them perpetuates a climate of fear. In such a contested society "communal politeness ritualizes the tension and makes it manageable" but the "other" is omnipresent, leaving a very uneasy peace. The aim of conflict resolution, under conditions spawned by a theology of separation, is not to agree on a collective memory, but to forge an "agreed society" in which a new history may eventually flourish. To argue over whose version of history is accurate gets you into the predicament of the two characters in the tragicomedy *No Man's Land*. While they go back and forth on who started the war, opinions change as often as weapons change hands. Presented with an opportunity to acknowledge their mutual predicament, they cannot overcome the ludicrous identity politics that seems so out of place against the backdrop of a wounded comrade whose fate has been sealed by a pressure-sensitive mine. NATO peacekeeping forces standby helpless, no technological wizardry can assist, and the squabbling parties vie for victimhood as they are both poised to kill. As Wilson reveals, we are all inclined to mimic the ancient tragedy as we identify with Abel, the victim, while we are closer to Cain, "the modern man, the person wedded to the tools and the new economy; the man prepared to kill and deny that action in order to get his way."

To make sense of relationships in which most social spaces have been colonized by communal fears requires organizational structures that permit mutual critique without recrimination, leeway for self-critique without reprisal. In the ethnic frontier of Northern Ireland, such an ecumenical atmosphere can be distilled from the social message of the Gospels and the openness to the other that typified the life of Jesus Christ. This relational theology, as Wilson calls it, must aim at creating social structures that relieve one from resolutely identifying with a particular tradition. This does not mean that the past is to be ignored, it means that a future of new relationships must be anticipated.

The theoretical position that the politics of memory is focused on the future also underpins Peterson's and Djikic's essay. The title "You can neither remember nor forget what you do not understand" is the conclusion of this very detailed and analytic approach to the complexity of memory. Peterson and Djikic boldly face the reconstructive and motivational aspects of memory and find in pragmatism an acceptable alternative to the determination of accurate representation. Their approach demonstrates how taking full account of the effects of motivation on memory does not mean that respect for the truth be abandoned. Their chief concern, however, is to analyze how the unwillingness to process anomaly and personal mistakes distorts memory, leads to a psychology of self-deception, which in turn produces disease, increased hostility to the world, and ultimately the adoption of a totalitarian style. Such a personality tries to force anomaly out of existence and thus sacrifices the creative side of the self. Willingness to face the threat of anomaly, however, means adherence to the truth as process.

The authors find the discussion of individual memories of traumatic events particularly relevant to the complexity of memory. Trauma is the emergence of the unknown and uncanny, and in large doses undermines longstanding presuppositions of predictability and stability. Representation of the uncanny, like the abuse of a child by the parent, is precisely what is meant by not being able to remember nor forget. A world in which we have been betrayed is not readily restored to normalcy. To understand and to linguistically produce a coherent account of such an event may elude us, since the original trauma was processed by primordial aspects of the brain, those that govern "fright and flight." Nonetheless, if a perpetrator and victim face off and the victim is still unable to get on with life, then the perpetrator's account is insufficient. Making the past "go away," the authors conclude, can never mean understanding in the scientific or existential sense; it means that "it does not rear its ugly head in the present, in the form of recurrent memory, or in the future, in the form of replication of the original trauma." Thus, Germans who are still Nazis and Russians who are still Stalinists neither remember nor forget.

Legal justice promises satisfaction that is rooted in the passion of vengeance. This source, however, is concealed in the rational architectonic institutionalized since the Enlightenment. In a whispering down the lane effect, there are hardly echoes of the spirit that formed the earliest impulse for justice. In his *The Common Law*, Oliver Wendell Holmes did not shy from unearthing these primordial foundations in his search for the fundamental principles underlying the conceptualization of law and the basis of liability in tort. While his analysis was restricted to English Common Law and Roman Law, he hinted at earlier stirrings in Greek antiquity, where we can find the literary expression of the evolution of the justice system that identifies the cultural gap between private retribution and public rhetorical mechanisms that institutionalized rational exposition and harnessed the psychological drive for revenge.

Holmes's analysis came as no surprise, since it merely articulated the cliché that law has its basis in antecedent customs. However, his conclusion that law cannot have an ameliorative social effect is sobering. Holmes's analysis of law alerts us to how fragile our hold on mutual responsibility may be. The basis of law appears to improve our mutual relations, that are always in peril because of self-interest, but it can only be an inducement to moral reciprocity, the institutional promotion of the proverbial reasonable man who acts with forethought and prudence. The pragmatist, then, tells us that our institutional arrangements provide a tenuous grip on the resolution of and provision for justice. Kaplan and Rinella's "Justice Perfected: Cinematic Exemplifications" reveals how the humanities complement legal structures and how, in particular, cinematic expressions can be interpreted as exemplary of poetic justice and the kind of psychological closure that institutions cannot provide. Their analysis of *Jean de Florette* and its sequel *Manon of the Spring*, films which embody the spirit of antique retributive practices, highlights the limits of reason and the need to embrace the kind of artistic expression that Plato found inimical to the State. Such artistic expression may be removed from legal institutions, but tragedy, as Aristotle promoted after Plato's denigration, contains philosophical intent, since it was occupied with probability and the articulation of what expectations and outcomes human action entails. While our present legal life may be historically informed by English common law, early Teutonic codes, and Roman noxal actions, the spirit of the law is rooted in the psychology of tragedy, according to Kaplan and Rinella. The totality of Greek tragedy can be interpreted as the basis of the legal caveat that we act at our on peril. And the refrain in the *Oresteia*, "we suffer into truth," has to be the fundamental expression of the spirit of the law that enlivens our legal system. *Jean de Florette* and *Manon of the Spring,* recall the tragic insight that our lives can spontaneously suffer reversals. This historical dialectic was inflated into a metaphysics by Hegel in the nineteenth century, but it offered no immediate solution to the problems faced by alienated consciousness, in its many manifestation, except the anticipation of the ultimate closure in absolute consciousness. So Cesar Souberyan (played by Yves Montand) was blinded by the same hubris that afflicted Oedipus: Certain that they were in control of the historical facts, they both willed and carried out plans that undermined their elevated social status. The ironic twists are poignant; and shamed by their ignorance, they inflict self-punishment. Similarly, their communities are polluted because of their complicity. What resolves the communal fracture is knowledge, knowledge that was suppressed and concealed by the intoxication of blind will power. Cesar and Oedipus suffered into truth, after they turned a blind eye to it. In Cesar's case, the memory of his misdeeds surfaces a generation later, after Manon, Jean's daughter and, as it turns out, Cesar's granddaughter, takes a simple non-invasive step that unravels the intrigue that destroyed her father. Cesar's ignominy literally kills him, but Oedipus lives long enough to curse the next generation. *Antigone* begins with a conversation between Ismene and Antigone lamenting the burden of their father's memory. The burden of memory for Manon is agitated by Ugolin's grotesque love for her. His offense is the greatest if we apply Dante's standard in the *Inferno*, his sin of violence against the neighbor was made worse through his deceit, obsequiousness and pandering.

The moral psychology of the ancient Greeks that begins in the epic tradition and is communicated through tragedy will always be available to supplement our culture of guilt, the Mosaic code that is marked by proscriptions, a lethargic legal system unable to satisfactorily address the vicissitudes   of life, and juristic consequences that are too often determined by ideology. This ancient code is based on having to make difficult decisions, often between two evils. So, if we are existentially prefigured to act at our own peril, as tragedy tells us, then we require more than a code that tells us what we ought not do. Manon's plugging of the Source is just the kind of action we should be prepared to take. It is the sort of non-invasive action that is the source of conflict resolution in the film *Diva*. The hero, here, after spending much of the film meditatively piecing together a gigantic puzzle of Hokusai's woodprint of Mt. Fuji, leaves his abode in an effort to ward off the threat of danger to innocents. He is not armed like a thick necked, renegade cop; he is armed with a mindfulness that was not obvious as he pieced together the gigantic puzzle. His rescue effort entails the slightest movement of an electrical switch suspended near an elevator shaft. Thugs who are armed to the teeth are undermined when this simple action causes them to lose their bal- ance. There is yet another cinematic hero who exemplifies the moral instruction and the "juristic" satisfaction embodied in Greek tragedy. Boo Radley, played by Robert Duvall in his first film role, whose reputation as a deranged shut-in fuels the children's imagination, emerges as an avenging angel to rescue Scout and her brother from the menacing grip of Bob Ewell whose deceit and chicanery undermined the wheels of justice. Here the community is complicit as well. While Atticus Finch has visually demonstrated the innocence of Tom Robinson, the jury can turn a blind eye when they ideologically pronounce their guilty verdict. Tom Robinson dies, but the final resolution agreed to by the Sheriff and Atticus is an acknowledgement that their best efforts to uphold the law cannot match the juridical satisfaction of Boo Radley's fateful intervention.

There are some narrative structures that do not benefit from literary invention, they are penned by the vagaries of life. Tim Giago's account of the acculturation of Native American children is such a story. Giago's story parallels the destructive wave of colonialzation that swept the African continent. Just as Wole Soyinka points out in regard to the uprooting of indigenous cultures in Africa, claims of religious superiority and the maniacal drive of modernity inspired the epistemic coloniality that caused aboriginal demise in the New World. This is a drama that is still being played out in the courts. While the case of slave reparations in the United States is stalled by rhetoric that not only argues that the welfare state has extended itself sufficiently, but that the antebellum South provided cultural and economic benefits to blacks that their distant homeland could not, Canada's courts are seeking compensation for aboriginals who suffered abuse at Indian residential schools. The 12,000 or so claims against the Canadian government could take over fifty years to resolve. At an estimated $1.5 billion for court costs alone, Canada has plans to resolve all claims within seven years.

The financial satisfaction provided by the courts is not as satisfying as invented literary solutions and it can easily fuel detractors who argue, in one form or another, that the benefits of modernity outweigh the denigration of uprooted cultures. As western academics engage in science and cultural wars it comes as poetic consolation that archaic cultures are now regularly invoked. Holistic models that challenge the conventional dichotomies of subject and object, mind and matter, fact and value have survived the epistemic colonialization of western science and religious totalitarianism. They now promise alternative worldviews to engage the tyranny of rationalism, which now extols the virtues of clinical self-replication. In the face of "what man has done to man," can this be regarded as a prudent application of scientific knowledge?

The memory of these worldviews allows us to reinvent ourselves. To suppress them is to invite Faust's cynicism, to ignore the demands of the future is to succumb to Margaret's self-pity. Reparations may be in order as a corrective in the wake of hegemonic worldviews, but absent monetary restitution, which arguably would involve logistical nightmares, turning to previously derided cultural models represents the sort of poetic satisfaction no institutional design could prescribe.

In recalling random child murders in Atlanta, Georgia, James Baldwin was able to speak as a survivor in *The Evidence of Things Not Seen*. In bearing the inexorable guilt of a survivor; in his case having been a Black child in a White country, he was able to instruct us about how the repudiation of memory affects us in our very being. What one chooses to remember or forget, he admonished, "dictates who one loves or fails to love." Suppressing memory can dictate "whether one plays poker, pool or chess." "What one doesn't remember contains the keep to one's tantrums or poise....is the key to one's performance in the toilet or in bed." Baldwin's visceral poetics recommends that love is the only help for recognizing what you do not remember, but in a rather Hegelian moment, he concludes that "memory makes its appearance in this life as this life is ending— appearing at last, as a kind of guide into a condition which is far beyond memory as it is beyond imagination."

Divided Memories: Collective Reckoning with a Criminal Regime

Heribert Adam

The Politics of Memory

Human memory is never an objective fact, a kind of fixed, stored datum that can be downloaded or accumulated for later use. What is being remembered and how events are recalled, depends very much on social conditions. Interests shape individual as well as collective memory. Memory, therefore, amounts to a contingent social construction.

As Ian Buruma (1999: 9) has rightly pointed out, "Memory is not the same as history and memorializing is different from writing history." If the two are lumped together, the distinction between fiction and fact, falsehood and truth, is lost. A history concerned with establishing factual events is to be distinguished from their interpretation. About this interpretive and moral truth, opinions can legitimately differ, particularly in divided societies. Since individual morals, feelings, and interests vary widely in a heterogeneous collectivity, it is problematic to assume a collective psyche. Without a collective persona, there can hardly be a collective memory. Only in a loose, metaphorical sense can we speak of a collective identity, a national character or a collective memory.

Collective memory constitutes the informal widely accepted perceptions of past events in which the collective identity of a people is mirrored. This identity is strongly influenced by the official definitions, rituals, and laws of the state. The memorials that a state erects, the national holidays selected, the museums subsidized, the speeches of politicians that celebrate or mourn the past and define a state's self-perception in laws and public institutions – all are contributions to collective memory that changes over time. Divided memories exist when sizable groups within the same state simultaneously attribute different meanings to the same history, just as individual witnesses to crimes or car accidents testify to the same event in surprisingly contradictory terms.

Ways of Remembering and Forgetting

It is difficult to generalize for all situations and all times. Perhaps the most useful generalization distinguishes between two kinds of remembering: a progressive and a regressive one. *Progressive memory* inquires into the causes of past suffering with a view to preventing a future recurrence of past misery. It amounts to political education in the best sense. Progressive memory results in politically literate citizens, whose current and future choices are guided by a historical awareness of their society, its misguided paths, wrong turns, and missed opportunities.

Retrogressive memory, on the other hand, locks people into vicious circles of past conflicts. History has become a set of mental shackles from which people cannot free themselves. They remember ancient battles, particularly lost ones, in order to reenact revenge. The quest for revenge blinds its adherents to alternative options. When individual and collective identity is tied to wounds, never to be forgotten, its adherents become prisoners of their past.

In short, the valid exhortation not to forget, should always be accompanied by the two questions: *what* is remembered and particularly remembering *for* what? Progressive remembering uses hindsight to draw lessons. It guards against repeating the mistakes of the past. Retrogressive remembering on the other hand, aims at continuing a battle in the hope of achieving a triumphant outcome this time. Nationalist mobilizers dwell on this hope. They manipulate with the mirage of victory, rescue from remembered humiliation, and wipe out past degradation by following the rallying cry of the unified collective. Theirs is the false language of sacrifice in order to be free from the shame of the past in an imagined glorious future, even if the utopia causes renewed pain to adversaries and followers alike.

A test for progressive or retrogressive remembering lies in the collective attitude towards the political crimes of the past. Again, there can be no universally valid rules as to how an emerging democracy should deal with the crimes of a previous regime. It seems useful to explore empirically how different democracies have coped with the problem of state-sponsored crimes, how victims are recognized or compensated, how the new order attempts reconciliation between warring factions, and how the repetition of an unsavory past is prevented.

Six forms of grappling with the past can be distinguished and compared in their historical context: (1) Amnesia (post-war Germany, Japan, Spain, Russia); (2) Trials and justice (Nuremburg, Proposed International Criminal Court); (3) Lustration, i.e., disqualification of collaborators from public office (GDR, Eastern Europe); (4) Negotiated restitution (Germany's reparations to Israel and compensations for forced labor, Canada's and Australia's negotiations about land rights of indigenous minorities); (5) Political reeducation; (6) Truth commissions (Latin America and South Africa).

Several of these strategies are frequently employed simultaneously or with different emphases over time. Of all cases, two countries are of particular significance: Germany, because of its unique past with Auschwitz as the universal paradigm of barbarism, and South Africa. The South African Truth and Reconciliation Commission (TRC) deserves critical scrutiny for three reasons: it is a novel experiment of restorative justice and nation building through reconciliation; the TRC is often recommended as an international model for similar conflicts elsewhere, from Cambodia to ex-Yugoslavia; achievements of the TRC are widely overrated outside South Africa, while largely dismissed inside. Among its flaws and problematic assumptions is the fallacy that "revealing is healing." Legislated reconciliation negates that only victims can forgive. The skewed composition of the TRC and its theological perspectives have affected its credibility. The quest for an official truth and common memory denies pluralist interpretations of history. Above all, the focus on gross human rights violations frees the many beneficiaries of apartheid from responsibility and obliterates the structural violence of racial laws for millions of victims not recognized by the TRC process.

Amnesia

In Germany, the postwar period up to the mid-sixties represents a typical example of official amnesia and private denial. Chancellor Adenauer, who himself was an anti-Nazi politician, nevertheless defended his heavily implicated aide, Hans Globke, with the demand in parliament, "to stop the sniffing for Nazis!" Instead of honestly dealing with the shame of the past, it was not to be remembered. The future and the rebuilding of the nation should be focused upon. Wallowing in a terrible past could not reverse it anyway. The past was considered a catastrophe, like a natural disaster, rather than the result of political divisions. The Nazi period was portrayed as an accident of German history. "In the middle of the 1950's," writes the historian Norbert Frei (1996:405), "a collective consciousness had emerged that attributed solely to Hitler and his inner circle all responsibilities for the atrociousness of the Third Reich." Germans as a whole were ascribed the role of apolitically seduced people whom the war and its consequences had made into victims themselves. To this day, the 8th of May is designated as "the day of liberation" by Allied forces, implying that Germans were mainly victims of Nazi rule. Daniel Goldhagen's "willing executioners" had shrunk to a small minority. The active complicity and passive collusion of a silent majority was out of sight and memory. The phrase of the "zero hour" (*Stunde Null*) dismissed historical continuity, insisting instead on a newborn society that had no relationship with the previous period.

In the communist German Democratic Republic (GDR) official anti-fascism denied all links with the Nazi past. Since the dark brown period had – in this economistic Marxist dogmatism – resulted from a capitalist crisis, the heroic rise of socialism in the anti-fascist struggle had also taken care of all fascist remnants and preconditions.

In the West, the theory of totalitarianism reigned supreme in the ensuing Cold War. The free West proudly distinguished itself from both the brown and red totalitarianism. The sociologist Helmut Dubicl (1992:276) argued that "the true scandal of German memorializing was not that the Nazi past was simply ignored, but immersed in the ideological competition between East and West." Both states accused each other of failing to draw the necessary conclusions from history. Each side blamed the other for perpetuating conditions in which freedom was denied.

There are two main explanations for the postwar amnesia. The most widely accepted version holds that the economic and bureaucratic reconstruction required the inclusion of Nazi collaborators, given the scarce skills available. German rearmament in the 1950s, for example, would have been impossible without falling back on the expertise of previous officers. Large sectors of the colluding population needed to be integrated into the new democracy and could not have been marginalized.

A second explanation, psychologically based, focuses on the subconscious reaction to collective trauma. A fragile collective identity – psychoanalytically speaking, a weak ego – had to protect itself against an unbearable truth by repressing and rationalizing it. Adorno pointed to the paradox that the factual collapse of the NS world had not been reflected in the psychic disposition of the population. With reference to Freud, Adorno draws the questionable conclusion that this proves the survival of Nazi mentalities: "What is missing when collective identities unravel, according to the theory of 'Mass Psychology and Ego Analysis,' is the phenomenon of panic. Unless one wants to dismiss the insights of the great psychologist, this allows for only one conclusion: that the old identifications and collective narcissism were not destroyed but continue secretly dormant in the unconscious and therefore particularly powerful" (cited in Perels, However, one could speculate equally persuasively that perhaps the Nazi identifications were not as deeply internalized and the consciousness of injustice was more widespread than the suspicions of Adorno allow. Otherwise the Allied democratic reeducation would not have run so successfully and smoothly. As critical studies in the tradition of *The Authoritarian Personality* have proven, this character type is more shaped by conformity pressure than by internalized ideological convictions. With the change of powerholders, the dominant attitudes of ego-weak characters also change. They replace easily one ideological doctrine with an opposite equally authoritarian master narrative. Therefore it is helpful to criminalize hate speech. While attitudes cannot be legislated, discriminatory behavior at least can be constrained by being outlawed.

It was not until the late 1960s that the children of the war generation revived questions about the past, spurred on by the student revolt against authoritarian traditions and general politicization. Debates about the statute of limitation of prosecutions after widely published trials of concentration camp guards under German jurisdiction together with moving personalized films about the Holocaust also evoked new interests. Yet another generation later, the meaning of the past has never been more intensely debated. Starting with the 1996 dispute among academic historians about the comparability and relationship between Stalinist and fascist terror (Wehler, 1988), and continuing with the Goldhagen controversy in 1996 (Wippermann, 1997), the Walser-Bubis argument in 1998 (Wiegel and Klotz, 1999; Rohloff, 1999) and the simultaneous controversial exhibition about the collusion of the German army in the war atrocities against the civilian population (Thiele, 1998; Hamburger Institut für Sozialforschung, 1999).

There is probably no other country that currently scrutinizes and redefines its collective memory so thoroughly. An eleven-year debate about a central Berlin memorial for the victims of Nazism (Reichel, 1999; Cullen, 1999; Jeisman, 1999) culminated in a sophisticated parliamentary debate in June 1999 with the decision that (a) the Eisenmann memorial should be built as proposed; (b) that it will be dedicated exclusively to European Jews; and (c) that it should also have an information and learning center attached to it. Earnest arguments split all parties, and the overwhelming supporting vote surprised everyone, including the head of the German Jewish Council, the late Ignaz Bubis. He had predicted that the memorial would never be built (interview, *Konkret*, 2/1999). The support of the political class for the challenging huge Eisenmann monument also revealed a substantial discrepancy in public opinion surveys. These had indicated a split population: 46 percent for and 44 percent against the memorial, with 93 percent of supporters in favor of its dedication to all Nazi victims. Parliament's decision to dedicate it exclusively to European Jews indicated that concern about negative foreign reactions outweighed local opinion.

Behind the German debate about whether the nation should define itself as a "normal" polity, stands the question whether the unified state should also shed the constraints on its "moral sovereignty." Full political sovereignty was restored with resocialization into Western democratic habits. Later in 1989, national unification within European rules and values was the final crowning achievement. A growing number on the political right and center now wishes to shed the moral inhibitions resulting from the Nazi legacy. Until the recent involvement of the German army in Bosnia and Kosovo, the country had shirked its responsibility for international human rights enforcement with respect to its unique history sixty years ago.

How should one evaluate this process of profoundly redefining collective memory? Is the decision for the Holocaust memorial the progressive acknowledgement of collective moral and political responsibility, although "Germans collectively do not bear criminal and moral guilt" (Neier,1998:228)? Is it an official rejection of the earlier Martin Walser warning about the "banality of the good," the instrumentalization of Auschwitz for ulterior purposes? Or is the victory of the seemingly progressive remembrance of shame merely the monstrous tombstone in the final burial of an embarrassing past, just as Walser had advocated to the applause of the establishment in the Paulskirche?

It would seem that the Berlin memorial, above all, fulfills the function of visibly exculpating the new "Berlin Republic" from the suspicion of past nationalist ambitions. With narcissistic self-congratulations, the debate lays to rest the Nazi legacy by demonstrating that the self-confident unified state has successfully come to terms with its shame – just as the victims wished. "The more unique the German crimes, the greater the own achievement of collective cleansing," comments the historian Gerd Koenen (1999:98) sarcastically. Hermann Lübbe speaks of "Sündenstolz," the German pride in their sins. Just as minorities the world over clamor for the "vicarious virtue" of victimization, as Ian Buruma (1999) has argued in an intriguing article entitled "The Joys and Perils of Victimhood," so the German political elite of all parties is now keen to demonstrate that it has mastered the much more intricate task of coming to terms with being the worst collective perpetrator in history. This negative uniqueness, the ritual acknowledgement of the Nazi break with civilization (*Zivilisationsbruch*), is now almost paraded as interesting a feature of a new national identity as the positive achievements of an economic miracle after total destruction in 1945. A shameful past as nationalist exhibitionism would be merely the other side of the dubious coin of denial and amnesia.

Helmut Dubiel (1999:228) in his study of parliamentary debates diagnoses a correlation between "the inability of Germans to accept collective responsibility for their history and their underdevelopment of democratic virtues." However, neither was the postwar German amnesia a specificly German characteristic, nor does historical denial of collective infamy stand in a necessary relationship with the development of democratic culture. Britain, France, or Holland had buried their colonial crimes until very recently but are considered model democracies nonetheless. The U.S. still lacks a single national memorial to slavery or to the near genocide of the aboriginal people. Nations memorialize their own suffering but not what they inflict on others. The Washington memorial of the Vietnam War lists all the names of Americans who lost their life, but not a single Vietnamese name. In Japan, history textbooks do not mention the atrocities of the Imperial Army in Korea and China. "The Rape of Nanking," the title of Iris Chang's English bestseller about the murder of 30,000 inhabitants, has not been published in a Japanese translation and is bogged down in arguments about its accuracy. The Tokyo government refuses a clear apology even to Chinese or Korean state visitors, despite the worldwide feminist concern with thousands of so-called "comfort women." Recently the official designation "capitulation" was renamed the more neutral "end of war." National guilt is widely considered to be absolved by the first atomic bomb dropped on Hiroshima and Nagasaki.

After political transformation many nations rationalize their guilt with new myths. In Austria, collective memory redefined the popular enthusiasm for Hitler into "forced unification" (*Zwangsanschluss*), thereby portraying collusion as victimhood. In France, only the recent trials against collaborators of the Vichy regime have undermined the popular myth that half of the French population had joined the underground resistance against the German occupiers. Spain has totally avoided coming to terms with its forty years of Franco dictatorship because it would reopen the wounds of the Civil War. Paradoxically, Germany has apologized for Guernica and paid compensation, but not the Madrid parliament. Turkey still cultivates its cherished taboo that the Armenian genocide never happened and is an invention of foreign propaganda.

The 80 to 100 million victims of Stalinism still wait to be rehabilitated and even properly recognized. When Stephane Courtois edited *Livre noir du communisme* (*The Black Book of Communism*) on the eightieth anniversary of the October revolution, it met with a hostile reception on the left, similar to the earlier exposure of communist crimes by Arthur Koestler, Alexander Solzhenitsyn, Robert Conquest, or François Furet (See Möller, 1999). Recognizing that Marxist-Leninism had a rational, humanitarian goal while Hitler's biological master narrative was by definition irrational, should not preclude comparisons with the racial genocide here and class genocide there. Nor are the fascist crimes relativized or trivialized by comparing them with the terror of Stalinism. Comparing does not mean equating.

The sketch of collective responses to past state crimes allows some general conclusions. Grappling with the past is not a necessary precondition for a functioning democracy. As Michael Ignatieff (1998:170) has written, "All nations depend on forgetting: on forging myths of unity and identity that allow a society to forget its founding crimes, its hidden injuries and divisions, its unhealed wounds. It must be true, for nations as it is for individuals, that we can stand only so much truth. But if too much truth is divisive, the question becomes, how much is enough?"

It is commonly assumed that public interest in a shameful past fades away among later generations. They carry no personal guilt, unlike their parents who engaged in denial because they were psychologically incapable of admitting the enormity of their own collusion with state atrocities. Paradoxically, public interest in and recognition of national crimes seems to increase over time. Subsequent generations feel free to accept collective responsibility for the sins of their ancestors although motivations differ in each context and divided memories prevail.

In their eagerness to prevent the gruesome past from haunting the future, well-meaning social engineers are intent to create "a common history" between hostile groups. In their most extreme form, they repress airing of past hostilities, as Tito did with the enforced slogan "Brotherhood and Unity." Such totalitarian designs are the surest recipe for renewed conflict: "By repressing the real history of the interethnic carnage between 1941 and 1945, the Titoist regime guaranteed that such carnage would return" (Ignatieff, 1998:185). Only a pluralist interpretation of history may achieve a shared truth at best or reinforce divided memories at worst. History as an ongoing argument is still preferable to the myth making of official collective memory.

Trials and Justice

Prosecution of perpetrators of gross human rights violations requires clear victors and vanquished. Where there is a stalemate – as in South Africa or in Chile between democrats and the military – historical compromises and amnesties are negotiated. Prosecutions would most likely provoke new violence and even endanger the survival of the emerging democracy.

Apart from the morality of pursuing justice for its own sake, there are good pragmatic reasons for trials of political criminals. Aryeh Neier (1998:213), one of the most ardent advocates of punishment, has expressed the most convincing reason: "When the community of nations shies away from responsibility for bringing to justice the authors of crimes against humanity, it subverts the rule of law." If the victimized see no one held accountable, they may seek revenge on their own and continue the cycle of violence. Prosecution of individual perpetrators also counteracts the misleading notion of collective guilt. Individualizing guilt does not smear the name of an entire group. Finally, indictments by the proposed International Criminal Court (ICC) cannot be accused of "victor's justice."

However, there are also clear pitfalls to be avoided. If a sovereign state can head off ICC prosecution by bringing alleged war criminals before its own courts, a fair trial depends very much on the independence and quality of its judiciary. This spectrum can range from biased judges of the old order (as alleged in South Africa) to an internal "victor's justice" where the judiciary has been purged and replaced with partisans of the new regime.

The ICC would be emasculated if prosecutions could only be launched with the consent of the states involved where the crime occurred or the alleged criminals live. A similar paralysis would ensue if vetoes by Security Council members could indefinitely block prosecution. NATO's unilateral military intervention in Kosovo without UN approval already responded to this predicament. NATO's "military humanitarianism" postulated that gross violations of universal rights within a sovereign state necessitates outside intervention in the same way as an aggression against a foreign territory would justify war in self-defense. The NATO action, Jürgen Habermas argued, anticipated a world citizenship that unfortunately does not yet exist as an enforceable order.

If the ICC were to be the first practical indicator of a more effective world order for universal human rights, it would be even more imperative to prevent "core" crimes rather than merely punish violators afterwards. It is doubtful whether the threat of indictment is sufficient to restrain future Pinochets or Milosovics. In fact, the opposite might happen. Faced with the prospect of being imprisoned in The Hague, future dictators may cling to power strenuously, resulting in more victims, rather than abdicate or remove themselves into unsafe exile.

A great step towards prevention of crimes against humanity could be the establishment of a similar international tribunal (or the inclusion of the task into ICC duties) to which aggrieved minorities could appeal for redress. The world lacks an impartial forum to which oppressed groups can formally turn for action against their government. With the realistic prospect of justifiable relief by an international body, armed resistance and civil war would be effectively discouraged. Should a sovereign state refuse to heed the verdict of the tribunal on the treatment of minorities, a variety of sanctions against the outcast could be meted out. The state's chief representative could even be indicted themselves for contempt of court. While the European Court in Strassbourg already hears complaints against unjust treatment by European governments and the International Court of Justice pronounces on inter-state disputes, aggrieved national minorities need to be offered a similar legal alternative to taking up arms.

Lustration

The term lustration is frequently meant to describe all actions against former regime affiliates, from violent or lawless purges to formalized procedures, to a mere "ceremonial cleansing" of the new order (see Karstedt, 1998: 15-56). In this analysis lustration is used in a narrower sense to define the regulated screening of collaborators for disqualification from public office. Victors establish categories of guilt and responsibility to which varying sanctions correspond. Typical examples would be denazification procedures in postwar Germany and "destasification" after reunification.

Attitudes of the general public show remarkable similarities between the two cases fifty-five years apart. Susanne Karstedt (1998) in a perceptive comparative analysis of polling data notes an initial strong approval of punishment of the top decision makers and beneficiaries, but a readiness to exempt ordinary party members and recipients of orders in the lower echelons. This reaction reflects and reinforces the notion of a "betrayed people." A small clique can be blamed while the collusion or silence of ordinary people is transformed into their being victims as well. With time, the call for indictment of the leadership fades and a general atmosphere of closure of the past takes hold.

Lustration is only possible where extensive files of the previous regime reliably document collaborators. Disqualification for public office also presupposes the availability of sufficient skilled substitutes. This was the case with the reunification of East and West Germany where the Eastern part was taken under the economic and bureaucratic tutelage of the West. In South Africa, the continued employment of apartheid administrators in the civil service for a while was not only part of the negotiated settlement but also a necessary in the absence of sufficiently trained personnel of the new order.

Restitution and Compensation

Even established democracies pay reparations to victims mainly under political pressure but rarely out of moral commitment or guilty conscience. Only more than thirty-five years after the establishment of internment camps for Japanese Canadians during World War II did the Canadian government finally pay a meagre average amount of $20,000 to the survivors. Reparations amounted only to a symbolic restitution of their expropriated property.

The Chinese Canadian National Council has been lobbying the Canadian government in vain since 1984 for redress of the Chinese "head tax." This racist legislation, enacted July 1, 1923, imposed a special tax on Chinese immigrants only. It was aimed at deterring further Asian immigration, considered to be the "yellow danger" at the time. However, since wealthy Asian immigrants are now courted by the Canadian government and only a few hundred head-tax payers survive, the government can ignore calls for compensation of the $23 million extracted by the head-tax. The diverse Canadian Chinese community itself does not like to be reminded of its unwelcome past in the country which many now consider a home of unlimited opportunities in which they no longer need their "grandparents money."

Another dynamic is at work with regard to the long-standing grievances of native people. Canadian courts have found the main churches and the federal government "jointly liable" for horrific sexual abuses of thousands of aboriginal children. They were sent to religious boarding schools as part of a government effort to assimilate native youth. Hundreds of former students have filed individual and class action lawsuits, seeking damages for their suffering, mostly inflicted by Roman Catholic and Anglican church officials. In the case of land claims and hunting and fishing rights by aboriginal groups in both Australia and Canada powerful moral pressure is exerted. The 3 percent scattered Canadian native population possesses neither the voting strength, physical power nor the economic clout to force the national government to recognize its historical grievances. Yet despite strong opposition from influential oil, mining, and forest companies, Canadian courts have recognized aboriginal land claims and forced governments to enter into good faith negotiations about the transfer of large tracts of crown land to native jurisdiction. Preferential fishing and hunting rights have long been granted, despite strong local voters opposition and concern for conservation measures. Australia has even instituted a symbolic national "Sorry Day" to create a collective memory of the country's illegitimate conquest by foreign settlers.

, At work here is the moral politics of embarrassment. A state is forced by relatively powerless groups into a clear choice: either to forfeit its claims of a model democracy, based on the rule of law, or to live up to broken treaties and admit historical injustice. Since Canada proudly markets itself as an anti-colonial, multicultural model, it can hardly allow itself to be exposed as practicing open internal colonialism. With the help of legal assistance by sympathetic lawyers, even powerless minorities can exercise power over indifferent governments. The Canadian state even bears the costs of the court challenges against itself and finances research into further claims in the name of historical injustice.

The political interest of reintegration into the international community motivated substantial German reparations to Israel and individual Jewish victims at the beginning of the 1950s, despite disapproval of the majority of the electorate. Foreign policy considerations also play a major role in the as yet unresolved question of German compensation for an estimated 1 million out of 8 to 10 million survivors of forced labor in Nazi Germany. Paradoxically, it was globalization with the fusion of German and foreign conglomerates that made the German side vulnerable to boycotts abroad and adverse court judgments in the US. Like the Swiss banks and insurance companies who had to account for Nazi gold transfers, German industry is faced with huge claims by American lawyers of the influential Claims Conference. Ongoing negotiations, coordinated by the Chancellor's office, not only concern the amount of reparation paid into a Foundation Fund but above all, the legal exclusion of future claims, whether individual restitution should be paid to the needy only, whether national wage levels and differential living costs should be taken into account, and whether the compensation should be based on underpaid wages or the suffering of Nazi slave laborers.

Although the German government promises to treat all claimants equally, it can be expected that the strength of their lobby and the status of their government play a decisive role. Sinti and Roma, unorganized gays or Jehovah's Witnesses will surely be shortchanged in the end. Claims of U.S. citizens will be given greater weight than those originating from Eastern Europe. Constantin Goschler (1998:49) points out that only the end of the Cold War made these demands possible. "Individual Nazi victims play a minor role in the calculation of East European states in light of their own interests in German support and therefore receive less endorsement from their own government than comparable claims originating from the US."

Even in a state with a government of liberation, the liberated victims cannot be sure to receive material reparations. The South African government agonizes over the recommendations of the Truth and Reconciliation Commission (TRC) to pay 20,000 recognized victims a modest amount of R20,000 for six years. At the same time the TRC process illustrates the danger of establishing a hierarchy of victimhood.

Advocates of the TRC praise the involvement of broad sectors of society in providing information. The communal experience of public hearings, of being listened to and officially recognized as victims, is said to be as important for the healing of trauma as the testimony itself. Unfortunately, this broad involvement also raises false expectations. In South Africa, one hears disappointment in many communities that no follow-up took place, and particularly that the expected compensation for suffering has not materialized. "We have stimulated hopes and then abandoned the people," explains one commissioner self critically (Personal conversation, February 7, 1999). However, the South African TRC, with limited resources and a limited life span, had not been empowered to fulfill the expectations it raised. It could only make recommendations to government which was free to accept and, more likely, to "fudge" even the modest TRC suggestions. ANC leaders now argue that liberation should not be reduced to material benefits.

Speculations that "the palpable insufficiency of reparations could stoke fires of revenge or further victimize the victimized as trivializing their harms or suggesting a payoff for silence" (Minnow, 1998:132) do not apply in South Africa. Since a government of victims is responsible for non-payment it would be a rejection of their own representatives. Nor is anyone co-opted into silence. Those 20,000 recognized by the TRC as theoretically eligible for compensation are envied by the millions of ordinary victims of apartheid laws who did not fall under the legal category of "gross violations." Their suffering caused by the expropriation of the Group Areas Act, low wages under the discriminatory labor policy, and arrests under the Pass Laws, is comparatively trivialized by not being worthy of restitution under the TRC legislation. In short, by focusing solely on the illegal transgressions of illegitimate laws, the TRC legislation ignores the structural, legal violence of a racist system. The TRC concerned itself mainly with a select group of victims, Mahmood Mamdani argues, instead of beneficiaries.

Reeducation

Memory politics frequently includes conscious measures for reeducation, from rewriting of history books to exchange programs and the official redefinition of collective identity. At the height of the Kosovo war, Daniel Goldhagen recommended, as the only lasting solution, the occupation of Serbia and the resocialization of the population, as had happened successfully after the war in Germany and Japan. Others emphasize the importance of focusing on the suffering of the adversary rather than on own group pain in order to achieve empathy and tolerance through a shared history.

Education for multicultural understanding always deserves support but must not be overrated in its impact. Another educational method promises greater success: strengthening the self-confidence of adolescents, to develop their critical consciousness and rules of negotiated conflict resolution.

The lessons of Auschwitz do not lie in repeating empty rituals of remembrance or in indoctrinating collective guilt. Political education in the next century must go beyond Auschwitz by keeping alive an awareness of and sensibility to future injustice. By exposing the all-pervasive dispositions for racism and discrimination the lessons of Auschwitz are best preserved.

The ashes and corpses of previous victims are best honored by providing the living with insights about the causes of their fate. In Germany that should include all victims of Nazism, not only Jews. To be sure, Jews were the most numerous victims, and in the paranoia of the Nazis their most dangerous enemy. Only for Jews was a "final solution" designed. Yet it would seem wrong to dedicate the Berlin memorial exclusively to Jews, as the German parliament decided. Promises of similar memorials for the other victim groups elsewhere leads to rivalry and establishes a hierarchy of suffering. Germany again makes selections among victims. Above all, the false impression is created that the motivation for the murder of Jews was based on their particular behavior. Yet Jews as scapegoats were interchangeable.

Memorialization in the form of an official monument always suggests the Nazi past has been laid to rest once and for all. Some consider such finality an advantage. A truth commission, writes Minnow (1998:127) "fails to create potential closure afforded by criminal trials that end in punishment." However, continuing soul-searching should be welcomed rather than regretted. Political education is advanced by disputes over interpretations of past events that are easily relegated to oblivion with the closure of an authoritative judgment. The more controversial a memorial in the center of Berlin, the better for raising consciousness. It ought to hurt as a thorn in national self-satisfaction rather than please. The central German memorial cannot be, as the glib suggestion of Chancellor Schröder implied, "a place which one likes to visit."

The central memorial need not even be confined to Nazi victims. Fascist mentalities survive among an alienated minority in the form of xenophobia and violence against foreigners, particularly in former East Germany where hardly any foreigners lived before. To highlight this continuity, the memorial could open itself to the future and engrave the names of all foreigners murdered for racist reasons in the post-fascist state.

To be sure, this everyday racism amounts to individual deviance and not the state-criminality of the Nazis. It is important to stress this difference, because racism is frequently viewed as always originating from fascist social conditions. The East German skinheads, who harass "others," know that they will not be tolerated by the state. They embody a syndrome similar to hate crimes in London, Paris, or Toronto.

How and under what conditions such universal individual predispositions emerge and are successfully mobilized in a mass movement for genocide, could be illuminated with the unique Nazi crimes. In this way the "normal society" of the "Berlin Republic," because of its abnormal past could prove to itself and the world that it has effectively ceased to mourn all victims of discrimination.

Truth Commissions

Truth commissions were first established after the successors of the military dictatorships in various Latin American countries came under pressure to reveal the fate of thousands of alleged dissidents who had disappeared. The celebrated South African Truth and Reconciliation Commission (TRC) differed from its Latin American counterparts by being established as an act of Parliament rather than by presidential decree, holding open hearings instead of in camera investigations and making an amnesty dependent on full disclosure of perpetrators. The South African TRC sees itself in the tradition of "restorative justice" foregoing punishment in favor of reconciliation. Assuming that "revealing is healing" encounters between forgiving victims and remorseful perpetrators were meant to achieve the ambitious goal as the only alternative to continued strife.

Due to the international stature of the TRC's chair, Desmond Tutu, his hopes and predictions have even entered the academic literature as empirical facts. In this vein Gesine Schwan (1997:245) in her celebrated *Politik und Schuld* falsely credits the TRC with "having endangered pity, empathy and remorse on the part of perpetrators by being confronted with the unspeakable suffering of victims." That was the intention of the TRC hearings but in reality only occurred in rare cases. Interestingly, two of the worst killers, Eugene de Kock, dubbed "prime evil" by the South African media as commander of the special Vlakplaas police unit, and his predecessor Dirk Coetzee, fall into this category of remorseful converts (De Kock, 1998). However, in most other cases, judging from participant observation and recorded confessions, apartheid's assassins tried to save their skin by applying for amnesty or turning state witness without recognition of the moral turpitude of their actions (Pauw, 1997). The public shaming of confessing perpetrators presupposes a moral reference group that shares the shame. This is doubtful when exposed killers retreat into ethnic enclaves for whom they committed their crimes and whose dominant attitudes range from understanding to open sympathy.

Typically, perpetrators acknowledged suffering caused or even expressed coded regret but rationalized their deeds in terms of the political climate at the time or their assigned role in the apartheid machinery. Like their political leaders in the National Party, genuine acknowledgement of guilt or acceptance of responsibility was not forthcoming. None offered private compensation within their means.

Indifference towards the plight of victims was also displayed by black perpetrators on the other side, most prominently Winnie Madikizele-Mandela. Despite an embarrassing beckoning for a sign of remorse by the TRC chair, she finally complied only half-heartedly and reluctantly. The ANC leadership as a whole has yet to remove from office cadres within its ranks for admitted human rights abuses. The ANC only took collective responsibility for "excesses" in the heat of the struggle. In fact, Mbeki criticized the TRC for its "erroneous determination" that indiscriminate bombings or the taking of civilian hostages constitute human rights violations. The TRC findings were seen by the ANC as an attempt to "crimalise a significant part of the struggle of our people for liberation." The TRC was accused of elevating the ANC's unfortunate "collateral damage" in pursuit of a just cause to the moral equivalent of the defense of an unjust one. To its lasting credit, the TRC had always insisted that no such moral leveling was intended or indeed possible, but even in the fight for a just cause, Geneva Convention rules of justice have to be upheld.

The SA debate has confirmed Michael Ignatieff's (1998:176) insight from the Yugoslav conflict that it is relatively easy for both sides to acknowledge each other's pain. "Much more difficult – indeed usually impossible – is shared acknowledgement about who bears the lion's share of responsibility. For if aggressors have their own defense against truth, so do victims. People who believe themselves to be victims of aggression have an understandable incapacity to believe that they too have committed atrocities."

While truth commissions can confirm the factual truth of an atrocity, they usually fail to establish a common interpretative truth. This moral truth of who is responsible and why it happened is always heavily contested. Divided memories prevail because truth is tied to institutional and collective identity. Apportioning blame in a moral narrative, affects the standing of a political party or the self-respect of a people. Even if something is an obvious truth to any "objective" outsider, it is far from acceptable to an insider. For a member of the in-group the myth about the others or the goodness of their own is not just a tissue of lies that can be unmasked. This identity is a daily reality to be lived by, a lens through which the world is interpreted and a tool to make sense and give meaning to life. As Ignatieff (1998:173) has rightly stressed, "It is unreasonable to expect those who believed they were putting down a terrorist or insurgent threat to disown the idea simply because a truth commission exposes the threat as having been without foundation. People, especially people in uniform, do not easily or readily surrender the premises upon which their lives are based."

Particularly if truth is imposed from the outside, it is rejected. Foreigners therefore should refrain from interpreting history for indoctrinated locals, no matter how high their academic standing outside and how good their intentions. It is also wise to guard against internal exiles, people of the same ethnicity but little ideological credibility among their own group: human rights activists or cosmopolitan minds who are viewed as sympathetic to the enemy. If collective identity is to be successfully redefined, it must be communicated by credible ideologues of the inside. If a few respected opinion leaders can be won over to the painful truth, their standing alone assures susceptibility, or at least stimulates some initial doubts about dearly held positions. The South African TRC neglected to enlist such figures from the Afrikaner intellectual or religious establishment. Unlike the Chilean Commission with four members of the old and four of the new regime, none of the seventeen member South African TRC belonged to the formerly ruling National Party (The two Afrikaners on the Commission were members of rival parties and were isolated among the rest of the ANC-oriented staff). This skewed composition of the TRC, comprised of otherwise well-intentioned people with predominantly legal qualifications or theological training, nevertheless compromised the reception of its findings. It almost promises better results to appoint reasonable hardliners from both sides to argue about a shared historical truth in the calm of a committee room than to select presumable non-partisan, "objective," politically low-profile representatives of various stakeholders, as the South African legislation stipulated. Should ethnic fundamentalists achieve some minimal consensus, they can communicate their controversial compromise more effectively than even Nobel Prize-winning personalities. In fact, the more the outside world courts leaders or heaps praise on interlocutors, in order to strengthen their difficult reconciliation, the more suspect they become among their followers. Bestowing honor should wait until results have been achieved.

The South African historic compromise initially benefited from having a range of credible leaders on both sides. With little internal democracy and authoritarian traditions in both the ANC and NP, followers trusted their leaders blindly. Mandela and Slovo could sell a controversial negotiated settlement to their skeptical constituency on the basis of their hallowed record of suffering and militancy. The conservative, cautious de Klerk was given an overwhelming mandate to negotiate because nobody suspected his team would surrender all political power in exchange for preserving economic privileges.

However, more than sanctions and rising costs of minority rule, it was the very nature of racial domination that distinguished South Africa from Yugoslavia. Mobilized ethnic identity in the Balkans prevented reconciliation while discredited racial identity in SA facilitated compromise. Long before negotiations about the abolition of apartheid started, the system had been delegitimized from the outside as well as from the inside. Most Afrikaner intellectuals had defected from the ruling group and championed "reform."

Furthermore, the economic interdependence limited ruthlessness in apartheid South Africa. Terror was not applied indiscriminately against all members of an outgroup, as under fascism or the ethnonationalist strife against Yugoslavia, but mainly against political activists. The vast majority of "non-whites," though heavily discriminated against, could escape direct attacks on their life by being apolitical and complying with "the law." Apartheid ruled through a supposedly equal legal system rather than placing its victims outside the law as rightless persons, as fascism did.

Racial discrimination in such a context does not lend itself to the same group cohesion and collective trauma as ethnic mobilization does. Unlike Nazi ideology, based on imagined national blood bonds of common ancestry, apartheid needed to racialize culturally different whites in order to unify a weak demographic base but ethnicize blacks in order to divide and rule. This artificial and imposed social engineering had to fail because it lacked the freely embraced legitimacy of ethnonationalism elsewhere. When the Cold War ended, Eastern European leaders turned successfully to previously suppressed nationalism to fill the ideological vacuum. In South Africa, costly segregation could finally be abandoned because the elites of both sides benefited from reluctant co-operation. In short, the discredited racism lacked the appeal of a just cause because even apartheid advocates had come to see blacks as victims while the humiliated colonized eschewed vengeance in the name of nonracialism and reconciliation.

A once-powerful Afrikaner nationalism had become a victim of its own economic success through state patronage. Once a mild African nationalism claimed political power and civil service positions without threatening the accumulated wealth and relative cultural autonomy of its historic adversary, Afrikaner nationalism unraveled into heterogeneous interest groups and different identity definitions without a common enemy. Graves of ancestors, territory acquired in ethnic cleansing or conflicts over holy sites, as in other nationalist conflicts, would be the last issues on the minds of black or white South Africans. Instead, a thoroughly Americanized society worries about access to the latest consumer goods and capitalist frills and diversions. The white "haves" are silently thankful that black "would-be haves" now keep a huge mass of black "have-nots" reasonably pacified and, if necessary, under authoritarian control. It is this constellation, not a Christian ethic or democratic consensus, that enabled a truth commission to go through the ritual of grappling with the past in order to proclaim in vain a reconciled memory for the future.

Conclusions

Collective memory of human rights violations could be separated into two broad categories of cases to which appropriate responses differ: (1) historical injustice and (2) contemporary abuses.

1. Historical injustice compromises cases where blameless groups have been the victim of state aggression a long time ago. Few direct survivors exist and the claims of their descendants relate to the appropriate recognition rather than to the restoration of the situation before the event. Victims of Nazi atrocities, Japanese imperial expansionism, Stalinism and colonial conquest and slavery fall into this category. Punishment of guilty perpetrators is no longer possible. Repossession of expropriated property or forced resettlement of people after civil wars or ethnic cleansing would create new strife and injustices or is not feasible because of

interim economic development. In these cases, collective responsibility consists more of symbolic restitution than material compensation. Keeping the memory of the injustice alive and mourning the victims through political education about the historical crime best does justice to the collective legacy.

2. Contemporary abuses call for both justice through legal recourse as well as developing new institutions that facilitate reconciliation or, perhaps more realistically, peaceful co-existence. Particularly where sizeable antagonists share the same state (South Africa, Northern Ireland, Rwanda, Latin America), truth commissions together with trials of guilty perpetrators can affirm victims, contribute towards common norms, or even create constitutional patriotism. Where ethnonationalist groups do not support common nation-building (Balkans, Israel/Palestine) and where mutual atrocities engendered divided memories, separation in independent or semi-autonomous polities would seem the only feasible solution. Here, international trials for state criminals of recent abuses could also act as a deterrent. An international forum to which aggrieved groups can turn for redress would constitute an alternative to renewed violence.

Remembering cannot be the same for perpetrators and victims. Both can fall into the trap of false memory. For the perpetrators this usually encompasses rationalizations of past misdeeds ("following orders," "blinded by the atmosphere of the time," "no choice"). Denial can be expected, the greater the atrocity. The moral identity of a perpetrator is challenged by full acknowledgement, not to mention the material and legal consequences of full confessions. Even the guaranteed amnesties in return for full disclosure did not entice many South African perpetrators before the Truth Commission to admit their involvement in gross human rights abuses. A much more vexed case is the memory of bystanders, or more specifically the beneficiaries of a conquest or the descendants of aggression a long time ago. Theirs is no personal guilt, but in Karl Jaspers' famous distinction, they still bear responsibility. In the broadest sense responsibility can be defined as progressive remembering, the knowledge of the causes of privilege, the awareness of infamy committed in the name of the group they belong to through no fault of their own. Even guilt by association does not apply to them, because they had no choice. Therefore, a historically conscious, that is, a politically literate beneficiary of past injustice must, above all, develop an awareness of historical privilege. Responsibility means political consciousness. It is a precondition for restitutive measures.

No general rules can be discerned, how much and how long a collective of conquest should compensate its surviving vanquished. Nor can it be left solely to the victims and their descendants to determine how much repentance is enough, whether material or symbolic remorse is appropriate. Survivors are too tempted by greed. Exploiting past crimes, or instrumentalizing the guilty conscience of beneficiaries for selfish enrichment would be an all to understandable strategy. In any case, it is impossible to put an exact price tag on past suffering. Past injustice is also trivialized if victims can be bought off. Patient negotiations in good faith about a mutually acceptable compromise would seem the only feasible route to follow in the absence of an international court on ethical behavior by governments and business. In the end, threats of boycott, harmful publicity for the image of a multinational company or state and general shaming may suffice to reach a reasonable compromise. Moral education in ethical awareness always facilitates appropriate choices in genuine predicaments.

In the long run, conquered and conquerors both benefit from leveling their playing field, from a social injustice that equalizes or at least reduces the vast historically caused material gaps in education, income and quality of life. However, social justice policies or even preferential treatment in affirmative action strategies may be insufficient to satisfy historically disadvantaged groups. For many of their members, liberal equity policies smack of co-optation. They will not be placated with the upward mobility of their elite, which robs the majority of historical victims of their leaders and leaves ordinary members further impoverished. Policies of pacification usually fail if they only benefit the few. Even the pampered leadership often demands more than material rewards, namely symbolic recognition, an official acknowledgement and apology for historical wrongs, or even secession in the case of the Palestinians, Quebecois, or Sri Lankan Tamils. It may be worth specifying mutually acceptable conditions under which secession of people with divided memories may proceed, as the Canadian government has attempted.

If perpetrators and victims, have to live together in the same state, the victims too have to adjust their attitude. It is counter productive to cultivate self-pity. Memory that wallows in victimhood may well be disempowering. History cannot be reduced to victimology because the powerless are never entirely without power. By remembering defeat as well as resistance, suffering as well as survival against all odds, victims empower themselves as human agents. Self-pity is replaced with enabling for appropriate action for change. The most useful memorial for past injustice is keeping the debate about it alive rather than freezing it in a monument. Past victims are best honored by sensitizing a new generation for future injustice.

References

Adam, Heribert and Kogila Moodley. 1993. *The Opening of the Apartheid Mind.* Berkeley: University of California Press.

Adam, Heribert. Frederick van Zyl Slabbert, Kogila Moodley. 1998. *Comrades in Business. Post-Apartheid Politics in South Africa.* Utrecht: International Books.

Adam, Heribert. 1998. "Widersprüche der Befreiung: Wahrheit, Gerechtigkeit und Versöhnung in Südafrika," *Leviathan*, 18, 350-70.

Bergmann, Werner. 1998. "Kommunikationslatenz und Vergangenheitsbewältigung," *Leviathan*, Sonderheft 18, 393-408.

Buruma, Ian. 1999. "The Joys and Perils of Victimhood." *New York Review of Books*, April 8, 4-9.

Cullen, Michael S, ed. 1999. *Das Holocaust-Mahnmal. Dokumentation einer Debatte.* Zürich: Penta.

de Kock, Eugene. 1998. *A Long Night's Damage: Working for the Apartheid State.* Saxonwald: Contra Press.

Dubiel, Helmut . 1999. *Niemand ist frei von der Geschichte.* München: Hanser.

Frei, Norbert. 1996. *Vergangenheitspolitik. Die Anfänge der Bundesrepublik und die NS-Vergangenheit.* München: Beck.

Goschler, Constantin. 1998. "Offene Fragen der Wiedergutmachung," *Leviathan,* 18, 38-52.

Hamburger Institut für Sozialforschung, ed. 1999. *EineAusstellung und ihre Folgen.* Hamburg: IfS.

Ignatieff, Michael. 1998. *The Warrior's Honour. Ethnic War and the Modern Conscience.* Toronto: Penguin Books.

Jeismann, Michael, ed. 1999. *Mahnmahl Mitte.* Köln: Du Mont.

Karstedt, Susanne, 1998, "Coming to Terms with the Past in Germany after 1945 and 1989: Public Judgements on Procedures and Justice," *Law & Policy,* 20, 1, January, 15-56.

König, Helmut, et al. eds. 1998. "Vergangheitsbewältigung am Ende des zwanzigsten Jahrhunderts," *Leviathan,* Sonderheft 18.

Minow, Martha. 1998. *Between Vengeance and Forgiveness.* Boston: Beacon Press.

Möller, Horst, ed. 1999. *Der rote Holocaust und die Deutschen. Die Debatte um das "Schwarzbuch des Kommunismus."* München: Piper.

Neier, Aryeh. 1998. *War Crimes: Brutality, Genocide, Terror, and the Struggle for Justice.* New York: Random House

Pauw, Jacques. 1997. *Into the Heart of Darkness: Confessions of Apartheid's Assassins.* Johannesburg: Jonathan Ball.

Perels, Joachim. 1998. "Die Zerstörung von Erinnerung als Herrschaftstechnik. Adornos Analysen zur Blockierung der Aufarbeitung der NS-Vergangenheir," *Leviathan,* Sonderheft 18, 53-58.

Reichel, Peter. 1999. *Politik mit der Erinnerung. Gedächtnisorte im Streit um die nationalsozialistische Vergangheit.* Frankfurt: Fischer.

Schwan, Gesine. 1997. *Politik und Schuld.* Frankfurt: Fischer.

Thiele, Hans-Günther, ed. 1997. *Die Wehrmachtsausstellung. Dokumentation einer Kontroverse.* Bremen: Temmen

Wehler, Hans-Ulrich. 1998. *Entsorgung der deutschen Vwergangenheit.* München: Beck

Wiegel, Gert and Johannes Klotz, eds. 1999. *Gestige Brandstiftung? Die Walser-Bubis Debatte.* Köln

Wipperman, Wolfgang. 1997. *Wessen Schuld? Vom Historikerstreit zur Goldhagen-Kontroverse.* Berlin: Elefanten Press

The Value of Regret? Lessons from and for Germany

Jeffrey K. Olick

If a guiding motif of the long nineteenth century was that war is the continuation of politics by other means, politics today seems to have become the continuation of war by other means. Power has certainly not disappeared, nor even diminished, but it has often become more subtle: hegemony has become hegemonic. This cloaking and transformation of violence in symbolic forms, however, has increased the possibility for challenges that do not depend entirely on traditional material resources. "The struggle of man against power," Czech novelist Milan Kundera put it in *The Book of Laughter and Forgetting*, "is the struggle of memory against forgetting." Victors and victims are now entwined in ongoing struggles of claim and counter-claim, memory and counter-memory: contemporary politics continues past wars as discursive battles over their legacies. The question is whether these discursive struggles tend towards a resolution or generate new cycles of hatred and atrocity.

Mnemonic resistance has become a common strategy in the past few decades, when increasing numbers of individuals and groups have challenged official versions of the past and demanded redress for perceived contemporary and historical wrongs. Perhaps surprisingly, governments and societal elites have become more and more willing to respond to such claims, even when the claimant groups are not particularly powerful in traditional terms. Indeed, a general willingness to acknowledge collective historical misdeeds has disseminated throughout the world, leading to more and more frequent official and unofficial apologies to both internal and external victims. An expectation of acknowledgment has become a decisive factor in processes of "transitional justice" as well as in domestic and international politics more generally. What forms such acknowledgment should take, what acknowledgment means, have thus become central questions where this politics of regret has taken hold.

Of course, there is far from universal agreement that political regret is a positive development. In the late nineteenth century, the theorist Ernest Renan pointed out that forgetting is at the heart of national self-understanding. Friedrich Nietzsche warned that an excess of history can destroy our humanity: "The past," he wrote, "has to be forgotten if it is not to become the gravedigger of the present." Contemporary theorists of memory are fond of quoting Borges' short story, "Funes the Memorious," about a boy who, after falling on his head, loses the ability to forget. This inability to forget makes his life impossible. In virtually every setting, there are those—and not just former perpetrators—who argue that remembering certain aspects of the past can be toxic to collective identity and political legitimation. How, then, are we to think about this delicate balance between remembering and forgetting? And what modes of memory are least likely to produce the destructive side-effects these theorists identify?

Efforts to address these problems of collective memory—how societies deal with the legacy of toxic pasts—almost inevitably begin with the German case, where the problems of memory have loomed larger and more potently in public discourse than perhaps anywhere else. Whether one views contemporary Germany as illegitimately burdened with a past that won't past away or as appropriately shaped by difficult memories, politicians and scholars in many other places debating what to do after transitions from regimes of brutality have looked to the German case as something of a canary in the mineshaft of historical consciousness. What have the effects of historical consciousness been there? Have its various forms been beneficial or destructive? Nuremberg was certainly a decisive event in the history of political justice, but it was only the beginning of a longer discourse about guilt and responsibility in Germany and elsewhere. The German case is thus especially instructive for the question of what criteria to employ when deliberating about the best course of action because it provided both a wide palette of arguments as well as a concrete test of various solutions.

How did Germany manage the legacy of its toxic history? There is no one answer to this; different solutions vied with each other at the same time, and different ones took precedence in different periods, though always with an awareness of and in reaction to earlier arguments and solutions. It is a commonplace of later commentary, for instance, that the Federal Republic of Germany in its first period "suppressed" the Nazi past. Of course, exactly what we could mean by suppressing the past is rather complicated. Early leaders, particularly the venerable Chancellor Konrad Adenauer, defined the new state as the antithesis of its predecessor. The basic law was self-consciously conceived as a bulwark against the possibility of developments similar to those that had led to the demise of the Weimar Republic. From 1951 to 1953, West Germany negotiated with the State of Israel and Jewish organizations over an unprecedented reparations agreement, at the end of which—though over substantial opposition in his own cabinet and in public opinion—Adenauer agreed to payments and transfers valuing 1.5 bil-

lion marks, which climbed to over ten billion marks over the next several decades. West German leaders propagated an official philosemitism, participated
in commemorative rituals, condemned the so-called uneducable, and claimed to
have learned the lessons of the past, which led them now to a rhetoric of "mili-
tant" democracy, strong commitment to the Western alliance, and general posture of "reliability" as a lesson of the past. In what sense, then, does this add up
to a "suppression" of the past?

Critiques focus particularly on the ways in which both ordinary Germans and
their political leaders ranked their own suffering above that of Jews and others
who had been persecuted by Nazi Germany, failed to acknowledge varieties of
perpetration beyond a narrow clique of political leaders and those directly involved in atrocities (referred to as Hitler and his henchmen), and refused to dis-
cuss the specifics of the crimes, preferring instead a vague passive grammar in
public—"the crimes that were committed," or "what happened in those years"—and
silence regarding personal experiences. Most important, critics charge, was the
failure to undertake a genuine denazification of public life, haste to rehabilitate
burdened individuals, calls for a general amnesty—all under the umbrella of vehe-
mently rejecting not only accusations of collective guilt but really of any guilt at all.
Here is what Konrad Adenauer said in his first address as chancellor in 1949:

> Through the denazification, much misfortune and much harm was produced. The truly guilty of the
> crimes that were committed in the National Socialist time and in war should be punished with all severity.
> But as far as the rest, we can no longer distinguish between two classes of people in Germany: the
> politically unobjectionable and the objectionable. This distinction must disappear immediately. The war
> and the disorders of the postwar period have brought such hard trials and such tribulations for so many,
> that one has to summon understanding for many lapses and misdemeanors. The question of a general
> amnesty will therefore be examined by the federal government. When the federal government is deter-
> mined to let the past be past when it seems defensible, in the conviction that many have already paid for
> subjectively minor guilt, it is on the other hand also absolutely decided to draw out of the past all the
> necessary lessons in regard to all those who clamor against the state, may they be attributable to right
> radicalism or left radicalism.

After only a brief mention of recent anti-Semitic expressions, which he dis-
misses as bizarre and inexplicable (a mere four years after the liberation of
Auschwitz!), Adenauer turns to the more pressing problem of German prisoners
of war: "The fate of these millions of Germans, who now for years have born the
bitter lot of captivity, is so heavy, the suffering of their families in Germany so
great, that all peoples must help finally to give back these captives and displaced
to their homeland and families." As for the problem of ethnic expellees from the
Eastern territories, Adenauer almost threatens: "One must solve it if one does not
want to let West Germany become a hotbed of political and economic unrest for
a long period."

These last remarks raise the question of Adenauer's motivations. On the one
hand, Adenauer's own experiences as a so-called inner emigre who was indeed

persecuted by the Nazis and his own long political career before 1933, which included a Catholic Rhinelander's distaste for things Prussian, made accusations of collective guilt nonsensical to him, and generated his sympathy for German suffering. On the other hand, as his long-time advisor Herbert Blankenhorn later described it, "Dr. Adenauer said nothing for years on the topic of the Jews, because he wished to win over the German people in its entirety to the cause of democracy. If Mr. Adenauer had said in 1949 what we had done in the past, then the German people would have been against him." A bit of personal understanding thus combines with what many later critics charged was a debased and complicit *Realpolitik*.

A thorough rejection of this posture was the leading idea of the rebellious new generation coming to maturity in the 1960s. Precisely in the name of "daring more democracy," the so-called sixty-eighters rejected what Adenauer claimed to have done to secure the institutional and popular foundation for that democracy. In contrast to the language of reliability Adenauer and others purveyed in the 1950s, the student movement and the charismatic young Chancellor Willy Brandt placed morality over *Realpolitik*. The new generation accused their parents and the system they had built, saw only continuity where their parents had avowed caesura. When Willy Brandt went on his knees in Warsaw, the reversal of posture was complete. Indeed, at times this new regime and its intellectual gurus seemed to claim moral superiority not only over their predecessors, but over other nations as well, deriving from their unflinching confrontation with collective responsibility. Of course, one prerequisite for that unflinching acceptance of the burden of history is that it was just that—an historical burden rather than a present accusation.

This epoch of the moral nation cleared the way for a new rhetoric of normalization. In a first stage, SPD (Social Democratic Party) Chancellor Helmut Schmidt depended on the symbolic work of his predecessor Brandt as a justification for treating the matters as settled and now focused on the "normal" problems West Germany faced as a "normal" state. But with the change of power to Helmut Kohl's Christian Democrats (CDU) in 1982, a burgeoning neo-conservative movement took the lead. Here the concern was to make up for the apparent legitimation deficits of the welfare state in a time of growing demands and declining capabilities. This new intellectual and political trend turned to history as the solution to Germany's legitimation deficit, and Helmut Kohl and his advisors pursued a cultural program that sought to accept German history "with all its highs and lows," a favorite trope rung at every opportunity.

Here, the centrality of Nazism in narratives of German history—so often characterized as the telos of the national spirit—stood in the way of the proud identity and healthy patriotism sought by the new cultural politicians. In the process, the moral politics of the sixties was vilified. These Germans, literally and figuratively on their knees, were seen as reveling in national self-flagellation and forcing young Germans to walk around "in hair shirts in perpetuity," as another common trope put it. On numerous occasions, Adenauer's choice for integration and legitimacy over memory and regret was hailed as heroic realism. The vilification of the new left, however, often encouraged rather overdramatic terms—perhaps partly learned from the left's indiscriminate use of the fascist label—and extravagant claims about the necessity of Adenauer's compromises—namely that not doing so would have led to a civil war, though what form that might have taken in an occupied country is not clear.

Two general competing criteria of how to manage the legacies of the past should be apparent even in this brief account, though clearly emerging more over the course of a historical narrative than as abstract philosophical principles. Classical political ethics, as well as practical politics, pose a stark choice between retribution and utility. In the abstract, there are good reasons for defending each of these, and long traditions of doing so. But in practice, they often become mere justifications for less admirable positions: On the one hand, the victim's lust for revenge; on the other, the perpetrator's haste to bury misdeeds. But we know well the dangers of blood lust, where universal suffering breeds only particularistic sympathy. There is thus a wide moral gulf between quiescence achieved by suppressing the past, and real peace. A past not worked through because it seems to cost too much will indeed create the deficits neo-conservatives lament.

The absolute terms of the debate—dogma versus opportunism—are thus not, it seems to me, really supple enough to take seriously the different positions apparent in this short narrative from Germany, as well as in the many other cases in which equally serious parties advocate both different solutions—for example, purge versus amnesty—as well as see different criteria—for example, principle versus consequence—as ethical guides. For a more versatile framework, I turn to the great German sociologist Max Weber who, particularly in his essays on science and politics as vocations, articulated a subtler distinction between what he called an "ethic of conviction" and an "ethic of responsibility."

Weber articulated this distinction in very general terms, and sought to connect up his preference for an ethic of responsibility over an ethic of conviction with his wider historical account of the rationalization and disenchantment of the world. For Weber, an ethic of conviction, though perhaps admirably motivated, fails to recognize the contribution of science in the modern rationalized world. In this context, science for Weber means acknowledging the inescapability of value conflict and that ends and means are not integrally connected. For a follower of an ethic of conviction, the ought does not depend on feasibility, and this kind of a position thus denies the realistic framework of science. In contrast, the ethic of responsibility embraces the ethical irrationality of the world and recognizes that realizing values in politics often involves a so-called "pact with diabolical powers." Weber is careful—this is not dogma versus opportunism, or even ethical policy versus *Realpolitik*. Responsibility is an ethical principle, not the absence of one. But it is one that opts for compromise and small steps in the pursuit of political values. The efforts of the German sixty-eighters, on this account, follow an ethic of conviction. It is less clear whether Adenauer's policies and later nostalgia for them follow an ethic of responsibility.

While Weber unpacked this argument in general terms, it is important to remember that he developed it immediately following his work on the war guilt question in negotiations over the Treaty of Versailles and in reaction to revolutionary parties in Germany in 1918 who were ready to accept the war guilt thesis out of pacifist and other convictions. Weber rejected these positions as based on an ethic of conviction—and thus as blind to necessity, feasibility, and consequence—and exhorted students to understand the ethical obligation of the politician to be responsible. Again, this is not a call to *Realpolitik*, which would imply no ethical principle, but a call to pursue whatever value one advocates in a manner sensitive to the possibilities of realizing it and to the relativity, rather than absolute hierarchy, of possible outcomes. Nevertheless, Weber rejected the war guilt clause on the basis of an ethic of responsibility in pursuit of his liberal nationalist values.

The question for the present is whether there can ever be an ethically responsible politics of regret, or whether all such calls are ultimately expressions of an irrational moralism, perhaps well motivated but blind to reality. It is certainly easy enough to dismiss Adenauer's compromises as unprincipled *Realpolitik*: Adenauer was expert at exploiting geopolitics to end denazification, to rehabilitate the German soldier, to justify reintegration of Nazi civil servants and personnel continuities at the highest levels. It is, moreover, also easy—though certainly not as easy—to see the New Left as sanctimonious dogmatists, unable to recognize the difference between Hitler and Adenauer, the Third Reich and capitalist West Germany. No matter what the realities of the German case, however, there is still room for debate between those who would hang the associates of criminal regimes in the public square, purge the armies, exclude the complicit right down to the last postman, and those who prefer to let bygones be bygones, whether the victims agree or not. Does an ethic of responsibility always prefer the latter, as Weber's own position against the war guilt clause might suggest?

In the spirit of the ethic of responsibility, which places stock in science not to determine the choice of ultimate values but to help choose its most feasible means, our answer has to depend on an analysis of both the different possible ultimate ends and the various means available for pursuing them. Regarding the former, there seem to be a number of competing propositions. For Weber, the choice might have been between peace and the national interest, though Weber saw peace as bogus without vigorously defended national interests. For the present, we have to ask ourselves about both the relationship between peace and national interests as well as what exactly constitutes peace. In the first place, the salience of national identifications in the contemporary world has clearly declined, or at

least national principles face great and increasing competition from other principles of identification. Certainly Weber could reasonably speak in terms of the
interests of the nation as paramount. By Adenauer's time, and certainly by the
sixties, such values had already begun to appear exhausted, even anachronistic.
Today, with national societies divided as much against themselves as against
others, national interests cannot as easily justify amnesiac settlements in the name
of continuity. It is also clear in many cases—for instance in the debate over the
extradition of Chilean dictator Augusto Pinochet—that even the most narrowly
domestic disputes never really are. While borders and allegiances have always
been complicated, ever-new forms of such complication are arising at ever-greater
pace, indeed in part as the result of mnemonic battles.

In the second place—the question of what peace means—we can, I believe,
responsibly debate—at the level of ultimate values—whether peace means quiescence or requires something more in the way of reconciliation. In the aftermath
of the First World War, for instance, Walter Benjamin worried that the prolifera-
tion of memorials and commemorations provided a false consolation, ennobling
the "sacrifice" of dead soldiers in the service of ever new programs; real mourning, according to Benjamin, required keeping the wound open, not to motivate
new struggles, but to prevent the reality of the deaths from being swept up into
some future with which they had nothing to do. In a similar vein, Theodor Adorno
argued in 1959 that we must "work through" the past to "break its spell," rather
than try to "master" it with silence; only the former will produce enlightenment,
while the latter lays the foundation for Freud's "return of the repressed."

Along these lines, a good argument can be made that the German quiescence
of the 1950s did not serve the long-term interests of peace, with the comparatively great vigor of German protests in the sixties, terrorism in the seventies, and
xenophobia in the 1980s and 1990s as evidence. This is to say nothing of the
aggregate and collective psychic burdens on the perpetrators and their children,
which have surely produced peculiar symptoms. These are questions all societies seeking some kind of settlement with the legacies of the past must ask: What
counts as reconciliation?

The second major kind of question—after we decide the issue of what ultimate value we want to pursue responsibly—is the more technical question of
how we do that. As far as I'm concerned, far too little thought has been given to
the very limited capabilities of both the perpetrators and the victims, and many of
the present solutions either demand too much of both or pander to their baser
instincts. Simple amnesty, for instance, tramples the feelings of the victim, ask-
ing him to live in the house of the hangman without comment. In Talmudic
terms, this kind of a failure to do justice for the victims is termed a second guilt—
a failure to expiate the injustice after it has occurred, the perpetration of a second
harm. On the other hand, lustration, *Berufsverbot*, exclusion from society treat
all complicit individuals—regardless of the degree or nature of complicity—as

equally guilty. And who among us is not guilty of some prejudice, weakness, callow enthusiasm, and the like? In 1946, the philosopher Karl Jaspers distinguished four kinds of guilt—criminal, political, moral, and metaphysical. Criminal guilt is quite narrowly defined. Certainly more than the few dozen tried at Nuremberg bore some criminal responsibility for the past, but how much, what kind, and where do we draw the line? One can draw absolute distinctions only at a distance, for the reality of human complicity is much more complex. And who but the victims would be left after such a cleansing? Moreover, the same process of absolute distinction between perpetrator and bystander leads to a false heroization of the victims as well, one which denies their ordinary humanity through the same logic, now merely reversed, with which they were originally persecuted.

What of apologies, official or individual? Apologies can be either genuine or cynical. While a cynical apology, particularly if it is accompanied by, or lays the groundwork for, material restitution may help to assuage some of the wounds of persecution, it does not necessarily involve any real learning, and must therefore be rejected by the victims to whom it has been addressed. For indeed, an apology is always addressive in one way or another. And this leads me to the case of genuine apology.

On the collective level, an official apology, insofar as it is anything more than instrumental pandering, can effect a turn in the narrative basis of community and justify new directions. And this is important. But the connection between this collective level and the individual level is not straightforward. Official apologies often alleviate the burden on individuals, doing the work individuals and the institutions of civil society are unwilling to undertake. Such apologies thus stand in for rather than express genuine moral and political regret.

At the individual level, moreover, apology often is misconceived, demanding too much of both perpetrator and victim. In the first place, it presumes that the perpetrator repudiates his earlier self without qualification. There are very few of us, to say nothing of those who have been able to participate in atrocities in one form or another, who are really capable of this. Where an ethic of conviction would tell us to demand nothing else, an ethic of responsibility is more sensitive to human realities and does not base its solutions on wishful thinking or Utopian faith in the human capacity for redemption. In the second place, what can your child's torturer possibly say to you that would make a difference? An apology, after all, always involves some form of exculpation: times were different, I made a mistake, I didn't understand, etc. If it doesn't, it isn't an apology at all. It is repentance or confession, and thus is wrongly addressed to the victim, who is not in a position to grant the kind of absolution sought.

Do we really want to build our hope for peace on the abilities of ordinary people to forgive? Freud is often quoted as having said that we should always forgive our enemies, but not until after they've been hanged. Where whole societies are complicit, how many of them do we hang? And does doing so really end the cycle? The biblical proclamation that the sins of the fathers shall be delivered unto the third and fourth generations seems a moderate prediction in comparison to the historical record.

What, then, can be done in the time of perpetrator and victim? We must do something, but can what we do possibly produce reconciliation in the present? My argument is that such reconciliation is indeed rare. That does not mean that there is nothing to be done. But the question is for whom we are doing it. We certainly owe the victims all possible compensation and help to repair what is really unrepairable, though it is in practice often unclear where the limits of victimhood lie. And—at risk of sounding like the sanctimonious Kantian who advocates punishing the criminal to restore the criminal's humanity—we owe it to the perpetrator and to the perpetrator's children to make clear exactly what he or she did wrong, though that effort is most often in vain. But for me, the relevant collectivity, the only one that can be healed, that can learn the lessons of history and make something of them, is the next generation. What can we do so that the children of perpetrator and victim can come together in a community in which guilt and suffering alike will not be born as marks of Cain through the generations? Suppressing the past even with the best intentions, it seems to me, mistakes quiescence for peace, burying the problem close to the surface where it will return to haunt later generations.

Whatever material and criminal solutions we pursue in the present, we must engage in testimony as a legacy for the future. This means listening to both victims and perpetrators, and not in order to judge absolute truth or even to sympathize with either, but to learn from their experiences and perspectives. For only through developing realistic images of both sides—which means both interested testimony and disinterested historiography—can we avoid turning ordinary victims into martyrs and ordinary perpetrators into psychopaths, as so many commemorative images and claims do. The excuses of the perpetrators are an important part of their testimony here, not because it leads us to exculpate them, but because it provides a record on the basis of which their children can understand their culpability as well as their humanity. For the victims as well, realism is also crucial because only a realistic depiction will aid them in avoiding the well-documented guilt of the second generation, in which children feel their own trials and tribulations are inconsequential because they can never be compared to the suffering of their parents, or in which the legacy of martyred generations keeps the flame of hatred burning.

The closest approximation we have had of such a procedure is the South African Truth and Reconciliation Commission, which has offered amnesty to perpetrators who will testify honestly about their involvement. Sometimes this does indeed seem to have led to reconciliation between perpetrator and victim, though just as often it has not. But it remains to be seen whether perpetrators and victims will be able to produce a civil discourse on the basis of such confrontations. For the moment, perhaps forbearance is all that is possible, or even desirable, though the Commission's designers hoped for more.

But the real success of the Commission, it seems to me, has been that it has established a record for the future. This works at both a personal and a collective level. The understandable love of children for their complicit parents will not, after such testimony, be able to blind them to the facts of perpetration. The victims have finally received an acknowledgment of their humanity in the opportunity to confront their persecutors, but in such a way that prevents them from denying the humanity of the perpetrators in turn. The children of the victims thereby have the opportunity to see the children of the perpetrators not as the fruits of monsters but as human beings struggling, though from a different perspective, with the legacies (and they are always plural) of the past. This has also been a unique opportunity for whites and blacks to confront each other face to face as citizens in a society in which contact between the races is sharply constrained by geographical, social, and economic distance. Whatever emotional powers were released in this crucible, it was one that required acknowledgment from both sides, thus providing a precedent for future civil discourse and indeed disputation.

At the collective level, the South African process has been remarkable as well, particularly when Nelson Mandela refused to dissent from the final report in which the African National Congress was condemned for various criminal activities. This is the most realistic political justice I have heard of, one where recognizing clear lines of historical perpetration has not led to the canonization of saints, martyrs, and psychopaths but instead to a realistic depiction of a sick society in which lines of admirable and despicable behavior were not as clearly drawn as victor's justice would like.

The South African case is certainly unique, not just for the solutions pursued but for the circumstance that have allowed them. The victims there are the majority, the transfer of power was more or less smooth, many basic institutions continued to operate if with changed personnel. These conditions do not obtain in all cases. They certainly did not in Germany in 1945. But even there, and in similar circumstances, we must ask whether present threats to the collectivity—in the German case, that of the potential spread of Soviet domination—serve as an alibi for past actions and for present solutions. Perhaps confrontation with the past is not always wise in times of emergency. But there is a big difference between trying to destroy the truth by burying it, and attempting to provide the foundation for a postponed confrontation. Even in the case of East Germany, where opening the files of the secret police revealed often deeply personal violations, it doesn't seem to me we can really maintain it would have been better—yes, certainly easier!—not to know. However much we might empathize with the desire to escape from freedom, as Erich Fromm put it in a different context, we cannot use this as a foundation for political ethics.

An ethic of responsibility in pursuit of genuine peace and reconciliation opens up alternatives to the seemingly intractable choice between imposing retributive convictions and bowing to the pressures of *Realpolitik*. Nowhere was this clearer than in the debate about whether or not to allow the extradition of Pinochet to Spain. As it was framed, the choice was one between punishing a dictator at all costs or helping secure a new, more peaceful regime and avoiding the Pandora's box of international encroachments on sovereign governments. A third choice, however, would have been consistent with an ethic of responsibility: Do not allow the extradition but go ahead and try Pinochet in absentia. It certainly would be better if Chile would sponsor its own forum for truth telling (and they have made some gestures in this direction), but there are real impediments to such an endeavor. In lieu of such an effort, however, other countries or better yet international agencies can provide a forum for testimony of all kinds. If Pinochet or his supporters choose not to provide a defense, it is at the cost of not preserving their perspective and not engaging in a moral discourse.

This is not a call for a pure historiographical or juridical determination of right and wrong but for the disputational production of collective memories, including some kind of adjudication (legal and scientific) of acceptable and unacceptable versions. The difference here between history and collective memory is crucial, but that difference is only partly epistemological—historical truth versus mnemonic invention. It is more importantly a question of relevance and centrality. When post-transitional societies make the past a matter for historical analysis rather than for political discourse, they treat interest in it as irrelevant and marginal. They thereby allow old subjectivities to remain within their particularistic horizons. One might object that a commission charged with soliciting and reconciling private memories, competing group memories, partial perspectives, and collective mythologies in order to create a truthful collective memory—perhaps a truths commission rather than a Truth commission—lacks not only legal but moral jurisdiction. But is it irresponsible to assert moral jurisdiction in the name of humanity where suffering is so universal? Not so long as doing so remains moral and factual rather than juridical or political, and so long as we place our own experiences up to the same measure of disputation and inquiry (this latter fear has provided another argument against extradition—that it would set a precedent which would allow American leaders to be extradited; but without the power of extradition and the force of punishment, much of the force of the objection disappears).

Punishment is thus not the only foundation for reconciliation; it is never sufficient and only sometimes necessary for the creation of justice. That is not to say that individual punishment or collective legal responsibility are irrelevant. But such punishment cannot be the ultimate measure of how a society has "dealt" with its past. This is one of the lessons of Nuremberg, the legacy of which has not been unequivocal. Nuremberg certainly was an important early stage in forcing a certain truth to be told, and the moral principles articulated there have been important precedents for much subsequent thought on such matters, if the legal embodiment of those principles has been ambiguous and sometimes even dubious. But it had its costs as well, providing an alibi for an expertly equivocating population that was eager to lay the blame on a narrow "clique," and providing some basis for accusations of a victor's justice particularly against the Soviet Union (whose moral right to sit in judgment was questionable, not to mention the much less potent accusations against the Western allies for their own failures in the conduct of war).

Nuremberg also enabled some of the false distinctions between two classes of people Adenauer had referred to, though my observation stems more from a concern that lesser forms of culpability be acknowledged rather than from Adenauer's concern that they not be seen as accountable at all. The latter is indeed what happened to the denazification process, in which early efforts to classify every adult in terms of his or her political involvement produced a vigorous business in so-called "*Persilscheine,*" or whitewash certificates. It was perhaps right that this process was abandoned, though probably not for the reasons Adenauer and the German political class in general wanted. The problem was that the goal of the so-called *Spruchkammer* (testimony chamber) was a classification of guilt and certification of innocence rather than truth telling, however partial that can ever be.

These, then, are just some preliminary thoughts on how a politics of regret can be founded on an ethic of responsibility rather than on an ethic of conviction—not retribution for retribution's sake, but that important combination of knowledge and ac-knowledgment that lays the foundation for reconciliation not between victim and perpetrator but among their children. There is a big differences between delaying confrontation with the past and hindering it in both the present and for the future. The former may serve the present interests of *Realpolitik*; the latter, however, is the only way to meet our responsibility to the future where memory and power have become interchangeable, the hallmark feature of our properly regretful age.

Nameless Memory: Levinas, Witness, and Politics

James Hatley

"Justice is the way in which I respond to the face that I am not alone in the world with the other."

Elemental Violence and Indecent Societies

The memory of violence, particularly of mass violence, can be personally, politically, and historically demoralizing. For this very reason, the fostering of memory often becomes the goad to yet further brutalities, to the nurturing of grudges through decades, centuries and even millennia, whose call for bloody retribution refuses to be stilled. Like the outrageous acts at the heart of Greek tragedy, historical wrongs open up wounds in time that are seemingly beyond repair. With this issue in mind, Rajeev Bhargava reminds us that there are moments in history and particularly in our not so distant history—whether they be the Shoah[1] enacted in Europe, or apartheid in South Africa, or the massacres of Sikhs and Hindus in Dehli—when violence has become so endemic to a society, or has been carried through by one group within it with such radical impunity, that it can be argued the very order of human relationships has reverted to a state of "barbarism."[2]

To speak of justice in the context of such a situation of basic indecency becomes problematic—the very depth and breadth of wrong inflicted renders ludicrous any human attempt to punish it, to exact reparations, or to reconcile perpetrator with victim. What these moments of violence stir up is so irremediable, so cruel and pitiless, that those who are caught up in them have seemingly escaped the rule of reason itself. Such extraordinary wrongs call for, in Bhargava's mind, an extraordinary notion of justice, one in which the first duty of the just is to insist on minimum procedures that restore all members of a society to political discourse.[3] Before one can even settle on a notion of what constitutes a substantial notion of justice, before one can even speak *of* punishment, reparation or reconciliation, those who enforce and follow the laws must be willing to speak *with* one another, to hear one another's voice. Without having met this minimum condition, Bhargava argues, to speak of justice in its more accepted and principled sense is a senseless act.

In a similar vein, Emmanuel Levinas, whose thought witnesses his own experience as a Jewish survivor of the Shoah, writes in his midrashic essay, "Damages Due to Fire," on how Auschwitz is a signifier for an elemental violence that leaves all rational attempts to limit its outcome, or respond to its loss, at a loss. In such an event, Levinas states, "We are entering the realm of total disorder, of sheer Element, no longer in the service of any thought, beyond war. Or perhaps we are entering the abyss from which all these uncontrollable forces emerge. An abyss that yawns during exceptional periods. Unless it is always ajar, like a madness which sleeps with one eye open in the heart of reason."[4]

Levinas's point that violence leads beyond war is an important one. In war, the inflicting of damage upon one's enemy, even if it is unjust, continues until the goals for which war is being prosecuted are reached. Within the cunning game of move and countermove that characterizes war, a realization is at work that either side might lose and so both sides must end up abiding by certain minimal covenants. In Bhargava's terms, war can remain minimally decent, even if destructive. But Levinas notes that in elemental violence, a possibility always sleeping within the notion of war with "one eye open," a disorder beyond the limits of intentionality, of a play of forces for purposes one can rationally delimit, comes into being. In this violence, a dynamic is at work in which any inflicting of damage against the other provokes the intensification, the escalation of yet further damage to be inflicted.[5] In violence, as opposed to war, damage can never be inflicted enough. In the throe of this dynamic, the very practice of war as damaging the other's means in order to achieve one's own goals slips into a conflagration of violence. One no longer merely resists the other's intention to resist one's own intention but becomes fixed upon crushing the other's humanity and his or her world. In violence, the other is no longer an opponent to be dealt with but a cipher to be crushed, to be annihilated, no matter what the cost. The enemy is not merely to be defeated—rather he or she is treated as if it would have been better if he or she had never existed.

Put in more concrete terms, in violence one treats the other as if he or she were faceless, or one is treated so by the other. Is this not the indecency of which Bhargava speaks in his own essay, the characteristic of a society, in which one no longer admits one is called to listen to another's voice, to be questioned by the impact of one's actions upon another's face? For Levinas, Auschwitz is one name of the event of such indecency.

Faceless and Nameless: When Justice Confronts the Unjustifiable

But even if one accepts the claim that there are historical moments when vio-lence exceeds all reasoned limits, does it necessarily follow that an extraordinary sense of justice is called for in the aftermath of such violence? In this regard, Bhargava makes a distinction between asymmetrical and symmetrical moments of indecency.[6] In some events, such as many civil wars, Bhargava contends that the insistence on treating others as voiceless and faceless infects all factions of a society. In these particular circumstances, truth commissions, such as those founded in the aftermath of apartheid, may be more effective in returning a soci-ety to justice than an insistence on bringing all those who participated in violent actions to trial and punishment. One cannot put an entire country in prison. But in events such as the Shoah, National Socialism's treatment of Jews is asym-metrically indecent—generally Jews and those who supported their cause were not consumed by the same drive to annihilate Nazis that Nazis were to annihilate Jews. And the allies, for all their shortcomings, also generally supported and carried through at least a minimal notion of human rights in their pursuit of the war.[7]

In the instance of the Shoah, critics could certainly point to the manner in which the trials at Nuremburg, as well as the patient and long-lasting search for war criminals in the decades following them, has done much to restore a sense of decency to Germany and to the relationship between Christian Europe and its surviving Jewish population. While the innovations in international law that formed the basis of the Nuremburg prosecution may have seemed extraordinary at the time, they increasingly have become a part of the ordinary rule of international law, as the suddenly more effective efforts to prosecute the seemingly impunious Agusto Pinochet, the former dictator of Chile, have recently demonstrated. If anything, could it not be argued that rather than relenting and loosening the call for punishment and reparation, the insistence upon these measures at Nuremburg and afterward helped Germany to regain its status as a decent society, one that has gone and continues to go to great lengths to acknowledge its former injus-tices?

Perhaps it would be better argued, at least in situations of what Bhargava terms asymmetrical violence, that more good is accomplished by immediately imposing the sanctions of law upon an indecent society and rooting out its perpe-trators Still, as Levinas points out in his essay "Transcendence and Evil," humanity's legacy of violence leaves it mired in a justice that necessarily fails to be just enough, no matter how assiduously it prosecutes the unjust and consoles the persecuted. The very sting of evil is how it leaves us burdened with the memory of "the unjustifiable."[8] For even if justice can serve to restore rights to peoples once afflicted and to put into proper historical and political perspective the arrogant self-aggrandizement of the unjust, justice cannot undo the most radical effects of violence. For those victims who survive, the memory of betrayal remains no matter how much the perpetrator may be punished, and for the victims who did not survive, the loss of their lives and of entire societies and their future descendants cannot be undone. No matter how much justice may strive to restore equity to political and historical life, the effects of violence will continue to be suffered. There is no meaningful way to command that suffering cease, no matter how much we may desire it so. The very scandal of evil, Levinas reminds us in yet another essay, is how it submits one to useless suffering, to a suffering for which no reason can be found that would justify its impact upon the other who faces me.[9]

How then should one remember the unjustifiable, the submission to suffering for which no remedy can truly be given? In his book of essays *Proper Names*, Levinas broaches this subject in one selection, simply titled "Nameless," a name which he paradoxically employs as the most (im)proper name of those who perished in the elemental violence of the Shoah.[10] In his invocation of this name without name is found a fundamental ambivalence. On the one hand, namelessness might signify for Levinas how my memory of the Shoah's particular victims calls me beyond their naming. I do not invoke the other, but instead I find I have always already been subjected to the other's invocation of me. For Levinas memory of the other ultimately engages me in a past that could never have been mine, what Levinas, in *Otherwise than Being*, terms the immemorial. Before the nudity of the other's face, before his or her vulnerability to being wounded, I find myself traumatized by a suffering that calls me near but that I cannot really share. No matter how deeply I might empathize with the suffering of this other, my feeling of empathy is always interrupted by the realization that it is this other and not I who has undergone that suffering. For Levinas, the memory in which we are called to the other from out of the other's time is not in the first instance an engram, or some representation of the other in consciousness, but an enigma, a calling into proximity that cannot be represented, cannot be given in any presence at all, the immemorial. Memory at its heart is a being addressed, a being submitted to others in their vulnerability and in their faces. To remember in this mode is to be rendered humble—the other calls us to his or her face, before we could have ever had the means to name it, or to dispose of its pain.

In refusing to name the other directly, in referring enigmatically to the other as he or she who is without name, Levinas, it could be argued, gives witness to the transcendence of the other out of whom my memory of her or him—in its more normal sense—has been given. In the background of such a gesture echoes the Biblical refusal of The Name (*HaShem*), of G-d, to be named—"I AM THAT I AM." Following up this emptying out of G-d's name in a more human vein, Levinas offers a notion of a transcendent yet human responsibility, in which I undergo its inescapable weight before the human other to whom I am responsible could even have been named. I do not name her or him but instead find myself named as a singular locus of responsibility, as the one for whom no one else can assume my burden of response.[11] To paraphrase the words of Hillel: *If not me, then whom? If not now, then when?* Further, for Levinas, my responsibility to the other, whether it be one of the Six Million[12] *or* a Nazi perpetrator, is not attendant upon my first determining whether she or he deserves my responsibility. Whether I find it reasonable or not, I have always already been elected to responsibility. Levinas goes so far to speak of this election as making me hostage to the other. Such is the situation in which a world of animate souls who are created, who are responsible in a manner that always already transcends their ability to account for their responsibility, find themselves. And such is the situation I would find myself in, if I am to hear the memory of each of the Six Million and more who call me into responsibility.

But, on the other hand, to be nameless can also signify to have been rendered faceless, to have been treated *as if* one had never been worthy of being responded to, as if the very naming of one's name was beyond even the bother of having been acknowledged. One is treated *as if*, even if one had existed, one still would not have mattered enough to have engaged the other's response to one's existence.[13] Thus, Primo Levi finds himself violently shoved back into his barracks at the Monowitz Work Camp, not because he asked an inappropriate question of a Nazi guard but because any question at all on his part would have been inappropriate.[14] In this gesture of dismissal, his countenance is rendered without question, without address and so without face. Over and over in the death camps the strange game took place of treating its inmates *as if* they were not even capable of being addressed by those who were plainly ordering them about. It was *as if* orders were being given whose very order was to deny that they were an order. And that not even the air had heard them.[15]

The radical pitilessness of this rejection of the other, which calls to mind Levinas's discussion mentioned above concerning elemental violence, is stunning and weighs heavily in any remembrance of the Shoah. For beyond the damage inflicted in the act of physical violence, as Philip Hallie reminds us in his analysis of the Jews saved at Le Chambon, is the undermining of one's very soul, of one's animation, by the betrayal that occurs when the other gazes into one's own face, *as if* it were no face at all.[16] Pitiless cruelty undoes the soul of the victim, as well as the victimizer, in a manner that should not be ignored. Levi makes this clear when he argues in *Survival in Auschwitz*:

> In this Ka-Be, an enclosure of relative peace, we have learnt that our personality is fragile that it is in much more in danger than our life; and the old wise ones, instead of warning us "remember that you must die," would have done much better to remind us of this greater danger that threatens us.[17]

The memory of such betrayal is the greatest ill that is left in the wake of events of elemental violence. More disturbing than the undergoing of death is the suffering of de-animation, of becoming, against the very grain of one's will, one of those who were called the *Muselmann*, the "Moslem" in the degenerate argot of the death camps,[18] or what Levinas more circumspectly terms the "servile soul."[19] It is not surprising that some of those who survived the Shoah and then dedicated their lives to writing about it and its attack upon the human face have committed suicide or wrestled with severe mental illness or both—the names of Primo Levi, Paul Celan, Nelly Sachs, and Taduesz Borowski come to mind.

The toxicity of such remembrances for the generations who follow should not be underestimated. Levinas himself speaks of them as a "tumor in memory" and "a gaping pit" that "nothing has been able to fill, or even cover over."[20] Not even the justice of Nuremburg, or the restoration of a Jewish state in Israel can sufficiently address the loss this memory entails. In regard to the power of such memories to demoralize humanity, Levinas asks,

> Should we insist on bringing into this vertigo a portion of humanity whose memory is not sick from its own memories? And what of our children, who were born after the Liberation, and who already belong to that group? Will they be able to understand that feeling of chaos and emptiness?[21]

Those who would institutionalize such memories, Levinas warns, face a double bind: on the one hand, these memories can undermine the very will to live; on the other hand, those who live without these memories unwittingly participate in the perpetrator's injustice. In our forgetfulness of the Nameless, the persecuted are left faceless, *as if this had meant nothing at all*. Further, without being submitted to the memory of the persecuted with all its abjection, succeeding generations become inattentive of and inured to the very extremity of violence that is part and parcel of their historical situation. The memory of the Shoah, as the memory of other moments of elemental violence, is chastising—it reminds us that what is at issue within history is disrupted in a manner that justice itself cannot directly articulate. Beyond the logical confines of war, of pursuing destructive means for reasonable ends, lies the disaster of pitiless aggression, of a violence that is gratuitous and without precedent. How are we to live with its memory?

Otherwise than Being: A Strategy of Remembrance

As Elizabeth Weber, among others, has suggested, the philosophical writings of Levinas continually evoke the plight of those suffering in the Holocaust.[22] Levinas himself explicitly dedicated his last philosophical work, *Otherwise than Being*, to the "*memory* [italics mine] of those who were closest among the six million," as well as to the "millions on millions" of other creeds and nationalities who were and continue to be "victims of the same hatred of the other man, the same antisemitism." The central theme of *Otherwise than Being*, which treats the question of *my* responsibility to the other, even the other who would murder *me*, can be argued to have stemmed directly from its dedication. In working out this theme, many of the book's most significant terms, notably those of the face, suffering, obsession, trauma, persecution and substitution find their sense through an analysis of paradigmatic scenes that each in turn recall the victims' being submitted to the violence of the Nazi interregnum.

To speak of this philosophical work as a remembrance of the Shoah may at first glance seem odd. For nowhere in the text of *Otherwise than Being* does Levinas directly give a factual or historiographical account of what occurred. As could be expected in a work of philosophy, his reference to the suffering undergone in the death camps, as well as in day to day life under National Socialism, is so circumspect that one might even be tempted to accuse him of having avoided memory rather than cultivated it. But in Levinas's defense, as well as in the defense of the poet most honored by Levinas, Paul Celan,[23] it can be argued that the responsible memory of radical suffering, of elemental violence, calls for reticence and discretion. Philosophy, or at least the sort of philosophy Levinas would write, it turns out, may provide an important mode of discourse for memory requiring these traits.[24] The danger of any remembrance of the other's suffering is that one might facilely appropriate it, making of it a fetish propping up one's own desires and projects, protecting one from, rather than exposing one to, the anguish that lies in the other's face. In its more normal and confident mode, as Levinas points out in *Totality and Infinity*, memory "assumes the passivity of the past and masters it."[25] Memory is capable of recapturing and reversing and suspending what is already accomplished—memory provides the ability of humans to put what seems doomed to be into question after all. But in being directed to the suffering of the other, memory now finds itself without its normal resources, without the confidence of its own assumption of time but attentive to a time that could never have been its own—the immemorial discussed above as it is revealed in the face of the other.

Attentive to the suffering of the victims of the Shoah, Levinas can be said to engage in a strategy of remembrance in *Otherwise than Being* possessing at least the following elements:

1. The memory of the Shoah should emphasize not the unprecedented nature of the evil it involved (although this is not to be denied) but the unprecedented nature of the good it calls for.

2. The memory of the Shoah is in the first instance a witness, which is to say a suffering of memory for the sake of the other.

3. Theodicy that would justify the suffering of the afflicted is a blasphemy against the human.

4. Any political articulation of memory is always already under the burden of a prior commitment to goodness, to the fundamental inability to escape the face-to-face relationship in all human affairs.

In order to better understand how Levinas's work functions as an act of memory, these points will be treated in turn.

Accounting for Goodness

As Levinas puts it, "when the perishability of so many values is revealed, all human dignity consists in believing in their return."[26] Precisely the danger inherent in the memory of violence, as Levinas explains in his Preface to *Totality and Infinity*, is that it tempts one to believe one has been "duped" by the very notion of morality.[27] Yet in his memory of the Shoah Levinas is most moved by how human beings remained who did not succumb to "the virile virtues of death and desperate murder"[28] but continued to insist they were responsible *no matter what the consequences*. In their actions is revealed for Levinas a responsibility without precedence, a concern for others that is gratuitous and beyond any reasonable justification. In his argument, Levinas strives to make room within Western thought for the expression and memory of such moments of unequivocal responsibility. In doing so, Levinas insistently questions a tradition of virile virtues, and by implication, of a virile justice that remains inextricably linked with the world defined as *polemos*, of force contending with force.

In response to those who ask for some explanation of how people become murderous,[29] Levinas replies that this transformation is far more understandable than the one in which human-beings are inspired by the other's face to nonviolence even as they are tempted to violence, to a peace that is not equanimity but a cellular irritability for the sake of the other. The murderer accomplishes his or her deed within a working notion of empirical, measurable force. For her or him, history is reduced to an arena of competition between various powers, whose meaning lies in winning that competition. But those who refuse murder can only do so by moving beyond the inflicting of force in return for force to acknowledging that, in the first instance, they are called to an irenic order in which they are responsible for all others, regardless of how the other comports her or himself. Not competition but responsibility most truly denotes what is decisive about being human. But humans must assume this responsibility, Levinas points out, in spite of the fact that in Auschwitz "God let the Nazis do what they wanted."[30]

At the core of Levinas's response to evil is an insistence not only upon the justice of goodness but also and in the first instance upon its gratuitousness, its transcendence of any reason that might be articulated for its having been given as the good. Responsibility for the other cannot be justified, *as if* I had the leisure to determine whether the other requires my attention, but is always already assumed. Responsibility would have no moral urgency, if it were merely the outcome of a rational deduction. Two important corollaries follow from this characterization of the good: First, that one is called to suffer "uselessly," which is to say, without recourse to some rational scheme that justifies suffering, that gives me the reason why I and others must suffer; and Second, that any political question that might arise concerning how the Shoah, the Nameless, the Six Million, the *Haftling* might be justly remembered can only be posed in the aftermath of a confrontation with one's singular responsibility to the other. Politics cannot take the place of ethics. One must remember that at the core of one's justice lies a resistance to injustice "having no other source but one's own certainty and inner self."[31]

Memory as Witness

Levinas's very approach of the other hints at a memory of the other, as discussed above, which begins with one's responsibility to the immemoriality of the other's face, the other's suffering. The truth elicited by the other's proximity cannot be met, in the first instance, by pointing out the other's qualities or substance or being, *as if* he or she were a merely a node of reality to be indicated, but by a radically subjective undergoing of one's exposure to the other to whom one responds. Echoing a core sense of the Hebrew *emet*, my saying of the truth must be *true* to the others I address—truth without the ethical relation is emptied of its animation, its honesty, its *sincerity*. Thus, truth requires in the first instance my *saying* to the other's face that I am sincere about what will be *said*. Levinas speaks of this saying as occurring before even a word could have been uttered, in the very sign of recognition that announces itself in the Hebrew *hineni*, "here I am—for you."[32] Put in other terms, I can only speak the truth if I become a witness to it. In Levinas's words

> The witness is not reducible to the relationship that leads from an index to the indicated...It [witness] is the bottomless passivity of responsibility and thus sincerity. It is the meaning of language, before language scatters into words, into themes equal to the words and dissimulating in the said the openness of the saying exposed like a bleeding wound.[33]

Truth can only be witnessed in sincerity, in an exposure of myself before the other to the point that I must expose even that exposure. Truth does not allow me the time to justify where I stand in regard to it but finds me already responsible to announce it to the other *and to continually be questioned by whether that announcement has been vigilant enough concerning its own self-imposed blindness, its own propensity to forget the face of the other in one surreptitious manner or another.*

It would seem then that the first responsibility of one who would remember the Nameless is not to point out where or how they suffered, to indicate their suffering *as if* it were a cipher to be named, but to be unconditionally disposed to rendering attentively one's account of this suffering to the very face undergoing it. As I have argued in *Suffering Witness*, the tone of one's witness, of how one's saying registers the proximity of her or him for whom one bears witness, is extraordinarily important.[34] But when those who would give witness are called to a face whose suffering has been undergone in the very act of its being rendered faceless by the perpetrators of the Shoah, the witness has a very difficult, exacting task to fulfill—in what tone should this witness be given? In shame for the face's degradation, or in awe of its transcendence?

One might say that finding the proper tone is impossible. Here the ambivalence referred to above in Levinas's very naming of the Nameless as such disorients the attempt to remember the Nameless. For the very face of the Nameless turns out to be the collapse of the face, a suffering of the blow of the persecutor to the point of becoming the servile soul, of dust and ashes rising up from the crematoria, of the hollow in time left by generations who will never have been born. What should be not forgotten in the suffering of the other is that there is no triumphant glory or dignity in that suffering that would somehow allow the witness to trivialize or turn away from the unrelenting passivity, the unrelievable impoverishment of suffering. Degradation of the other, particularly when it is not attended to as degradation, becomes scandalous.

In *Otherwise than Being*, Levinas's response to this ambivalence is to focus the very account of what it means to be a self—to be *my*self—on the moment of my being rendered faceless by the other who attacks me with pitiless aggression, the scene of what Levinas terms "persecution." In this pivotal analysis, Levinas strays as close to a deictic moment of memory as he allows himself, at least in his philosophical writings.[35] Levinas constructs the scene in a manner that inverts his widely discussed account of the face-to-face relationship in *Totality and Infinity*.[36] There the face of the other, who is vulnerable to my power and yet whose vulnerability precisely resists my power in a manner that transcends any force I might use against her or him, both tempts me to and yet prohibits me from murdering the other. It is, in that particular scene, *as if* I had been placed in the position of the Nazis manning the death camps. But in *Otherwise than Being*, the face of the other is now revealed in the opposite position as the one who would persecute me, *as if* I were before the Nazi guards and other camp personnel who would render me faceless, who would strike me down to the point that it would de-animate my soul.

Levinas's analysis of this scene finds that my very undergoing of the other's blow resists the other's violence by calling attention to how that violence leaves not only my face but also the face of the other in disarray, consumed in violence, suffering beyond any possibility of relief. In this witness, the other is revealed as a perpetrator, as one who would de-animate others. But this revelation does not occur by any action on my part, such that I would point to the other's face in order to indicate to her or him, for instance, that it has become a pitiless mask. In fact, such an action would only return force for force. My pointing at the persecutor's face in this tone would only serve to render her or him as a cipher, a thing to be gawked at and mocked. But in undergoing the other's blow, in facing the other even as her or his blow leaves me suffering and in shame, I reveal for the other how what he or she would pretend is *pitiless* is in fact *pitiful*. In Levinas's words: "The face of the neighbor in its persecuting hatred can by this very malice obsess as something pitiful."[37]

For Levinas, pity does not imply condescension but compassion, a taking of responsibility for the irresponsibility of the other. In becoming pitiful, the face of the perpetrator no longer motivates me to outrage, to a returning of violence with violence, but opens up what Levinas terms "expiation." Yet, this move from outrage to expiation, from violence to peace, should not be interpreted as making of suffering "some kind of magical redemptive virtue."[38] My suffering does not cease in its revelation of my responsibility for the other's responsibility but is magnified in a manner that animates even as it burdens me. As Levinas puts it in another essay: "The condition of being the victim in a world of disorder, which is to say, in a world where the good does not triumph, is suffering."[39] I am revealed in this moment of suffering for the other not as "a constituted, willful, imperious subject"[40] but as one who is impoverished and humbled. But I am also revealed as one who is called without reserve to the work of establishing justice upon the face of the earth, of sustaining a human order in which "pity, compassion, pardon and proximity"[41] can find themselves at home. While I may not be captivated by a notion of goodness that triumphs, I am even more dedicated for that very reason to sustaining goodness in my treatment of others, to opening up the possibility of justice in spite of how Auschwitz cannot be undone.

Useless Suffering

To find oneself living in a world in which good is not triumphant is to find oneself tempted rather than consoled by theodicy. In theodicy, those who would witness the suffering of others, particularly those submitted to elemental violence would provide some consolation for those who have suffered. But such consolation, Levinas warns, is always bought at the price of my indicating to the other how "good" it was that he or she suffered. In this strategy, rendering the other faceless becomes somehow part of G-d's plan, of the scheme of the good, and so of my treatment of the other. To define goodness in this way no longer honors its height, its allergy to all moments of de-animation, to all acts that render humans as faceless and consume them "as if they were bread."[42] Suffering in the face of the other reveals theodicy to be a blasphemy against the human. Paradoxically to deny that good is triumphant in history is to argue for a goodness that is unprecedented in its scope, that is gratuitous, that is transcendent. Goodness is not the opposite of evil, is not at war with evil, but prior to it absolutely.

But to live in a world where goodness is without precedence also demands, as I have argued in *Suffering Witness*, that we live in quandary.[43] For our witness of those who have been submitted to consuming violence must suffer how their suffering cannot be undone, even if in goodness we would do whatever we might to be addressed by that suffering. No matter how much we witness the suffering of the other, that witness is not enough. And yet witness continues to be an urgent responsibility, *in spite of its failure*. And in giving witness to the insufficiency of our witness, we acknowledge how the unjustifiable has occurred and how we continue to offer ourselves as "an imprudent exposure to the other."[44]

Justice and the Memory of the Nameless

But even if theodicy is morally repugnant, the struggle for a justice that would console the afflicted and call the perpetrator to account remains a reality for he or she who is elected to infinite responsibility within the conditions of the finite, mundane, historical world. Precisely because goodness is not triumphant in history but remains gratuitous and without precedent, it depends upon human communities called to unrelenting yet animating responsibility for the other to envision and carry out the social and political meaning of this call. The call to singular responsibility now finds the "I" of Levinas's text before a multiplicity of faces. One must respond not only to *the* other but also to *all the other* others.

For Levinas, this movement from duality to plurality, or what he terms the "third," is synonymous with the movement from ethics to politics. In the political realm, one is called upon to address all the other others in order to makes sense of how one might most fairly work out one's responsibility to the particular other. In becoming attentive to the various and competing claims to one's responsibility, one is brought to the question of how one is to be just. But the posing of this question is never relieved from the insistent and unlimited election to responsibility for *the* singular other that characterizes the ethical relation. Justice cannot replace ethics but remains in an ambivalent and tense relationship with it. In Levinas's words,

> Justice is impossible without the one that renders it finding himself in proximity [to the other's face]. His function is not limited to the "function of judgment," the subsuming of particular cases under a general rule. The judge is not outside the conflict, but the law is in the midst of proximity...This means nothing is outside the control of the one for the other.[45]

In the movement from ethics to justice, those issues raised in the early part of this essay concerning the adjudication of guilt, the punishment of perpetrators, the imposing of reparations, and the restoration of victims to their full participation in the political and social order after times of elemental violence, now become preeminent. But for Levinas, as for Bhargava, the restoration of principled justice (of a justice that subsumes particular cases under a general rule) is itself always put into question by the overwhelming necessity that it occur in a social order in which attending to the other's voice is a preeminent part of the ongoing practice of that justice. For this reason, both thinkers in their own way envision a justice that is hyper-aware of the very manner in which language itself structures our social and political identities and commitments.

For what the victim, as well as the victimizer, confronts in a return to a world in which justice finally is have its say, is that the very language in which justice's saying must be said is still under occupation by the tones of address, by the manners of approaching others—whether they be individuals or groups—that characterize elemental violence. The words inflaming hatred and imposing de-animation of the other, still circulate, still distort the manner in which persons take part in justice, no matter how principled it may strive to be. Those who survive their persecution need more than to witness the punishment of their perpetrators, or to be granted privileges or money by way of reparation. They also need to hear how the language that is spoken in the social order in which they participate now suffers to carry the tones of their speech as well.[46] For in opening up language to the voice of the victim, the victim is restored to a responsibility for how the social order as a community articulates truth and searches for the best response to it.

In the case of the Shoah, of the Nameless, the struggle to render justice demands that its subjects in some measure move from the traumatic memory of the immemorial found in writings of witnesses such as Primo Levi's *Survival in Auschwitz* to some form of more objective and indexical memory, such as that developed in Lucy Dawidowic's historiographical work, *The War Against the Jews*.[47] Most of the human community who now stands ready to witness those who suffered in the Shoah, including the author of this essay, can only do so through the mediation of written or oral accounts from those who were there, or from those who would research and interpret the actions and documents left behind by those who were there. In passing on one's witness to the other others, the call to *point out* the other's situation, to tell the truth about perpetrators and victims in a manner that not only suffers the other's face but also indexes it, becomes inescapable.

Further, this indexing must take place within language of some sort. In the transmission of the other's face as it was revealed within the confines of the death camps, the immediacy of the impact of that face upon one's witness must now find a way to be said within the welter of intentions and tones that characterize language as a social, historical and political phenomenon. In responding to the call to point out injustice, to remember in empirical terms what occurred to the Nameless, one is also called to become attentive to the manner in which the very language one would use to characterize the suffering of the other is itself at times at issue. For, in spite of our best efforts, language remains under the thrall of anti-Semitism, of the hatred of the other human, of a violence that would render faceless the other's face.

In *Suffering Witness*, I raised briefly the specter of one such occupation of language by the persecutor, when I pointed out how the poetry of Paul Celan brings into question a Christian tone in regard to Jews, which peals throughout European languages and literatures and which continues to have its dehumanizing effect, even after the ending of the overt persecution of the Shoah.[48] For this very reason, religious institutions such as the Catholic Church have undergone a sea change in their thinking about Judaism and have begun a very laudable although wrenching process of becoming aware of the innumerable ways in which the Christian characterizations of Judaism throughout centuries of preaching and writing has contributed to outbreaks of persecution. Although controversial for some Christian scholars and believers, James Carroll's deeply troubled and troubling consideration of how Christianity developed the notion of the Crusade and how this notion contributed to centuries of violence against the non-Christian other provides a praiseworthy example of how the search for justice must go beyond the mere question of punishing guilty parties and providing reparations for the aggrieved.[49] We must learn to attend to the very words in which we speak our judgments, since these words and their tones become the building blocks for the construction of our own identities, of our own mode of articulating our singular responsibility for all else that exists.

Levinas, in *Otherwise than Being,* often supplements the philosophical point he is making by the use of a particular term, allusion or metaphor taken from the Biblical and, in particular, the Jewish tradition. This gesture, in addition to hinting at uniquely Jewish resonances in the naming of the Nameless, also tacitly questions the continuing dominance of Christian tones and themes within the language of thought, often to the exclusion of other voices. One example of this implied critique is found in the analysis referred to above of persecution. The theme of that discussion and the conclusion to which it leads could perhaps be said, at least at first glance, to have a particularly Christian "ring" to it. Levinas's use, for instance, of how the victim's being struck by the perpetrator's blow resists the violence of the blow and the outrage it inspires, could remind one of Christ's own dictum that one should turn the other cheek, when the first is struck.

But Levinas both anticipates and detours this expectation of the Christian reader by citing not the Christian Gospels but the Hebrew Lamentations in his construction of the scene : "To tend the cheek to the smiter and to be filled with shame."[50] And, in quoting Lamentations, Levinas goes on to emphasize (by means of a parenthetical statement) that, in his analysis of being attacked by the persecutor, not "the exposure of the other cheek" to the persecutor's second blow but one's already suffering the first blow is sufficient to offer expiation, to move from violence to peace, from murderous virtue to irenic submission to the other. Levinas further complicates his implied reference to Christianity by concluding his sentence, as noted above, with a rejection of suffering as "some kind of magical redemptive virtue."

In his manner of phrasing the argument, Levinas does not exclude the possibility of still reading his text in a Christian tone of voice. Levinas himself points to the work of Jean Luc Marion, as well as Philip Nemo, as exemplifying Christian readings of responsibility and suffering that would fit well with what Levinas's own work argues.[51] And the fact that Levinas has inspired a significant following of Christian philosophers and religious thinkers throughout the world testifies to his efficacy as a philosopher who speaks across confessional differences to a universal audience. But Levinas also constructs his text in a manner that continually puts into question the troubling presupposition that Christianity and not Judaism, or any other tradition beside Christianity for that matter, articulates the preeminent account to the full structure of the soul's interior life, of living a life that is inspired by G-d's (or should one write "Christ's" here?) saving presence and (as often alleged by Christian apologists starting with Paul) not simply submitted to the letter of G-d's transcendent Law.[52]

Like Hermann Cohen before him, who authored a defense of Judaism as preeminently a religion of interiority, when pressed by German Christians to justify his adherence to Judaism or to admit the insufficiency of his religion and convert to theirs,[53] Levinas implies in his very manner of citation that, even if Christianity has its own manner of opening up the interior dimensions of the human soul, Judaism too is a religion of interiority. Levinas, in speaking more directly of how the memory of Shoah provokes Judaism into rethinking its significance, says the following:

> We must—reviving the memory of those who, non-Jews and Jews, without even knowing or seeing one another, found a way to behave amidst total chaos as if the world had not fallen apart—remembering the resistance of the maquis, that is, precisely, a resistance having no other source but one's own certainty and inner self; we must, through such memories, open up a new access to Jewish texts and give new priority to the inner life. The *inner life*: one is almost ashamed to pronounce this pathetic expression in the face of so many realisms and objectivisms.[54]

Both Christian and Jewish thinkers have remarked upon the need for Christianity, particularly after the violence unleashed in the Shoah, to relent in its insistence upon reading Judaism, *as if* its every word were nothing other than a preparation for a revelation that Christianity embodies and that Judaism remains sadly incapable of acknowledging. Levinas, even as he seeks to make an argument that does not require belief in his particular religious affiliation on the part of his reader, still frames that argument in a manner that calls Christian readers to reconsider their presupposition that Judaism remains ignorant of the final truth concerning the expiation of human evil, the meaning of the soul's struggle for redemption and reconciliation.

Justice and the Politics of Memory

In this manner, the very phrasing of Levinas's text becomes a mode of justice, although one not so much caught up in the articulation of the particular principles by which to judge human misdeeds as worried about how the impact of the other's face might find its way into both the interpretation and the application of those principles. In his articulation of a Jewish tone within his philosophical, as well as confessional work, Levinas makes room for his reader not only to remember but also to acknowledge the voices of the six million who succumbed to the Shoah, those among all the other others for whom his writing must inevitably offer its witness. And for this to occur, the impact of these other faces upon language itself, including the language of philosophy, as well as the stories we tell about our past, must be felt. Levinas's philosophical and confessional writing provide one approach, one philosopher's and talmudist's voice, in response to this work of justice.[55]

For Levinas, justice, if it is to be just, must become painfully aware of how its thematization of the unthematizable, its "comparison of incomparables," its pointing out the plight of the other's face to all the other faces, calls for "an incessant correction" of precisely how it has come to terms with the other's face.[56] Ultimately, justice calls upon philosophy, as a part of its discourse, "to conceive ambivalence, to conceive it in several times."[57] Philosophy, as it is practiced in a work such as *Otherwise than Being*, would offer counsel to those who would be just on how to hear in the accounts that become the text of justice how the unjustified still rings out within them, of how claims made in one voice might become problematic in another, of how suffering undergone is not a problem to be resolved but an enigma to be returned to incessantly, in cellular irritability, in nonindifference to the other, even if also in a critique given in disinterest, without regard for one's own advantage.[58] It is to have written one's history and one's justice in the tone of compassion, what Levinas would term "the wisdom of love at the service of love."[59]

In speaking of a discourse that becomes aware of times that cannot simply be reduced to one another, of voices that cannot simply be rendered in the same idiom, Levinas offers an implicit defense of the telling of the victim's and perpetrator's stories cultivated by the truth commissions springing up across the world's political landscape in response to all too many moments of elemental violence, of unconstrained indecency. In these acts of witness, as Bhargava, Minow, and others have argued, justice is moved beyond notions of punishment and reparation (which are not given up but tempered[60]) to one of restoration.

What exactly is being restored remains an important issue in the elaboration of this concept. As Minow concludes in her description of that process:

> The asking and the telling [which occur as truth commissions elicit the testimony of victims and perpetrators] unwind something more than complicity; a complicated process of identification and implication in the past must be confronted as part of the building a new relationship between all citizens and the state.[61]

Restoration involves more than simply getting all parties to agree in principle that the principles of justice matter; it also asks that members of a society *ac-*

knowledge[62] how the construction of a political memory responding to past injustices requires undergoing the impact of other voices, of other times, in a matter that fundamentally touches one's own outlook upon the world. One might say that what is restored here is the sociality of discourse, discourse in which each voice resonates with the voices of all the others with whom it shares its polity and so its political responsibility. In Levinasian terms, I am restored to a discourse in which the face of the other is already implicit in whatever I say. Phrasing it in this manner envisions restoration more asymmetrically than what is perhaps argued for by Bhargava or Minow: for Levinas, not just the interest of *all* persons but those of the *other* person must become my preoccupation, if justice is to become vigilant enough and wise enough to structure a society of peace.

   To ask the victim, *as well as the perpetrator,* to speak his or her story within a forum designed to listen attentively and responsibly to it, resists the dehumanization of all citizens that is at the core of violent regimes. It does so not only by restoring autonomy to former victims *but also their responsibility to all the other victims, as well as the perpetrators*. While Minow argues that the therapeutic outcome of letting victims speak, of bringing their memory back into the political discourse of the state, is of inestimable value,[63] Gutmann and Thompson point out there is strong empirical evidence that offering witness may not relieve the victim's trauma but actually leave her or him more burdened by it.[64] Here Levinas would intervene to remind us that the therapeutic effects of giving one's witness may not be as important to the witness as a renewed affirmation of how the suffering of the other's blows leaves the witness responsible—both to the perpetrator and to all the others with whom that perpetrator must now share a political order. As I have argued in another paper recently, truth commissions should not only hear the truth but also suffer it; to tell or hear the memory of wrongs suffered is not the relieving of a burden but the assumption of responsibility.[65] As George Kunz has argued, the integrity of one's psyche may have less to do with the restoration of power over its circumstances and more to do with the assumption of responsibility for the other's vulnerability than our current paradigms of mental health convey.[66]

   Ultimately, if there is to be peace, the political memory of violence must move beyond merely expressing an outrage for wrongs suffered. Yet, in being so called, those who would be just cannot forget these wrongs but must be ever attentive to how the memory of them can devolve into yet again rendering the other faceless: on the one hand, by instituting a justice in which I remain at war with the unjust, *as if* their wrong could be utterly wiped out; on the other hand, by instituting a memory in which the cries of the victims are yet again extinguished, *as if* their suffering could somehow be mastered. In this impossible tension, which demands a discourse of incessant correction, of a wakefulness for the sake the other's face for whose suffering I am always already responsible, justice must yet again mark out a course that leads to renewed listening to the other and to all the other others.

In the scene of persecution, Levinas names this new tone in my approach to the other as expiation. In it, justice fashions a response to violence that continues to suffer its injustice, even as it would call those who have participated in that injustice to acknowledgment of their role within it. The witness of the victim shatters the heart of the perpetrator and calls attention to those who would administer justice not only to the pitilessness of the perpetrator's face but also its pitifulness. In spite of "so many realisms and objectivisms" that blanch at the call for repentance, for an imprudent turning that leaves the soul exposing its very exposure to others, to the articulation of a responsibility that transcends political and historical terms, justice must strive yet again to make room for the *inner life*.

Notes

1. A name employed in this essay in lieu of the more widely used "Holocaust." Unlike the latter term, which implies a redemptive sacrifice, the former term, taken from the Hebrew for "total destruction" emphasizes the suffering and degradation involved in the attack of National Socialism upon Jewish culture and life.

2. See Rajeev Bhargava, "Restoring Decency to Barbaric Societies," in *Truth v. Justice: The Morality of Truth Commissions*, Robert Rotberg and Dennis Thompson, eds. (Princeton, NJ: Princeton University Press, 2000). While Bhargava employs the term "barbaric," I am more comfortable with his reference to "indecency" as descriptive of societies in which violence is practiced with impunity.

3. For Bhargava, one such procedure could be a truth commission, a body whose charge would not be to determine guilt in order to punish the guilty but simply to listen attentively to the various parties involved in a time of endemic violence, in order to determine *and acknowledge* what actually occurred.

4. Emmanuel Levinas, "Damages Due to Fire," in *Nine Talmudic Readings*, trans. Annette Aronowicz (Bloomington: Indiana University Press, 1990), p. 187.

5. For a more detailed discussion of the dynamic see James Hatley, "Beyond Outrage: The Delirium of Responsibility in Levinas's Scene of Persecution," in *Addressing Levinas*, eds. Eric Nelson and Kent Still (Evanston, IL: Northwestern University Press, forthcoming).

6. Rajeev Bhargava, "Restoring Decency to Barbaric Societies," pp. 58-60.

7. But one should also be careful of making this distinction too facilely, too absolutely. For actions on the part of the allies such as strategic bombing or the use of nuclear weapons, as well as the treatment of civilians by Russian troops during their sweep through central Europe, certainly leave in question whether indecency did not become after all symmetrical. Further, many citizens across the face of Europe who carried out or collaborated with Nazi violence remain forever uncharged and in many instances unremembered for what they did. The trials at Nuremburg could bring the worst perpetrators to justice but could hardly bring to trial, let alone imprison, entire neighborhoods and communities for their actions during the *Nazizeit*.

8. Emmanuel Levinas, "Transcendence and Evil," in *Of God who Comes to Mind*, trans. Bettina Bergo (Stanford, CA: Stanford University Press, 1998), p. 129.

9. See "Useless Suffering," in *The Provocation of Levinas*, Robert Bernasconi and David Wood, eds. (London: Routledge, 1988).

10. Emmanuel Levinas, "Nameless," in *Proper Names*, trans. Michael Smith (Stanford, CA: Stanford University Press, 1996).

11. Levinas terms this mode of being named, "election" and contrasts its pointedly to the verbalization of Being that is characteristic of the thought of Martin Heidegger. "The subject as a noun, a term, is someone...It is someone who, in the absence of anyone is called upon to be someone, and cannot slip away from this call. The subject is inseparable from this appeal or this election, which cannot be declined" (*Otherwise than Being*, p. 53). Rather than naming the other, we find ourselves named by her or him. (See also: *Otherwise than Bing*, ftn. 38, p. 190).

12. Another name Levinas gives to those who suffered in the Shoah.

13. See discussions of this point in my "Beyond Outrage: The Delirium of Responsibility in Levinas's Scene of Persecution," forthcoming in *Addressing Levinas*, Eric Nelson and Kent Still, eds. (Evanston, IL: Northwestern University Press).

14. Primo Levi, *Survival in Auschwitz*, trans. Stuart Woolf (New York: Collier Books, 1961), p. 25.

15. See the discussion of this point in James Hatley, *Suffering Witness* (Albany, NY: SUNY Press, 2000), pp. 87-95.

16. See Philip Hallie, "From Cruelty to Goodness," in *Vice and Virtue in Everyday Life: Introductory Readings in Ethics*, eds. Christina Sommers and Fred Sommers (Fort Worth, TX: Harcourt Brace College Publishers, 1997 (4th ed.)), pp. 15 ff.

17. Primo Levi, *Survival in Auschwitz*, p. 49.

18. See the glossary in Wolfgang Sofsky, *The Order of Terror: The Concentration Camp* (Princeton, NJ: Princeton University Press, 1997), p. 284. Primo Levi speaks of these figures as "the drowned" [*Survival in Auschwitz*, p. 82].

19. See his essay "Freedom and Command," in *Collected Philosophical Papers*, trans. Alphonso Lingis (Dordrecht: Martinus Nijhoff, 1987), p. 16.

20. Emmanuel Levinas, "Nameless," p. 120.

21. Emmanuel Levinas, p. 121.

22. See Elizabeth Weber, "Persecution in Levinas's *Otherwise than Being*. In *Ethics as First Philosophy*, ed. Adriaan Peperzak (New York: Routledge, 1995).

23. Levinas cites the following lines from Celan as an epigram for the chapter in *Otherwise than Being* in which the analysis of persecution discussed below is treated: "Ich bin du, wenn/ ich ich bin." ("I am you, when/ I I am").

24. While this claim remains tentative and at the margins of the discussion occurring in this paper, much more remains to be said about Levinas's own notion of what philosophy is and whether and how it might be called upon to give witness to and for others in the determination of justice.

25. Emmanuel Levinas, *Totality and Infinity*, p. 56.

26. Emmanuel Levinas, "Nameless," p. 121.

27. See Emmanuel Levinas, *Totality and Infinity*, trans. Alphonso Lingis (Pittsburgh: Duquesne University Press, 1969), p. 21. The analysis of war in this particular piece of writing is, to my mind, revised by Levinas's later remarks in "Damages Due to Fire."

28. Emmanuel Levinas, "Nameless," p. 121.

29. See "The Paradox of Morality," Interview of Emmanuel Levinas by Tamara Wright, Peter Hughes and Alison Ainley, in *The Provocation of Levinas*, eds. Robert Bernasconi and David Wood, pp. 176-77.

30. Emmanuel Levinas, "The Paradox of Morality," p. 175.

31. Emmanuel Levinas, "Nameless," pp. 121-22. One must keep in mind that what Levinas means by an "inner self" in this statement is not an autonomous self focused upon its own Being but a suffering self, a self whose interiority is articulated only through its submission to the other's exteriority, to a singular responsibility I could never have articulated alone.

32. See *Otherwise than Being*, p. 149.

33. See *Otherwise than Being*, p. 151.

34. See James Hatley, *Suffering Witness*, pp. 123-27.

35. See Emmanuel Levinas, *Otherwise than Being*, pp. 109-113.

36. See Emmanuel Levinas, *Totality and Infinity*, pp. 197-201.

37. See Emmanuel Levinas, *Otherwise than Being*, p. 111.

38. See Emmanuel Levinas, p. 111.

39. These words come from Sandor Goodhart's translation of a passage from Levinas's "To Love the Torah more than God." His discussion of this text, as well as a translation of a large portion of it, can be found in his *Sacrificing Commentary: Reading the End of Literature* (Baltimore, MD: Johns Hopkins University Press, 1996), p. 180. Goodhart's comments there do much to fill out the notion of a non-magical suffering referred to above.

40. Emmanuel Levinas, *Otherwise than Being*, p. 112.

41. Emmanuel Levinas, p. 117.

42. Psalm 14:4

43. See James Hatley, *Suffering Witness*, pp. 21-23.

44. Emmanuel Levinas, *Otherwise than Being*, p. 151.

45. Emmanuel Levinas, p. 159.

46. It should be kept in mind that the entrance of the victim's tone of speech into the discourse of justice would not, for Levinas, be heard as a moment of perverse self-actualization, *as if* one's identity were now to be established in one's victimization, one's *own* being wronged. In justice, the victim is called upon to be a witness, to giving his or her response to and for the face of the perpetrator, as well as the faces of fellow victims..

47. Lucy Dawidowicz, *The War Against the Jews* (Toronto: Bantam Books, 1976).

48. See James Hatley, *Suffering Witness*, pp. 178-91.

49. See James Carroll, *Constantine's Sword: The Church and the Jews* (New York: Houghton Mifflin, 2001).

50. Lamentations, 3:30.

51. See for example, Levinas's remarks in "Transcendence and Evil," p. 133.

52. See also Emil Fackenheim, *The Jewish Bible after the Holocaust* (Bloomington: Indiana University Press, 1990), in which he discusses Jewish and Christian approaches to reading

and understanding the Hebrew Bible and how, after the disaster of the Holocaust, Christians are called to a renewed appreciation of the efficacy of Jewish insights about Holy Scripture and its significance for Christians. In this regard, the testimony found in the book's appendix of Astrid Fiehland, a Christian minister, is particularly welcomed: "The intensive study of Jewish sources has sharpened our insight into how shallow and often enough negative our textbooks and even more recent theological literature, are among us on 'Jews', or 'Pharisees'...It is a serious and necessary step to listen to how Jews themselves understand their faith and their religious traditions" (p. 105).

53. See Michael Zank, *The Idea of Atonement in the Philosophy of Hermann Cohen* (Providence, RI: Brown Judaic Studies, no. 324, 2000), especially 3.4 *T'shuva* as the Center of Gravity of Jewish Thought, especially p. 150.

54. Emmanuel Levinas, "Nameless," pp. 121-22.

55. In a similar vein, Saul Friedlander charges historians to cultivate a writing that is not only indexical in nature but also attentive to how the individual voices of victims (and, I would add, perpetrators) alter accounts of the Nazi epoch, whether they be of the every day life of the death camps, or of political views of the "normal" citizen in the street, or of troop movements on the Russian front. In Friedlander's words:

> The reintroduction of individual memory into the overall representation of the epoch implies the use of the contemporaries' direct or indirect expressions of their experience. Working through means confronting the individual voice in a field dominated by political decisions and administrative decrees which neutralize the concreteness of despair and death.[Saul Friedlander, *Memory, History and the Extermination of the Jews of Europe* (Bloomington: Indiana University Press, 1993), p.132]

> This mode of doing history, in which facts are to be assiduously ascertained but must then be given their weight in regard to how they resonate in the voices of those who have suffered history, he terms "commentary."

56. Emmanuel Levinas, *Otherwise than Being*, p. 158.

57. Emmanuel Levinas, p. 162.

58. For Levinas, "disinterestedness" would imply the priority of the other's suffering to my intentions about her or him. My interests do not matter here, because before they could have been formed, I was already responsible for the other. The self, for Levinas is not in the first instance sovereign or autonomous but a having-been-subjected, a for-the-other. "Non-indifference," on the other hand, would signify how the priority of the other's suffering to my intentions about that suffering leaves me already burdened with the other's suffering. I could not have ever not cared about whether the other suffers, of how he or she is vulnerable.

59. Emmanuel, Levinas, *Otherwise than Being*, p.162.

60. For instance, Martha Minow argues that reparations remain a limited response to injustice, insofar as they "elevate things over persons, commodities over lives, money over dignity" Martha Minow, *Between Vengeance and Forgiveness: Facing History after Genocide and Mass Violence* (Boston: Beacon Press, 1998), p. 131.

61. Martha Minow, p. 131.

62. See Bhargava's discussion of this term in "Restoring Decency to Barbaric Societies," pp. 54-58.

63. Martha Minow, pp. 118-122.

64. See Amy Gutmann and Dennis Thompson, "The Moral Foundations of Truth Commissions," in *Truth v. Justice*, eds. Rotberg and Thompson, p. 30: "Officials for the Trauma

Center for Victims of Violence and Torture, a nongovernmental group that provides services in the Cape Town area, reported 50 to 60 percent of the victims they had seen suffered serious difficulties after giving testimony" [Cited from Suzanne Daley, "In Apartheid Inquiry, Agony is Relived but Not Put to Rest," *New York Times*, 17 July 1997, A10].

65. James Hatley, "The Malignancy of Evil: Witnessing Violence beyond Justice." In *Studies in Practical Philosophy: Witnessing*, eds. Shannon Hoff and Kelly Oliver. Forthcoming.

66. See George Kunz, *The Paradox of Power and Weakness: Levinas and an Alternative Paradigm for Psychology* (Albany, NY: SUNY Press, 1998).

Germany's Holocaust Memorial Problem– and Mine[1]

James E. Young

O nce, not so long ago, Germany had what it called a "Jewish Problem."
Then it had a paralyzing Holocaust memorial problem, a double-edged
conundrum: How would a nation of former perpetrators mourn its victims? How
would a divided nation reunite itself on the bedrock memory of its crimes? In
June 1999, after ten years of tortured debate, the German Bundestag voted to
build a national "Memorial for the Murdered Jews of Europe" on a prime, five-
acre piece of real estate between the Brandenburger Tor and Potsdamer Platz, a
stone's throw from Hitler's bunker. In their vote, the Bundestag also accepted the
design—a waving field of pillars—by American architect, Peter Eisenman, which
had been recommended by a five-member *Findungskommission*, for which I
served as spokesman.

Proposed originally by a citizens' group headed by television talk-show personality and journalist Lea Rosh and World War II historian Eberhard Jackel, the
memorial soon took on a fraught and highly politicized life of its own. Although
I had initially opposed a single, central Holocaust memorial for the ways it might
be used to compensate such irredeemable loss, or even put the past behind a
newly reunified Germany, over time I began to grow skeptical of my own skepticism. Eventually, I was invited to join the five-member *Findungskommission*
charged with choosing an appropriate design for Germany's national memorial
to Europe's murdered Jews, the only foreigner and Jew on the panel. Here I
would like to tell the story of Germany's national Holocaust memorial and my
own role in it, my evolution from a highly skeptical critic on the outside of the
process to one of the arbiters on the inside. I find that as the line between my role
as critic and arbiter began to collapse, the issues at the heart of the Germany's
memorial conundrum came into ever sharper, more painful relief.

Along with a private citizens' initiative they had organized, Leah Rosh and
Eberhard Jaeckel at first hoped to place their memorial on the Gestapo-Gelande,

a scarred wasteland and former site of the Gestapo headquarters in a no-man's land near the wall in the center of Berlin. But the "Gestapo-terrain" had long been enmeshed in a complicated debate over its own future and how to commemorate all the victims of the Gestapo in a single place.[2] With the fall of the wall in 1989, however, the project gained the backing of both the federal government and the Berlin Senate, who recognized that such a memorial might serve as a strategic counterweight to the *Neue Wache*. Shortly after, the government designated an alternative site for the memorial, also at the heart of the Nazi regime's former seat of power. Bordered on one side by the "*Todesstreifen*," or "death-strip" at the foot of the Berlin wall, and on the other by the Tiergarten, the former site of the "Ministerial Gardens" was still a no-man's land in its own right, slightly profaned by its proximity to Hitler's bunker and the Reichs Chancellery. But in its 20,000 square meters (almost five acres) at the heart of a reunified capital, it would also become one of Berlin's most sought-after pieces of real estate—and was thus regarded as a magnanimous, if monumental, gesture to the memory of Europe's murdered Jews.

In 1994, about a year after the dedication of the *Neue Wache*, a prestigious international competition was called for designs for Germany's national "Memorial to the Murdered Jews of Europe," and some 528 designs were submitted from around the world. Submissions ran the gamut of taste and aesthetic sensibilities, from the beautiful to the grotesque, from high modern to low kitsch, from the architectural to the conceptual. There was, for example, Horst Hoheisel's proposal to blow up the Brandenburger Tor, as well as Dani Caravan's proposed field of yellow flowers in the shape of a Jewish Star. Berlin artists Stih and Schnock proposed a series of bus stops whence coaches would take visitors to the sites of actual destruction throughout Berlin, Germany, and Europe. Other designs included numerous variations on gardens of stone, broken hearts, and rent Stars of David. Round, square, and triangular obelisks were proposed, as well as a gigantic empty vat (130 feet tall), an empty vessel for the blood of the murdered. One artist proposed a Ferris wheel composed of cattle cars instead of carriages, rotating between "the carnivalesque and the genocidal."[3]

The jury was composed of some fifteen members, experts and laypeople, appointed by the three sponsoring agencies now involved—the Bundestag, the Berlin Senate, and the original citizens' group. Though the deliberations had been shielded from public view, many of the jurors subsequently told of rancorous, biting debate, with little meeting of the minds. The citizens' group resented the intellectuals and experts on the jury, with what they regarded as their elitist taste for conceptual and minimalist design. "This is not a playground for artists and their self-absorbed fantasies," Leah Rosh is reported to have reminded her colleagues on the jury. Meanwhile, the intellectuals sniffed at the layjurors' middle-brow eye for kitsch and monumental figuration, their philistine emotionalism;

and the Bundestag's appointees glanced anxiously at their watches as the right political moment seemed to be ticking away.

In March 1995, organizers announced the jury's decision: first prize would be shared by two teams who had submitted similarly inspired designs—one led by Berlin artist Christine Jacob-Marks and the other by a New York artist living in Cologne, Simon Ungers. Of these two, only that proposed by Jacob-Marks would be built, however, possibly with elements incorporated from the other, and an additional eight projects would be recognized as finalists in the competition. Jacob-Marks's winning design consisted of a gargantuan, twenty-three-foot-thick concrete gravestone, in the shape of a 300-foot square, tilted at an angle running from six feet high at one end to twenty-five feet high at the other. It was to be engraved with the recoverable names of 4.5 million murdered Jews, and in the Jewish tradition of leaving small stones at a gravesite to mark the mourner's visit, it was to have some eighteen boulders from Masada in Israel scattered over its surface.

Its literal-minded and misguided symbolism seemed to have paralyzed a jury as unable to resist it as to love it. Since eighteen is the Hebrew number representing *chai*, or life, the number of stones seemed right. But according to Josephus, Masada was the last stronghold against the Romans at the end of the Jewish revolt of 66-73 C.E. and also the site of a collective suicide of Jews that prevented the Romans from taking them as slaves. A German national Holocaust memorial with Jewish self-sacrifice as part of its theme? Within hours of the winner's announcement, the monument's mixed memorial message of Jewish naming tradition and self-sacrifice generated an avalanche of artistic, intellectual, and editorial criticism decrying this "tilted gravestone" as too big, too heavy-handed, too divisive, and finally just too German. Even the leader of Germany's Jewish community, Ignatz Bubis, hated it and told Chancellor Kohl that the winning design was simply unacceptable. Kohl threw up his hands in exasperation, pronounced the design as "too big and undignified," and obligingly rescinded the government's support for the winner of the Holocaust memorial competition. Germany's "Memorial for the Murdered Jews of Europe" seemed to have been sunk by its own monumental weight—and once again, Germany was left pondering its memorial options.

Between the announcement of the winner and its subsequent rejection, the organizers showed all 528 designs in a grand memorial exhibition at Berlin's Stadtratshaus. Good, I wrote at the time. Better a thousand years of Holocaust memorial competitions and exhibitions in Germany than any single "final solution" to Germany's memorial problem. This way, I reasoned, instead of a fixed icon for Holocaust memory in Germany, the debate itself—perpetually unresolved amid ever-changing conditions—might now be enshrined. Of course, this was also a position that only an academic bystander could afford to take, someone whose primary interest lay in the perpetuating the process itself.

My Holocaust Memorial Problem

After yet another year of stormy debate over whether a new competition should be called, whether a new site should be found, or whether the winners should be invited to refine their proposals further still, the memorial's organizers once again took the high road. They called for a series of public colloquia on the memorial to be held in January, March, and April 1997, which they hoped would break the memorial deadlock and ensure that the memorial be built before the Holocaust receded further into the history of a former century. Toward this end, they invited a number of distinguished artists, historians, critics, and curators to address the most difficult issues and to suggest how the present designs might best be modified. Among those invited to speak at the last colloquium in April 1997, I was asked to explore the memorial iconography of other nations' Holocaust memorials in order to put the Germans' own process into international perspective.

The first two colloquia, in January and March 1997, roused considerable public interest on the one hand, but as the exchanges between organizers of the memorial and invited speakers grew more acrimonious, a gloomy sense of despair gradually settled over the proceedings. The organizers, led by Lea Rosh, insisted that the "five aims" of the project remain inviolable: (1) this would be a memorial only to Europe's murdered Jews; (2) ground would be broken for it on 27 January 1999, Germany's newly designated "Holocaust Remembrance Day" marked to coincide with the 1945 liberation of Auschwitz; (3) its location would be the 20,000 square meter site of the Ministers Gardens, between the Brandenburg Gate and Potsdamer Platz; (4) the nine finalists' teams from the 1995 competition would be invited to revise their designs and concepts after incorporating suggestions and criticism from the present colloquia; and (5) the winning design would be chosen from the revised designs of the original nine finalists.[4]

Not only did the designs continue to come under withering attack by the invited experts but the aims of the project itself were now called strongly into question. Among other speakers at the first colloquium, historian Jurgen Kocka suggested that while there was an obvious need for a memorial to Europe's murdered Jews, the need for a memorial to encompass the memory of the Nazis' other victims was just as clear. Other speakers, such as Michael Sturmer, then questioned the site itself, whether its gargantuan dimensions somehow invited precisely the kind of monumentality that had already been rejected. Other critics focused more narrowly on the first colloquium's theme: "Why There Should Be a Holocaust Memorial in Berlin," concluding that with the authentic sites of destruction and memory scattered throughout Berlin, there shouldn't be a central memorial at all.

These vociferous challenges to the memorial were met by a seemingly stony indifference by the speaker of the Berlin Senate, Peter Radunski, who had been appointed to convene the proceedings. Since these criticisms had no place on the agenda, he said, they need not be addressed here. Lea Rosh's response was less measured. She opened the third colloquium with a bitter attack on what she called the "leftist intellectual establishment" responsible for undermining both the process and by extension memory of Europe's murdered Jews. The aim here was how to go forward, she said, not to debate the memorial's very raison d'être, which was already established. Her angry words, in turn, merely served to antagonize the critics and harden the positions of the memorial's opponents, who included many of Germany's elite historians, writers, and cultural critics, including Reinhart Koselleck, Julius Schoeps, Salomon Korn, Stefanie Endlich, Christian Meier, and eventually Gunter Grass and Peter Schneider.

By the time I spoke at the third colloquium in mid-April, both the organizers and a large public audience at the Stadtratshaus in Berlin had grown visibly and audibly agitated by the spectacle of their tortured memorial deliberations. Over and over again, the other speakers—senators, art historians, and artists—bemoaned the abject failure of their competition. All of which was compounded by their acute embarrassment over the incivility of it all, the petty bickering, the name-calling, the quagmire of politics into which the whole process seemed to be sinking. Bad enough we murdered the Jews of Europe, one senator whispered to me, worse that we can't agree on how to commemorate them.

When my turn to speak came, I began instead by trying to reassure the audience: decorum is never a part of the memorial-building process, not even for a Holocaust memorial. "You may have failed to produce a monument," I said, "but if you count the sheer number of design-hours that 528 teams of artists and architects have already devoted to the memorial, it's clear that your process has already generated more individual memory-work than a finished monument will inspire in its first 10 years." I then proceeded to tell the stories of other, equally fraught memorial processes in Israel and the United States, the furious debate in Israel's Knesset surrounding the day of remembrance there, the memorial paralysis in New York, Los Angeles, and Washington that had eventually resulted in several competing memorials, all of them contested. I could almost hear the collective sigh of relief.

In fact, here I admitted that until that moment, I had been one of the skeptics. Rather than looking for a centralized monument, I was perfectly satisfied with the national memorial debate itself. Better, I had thought, to take all these millions of deutsch marks and use them to preserve the great variety of Holocaust memorials already dotting the German landscape. Because no single site can speak for all the victims, much less for both victims and perpetrators, the state should be reminding its citizens to visit the many and diverse memorial and pedagogical sites that already exist: from the excellent learning center at the Wannsee Conference House to the enlightened exhibitions at the Topography of Terror at the former Gestapo headquarters, both in Berlin; from the brooding and ever-evolving memorial landscape at Buchenwald to the meticulously groomed grounds and fine museum at Dachau; from the hundreds of memorial tablets throughout Germany marking the sites of deportation to the dozens of now-empty sites of former synagogues—and all the spaces for contemplation in between.

Here I also admitted that with this position, I had made many friends in Germany and was making a fine career out of skepticism. Most colleagues shared my fear that Chancellor Kohl's government wanted a "memorial to Europe's murdered Jews" as a great burial slab for the twentieth century, a hermetically sealed vault for the ghosts of Germany's past. Instead of inciting memory of murdered Jews, we suspected, it would be a place where Germans would come dutifully to *unshoulder* their memorial burden, so that they could move freely and unencumbered into the twenty-first century. A finished monument would, in effect, finish memory itself.

On the one hand, I said, we must acknowledge the public need and political necessity for a German national Holocaust memorial; at the same time, we must also recognize the difficulty of answering this need in a single space. If the aim of a national Holocaust memorial in Berlin is to draw a bottom line under this era so that a reunified Germany can move unencumbered into the future, then let us make this clear. But if the aim is to remember for perpetuity that this great nation once murdered nearly six million human beings solely for having been Jews, then this monument must also embody the intractable questions at the heart of German Holocaust memory rather than claiming to answer them. Otherwise, I feared that whatever form the monument takes near the Potsdamer Platz would not mark the memory of Europe's murdered Jews so much as bury it altogether.[5]

These were persuasive arguments against the monument, and I am still ambivalent about the role a central Holocaust monument will play in Berlin. But at the same time, I said, I have also had to recognize that this was a position of luxury that perhaps only an academic bystander could afford, someone whose primary interest was in perpetuating the process itself. As instructive as the memorial debate had been, however, it had neither warned nor chastened a new generation of xenophobic neo-Nazis—part of whose identity depends on forgetting the crimes of their forebears. And while the memorial debate has generated plenty of shame in Germans, it is largely the shame they feel for an unseemly argument—not for the mass murder once committed in their name. In good academic fashion, we had become preoccupied with the fascinating issues at the heart of the memorial process and increasingly indifferent to what was supposed to be remembered: the mass murder of Jews and the resulting void it left behind.

The self-righteous and self-congratulatory tenor of our position had also begun to make me uneasy. Our unimpeachably skeptical approach to the certainty of monuments was now beginning to sound just a little too certain of itself. My German comrades in skepticism called themselves "the secessionists," a slightly self-flattering gesture to the turn-of-the-century movement of artists, many of whom would be Jewish victims of the Nazis. What had begun as an intellectually rigorous and ethically pure interrogation of the Berlin memorial was taking on the shape of a circular, centripedally driven, self-enclosed argument. It began to look like so much hand wringing and fence sitting, even an entertaining kind of spectator sport. "But can such an imperfect process possibly result in a good memorial?" parliamentarian Peter Conradi asked me at one point. I replied with an American aphorism that was altogether unfamiliar to his German ears: "Yes," I said, "for perfect is always the enemy of good." To this day, I'm not sure he understood my point.

And here, I realized, my own personal stake in the memorial had begun to change. The day after I returned from that third colloquium in April, Berlin's minister of culture, Senator Peter Radunski, called to ask if I would join a *Findungskommission* of five members appointed to find a suitable memorial design. Who were the other four, I asked. He replied with the names of the directors of the German Historical Museum in Berlin (Christoph Stoelzl) and the Museum of Contemporary Art in Bonn (Dieter Ronte), as well as one of Germany's preeminent twentieth-century art historians (Werner Hoffmann) and one of Berlin's most widely respected and experienced arbiters of postwar architecture (Josef Paul Kleihues)—all authorities he believed to be above reproach. We would be given free rein to extend the process as we saw fit, to invite further artists, and to make an authoritative recommendation to the chancellor and the memorial's organizers. I was to be the only true expert on Holocaust memorials, he said. And, as I then realized, I would be the only foreigner and Jew.

Before answering, I had to ask myself a series of simple, but cutting questions: did I want Germany to return its capital to Berlin *without* publicly and visibly acknowledging what had happened the last time Germany was governed from Berlin? With its gargantuan, even megalomaniacal restoration plans and the flood of big-industry money pouring into the new capital in quantities beyond Albert Speer's wildest dreams, could there really be no space left for public memory of the victims of Berlin's last regime? How, indeed, could I set foot in a new German capital built on the presumption of inadvertent historical amnesia that new buildings always breed? As Adorno had corrected his well-intentioned but facile (and hackneyed) "Nach Auschwitz . . ." dictum, maybe it was also time for me to come down from my perch of holy dialectics and take a position.

But as one of the newly appointed arbiters of German Holocaust memory, I would also find myself in a strange and uncomfortable predicament. The skeptics' whispered asides echoed my own apprehensions: a mere decoration, this American Jew, a sop to authority and so-called expertise. I asked myself: was I invited as an academic authority on memorials, or as a token American and foreigner? Is it my expertise they want, or are they looking for a Jewish blessing on whatever design is finally chosen? If I can be credited for helping arbitrate official German memory, can I also be held liable for another bad design? In fact, just where is the line between my role as arbiter of German memory and my part in a fraught political process far beyond my own grasp?

So when asked to serve on this *Findungskommission* for Berlin's "memorial to the murdered Jews of Europe," I agreed but only on the condition that we write a precise conceptual plan for the memorial. Perhaps the greatest weakness in the first competition had been its hopelessly vague conceptual description of the memorial itself, leaving artists to founder in an impossible sea of formal, conceptual, and political ambiguities. In contrast, we would be clear, for example, that this memorial will not displace the nation's other memorial sites, and that a memorial to Europe's murdered Jews would not speak for the Nazis' other victims, but may, in fact, necessitate further memorials to them. Nor should this memorial hide the impossible questions driving Germany's memorial debate. It should instead reflect the terms of the debate itself, the insufficiency of memorials, the contemporary generation's skeptical view of official memory and its self-aggrandizing ways. After all, I had been arguing for years that a new generation of artists and architects in Germany—including Christian Boltanski, Norbert Radermacher, Horst Hoheisel, Micha Ulmann, Stih and Schnock, Jochen Gerz, and Daniel Libeskind—had turned their skepticism of the monumental into a radical counter-monumentality. In challenging and flouting every one of the monument's conventions, their memorials have reflected an essentially German ambivalence toward self-indictment, where the void was made palpable yet remained unredeemed. If the government insisted on a memorial in Berlin to "Europe's murdered Jews," then couldn't it too embody this same counter-monumental critique?

Rather than prescribing a form, therefore, we described a concept of memorialization that took into account: a clear definition of the Holocaust and its significance; Nazi Germany's role as perpetrator; current reunified Germany's role as rememberer; the contemporary generation's relationship to Holocaust memory; the aesthetic debate swirling around the memorial itself. Instead of providing answers, we asked questions: What are the national reasons for remembrance? Are they redemptory, part of a mourning process, pedagogical, self-aggrandizing, or inspiration against contemporary xenophobia? To what national and social ends will this memorial be built? Just how compensatory a gesture will it be? How anti-redemptory can it be? Will it be a place for Jews to mourn lost Jews, a place for Germans to mourn lost Jews, or a place for Jews to remember what Germans once did to them? These questions must be made part of the memorial process, I suggested, so let them be asked by the artists in their designs, even if they cannot finally be answered.

Here I also reminded organizers that this would not be an aesthetic debate over how to depict horror. The Holocaust, after all, was not merely the annihilation of nearly 6 million Jews, among them 1.5 million children, but also the extirpation of a thousand-year-old civilization from the heart of Europe. Any conception of the Holocaust that reduces it to the horror of destruction alone ignores the stupendous loss and void left behind. The tragedy of the Holocaust is not merely that people died so terribly but that so much was irreplaceably lost. An appropriate memorial design will acknowledge the void left behind and not concentrate on the memory of terror and destruction alone. What was lost needs to be remembered here as much as how it was lost.

In addition, I suggested that organizers must be prepared to accept the fact that this memorial was being designed in 1997, more than fifty years after the end of World War II. It will necessarily reflect the contemporary sensibility of artists, which includes much skepticism over the very appropriateness of memorials, their traditional function as redemptory sites of mourning, national instruction, and self-aggrandizement. To this end, I also asked organizers to encourage a certain humility among designers, a respect for the difficulty of such a memorial. It is not surprising that a memorial such as Jacob-Marks's was initially chosen: it represented very well a generation that felt oppressed by Holocaust memory, which would in turn oppress succeeding generations with such memory. But something subtler, more modest and succinct might suggest a balance between being oppressed by memory and inspired by it, a tension between being permanently marked by memory and disabled by it. As other nations have remembered the Holocaust according to their founding myths and ideals, their experiences as liberators, victims, or fighters, Germany will also remember according to its own complex and self-abnegating motives, whether we like them or not. Let Germany's official memorial reflect its suitably tortured relationship to the genocide of Europe's Jews, I said.

Before proceeding, we also had to address two further concerns shared both by us, as members of the *Findungskommission*, and the memorial's opponents: Should it be a contemplative site only, or pedagogically inclined, as well? By extension, would this memorial serve as a center of gravity for the dozens of memorials and pedagogical centers already located at the actual sites of destruction, or would it somehow displace them and even usurp their memorial authority? Because we did not see Holocaust memory in Germany as a zero-sum project, we concluded that there was indeed room in Berlin's new landscape for *both* commemorative spaces and pedagogically oriented memorial institutions. In fact, Berlin and its environs were already rich with excellent museums and permanent exhibitions on the Holocaust and other, more contemporary genocides—from the Wannsee Villa to the Topography of Terror, from the new Jewish Museum on Lindenstrasse and the proposed Institute for the Study of Anti-Semitism, to the critical and insightful exhibitions at Buchenwald and Sachsenhausen.

The question was never whether there would be only a memorial or a museum. But rather: in addition to these already existing pedagogical houses of memory, was there room as well for a commemorative space meant for memorial contemplation and national ceremonies? Again, we concluded that in Berlin's constellation of memorial sites, there was indeed room for a central memorial node in this landscape, one that would inspire public contemplation of the past, even as it encouraged the public to visit and learn the specifics of this past in the many other museums nearby and throughout the country.

In fact, though still suspicious of the monument as a form, I also began to see how important it would be to add a space to Germany's restored capital deliberately designed to remember the mass murder of Europe's Jews. This would not be a space for memory designed by the killers themselves, as the concentration camp sites inevitably are, but one designed specifically as a memorial site, one denoting the current generation's deliberate attempt to remember. Of course, the government must continue to support the dozens of other memorial and pedagogical sites around the country. But these are, after all, already there. To build a memorial apart from these sites of destruction, however, is not merely the passive recognition and preservation of the past. It is a deliberate act of remembrance, a strong statement that *memory must be created* for the next generation, not only preserved.

Finally, I would have to reserve the right to dissent publicly over any final design that I could not stand by. I would agree to serve on such a *Findungskommission* even as I still held strong doubts that a resolution was even possible. I would suspend judgment on whether such a resolution was desirable until the end. If in the end, we arrived at nothing we could justify to the organizers, then my early skepticism would have been justified. But if we did find something in a collaborative effort with artists and architects, it would be our responsibility to explain our choice to the public. For if we could not justify it formally, conceptually, and ethically, then how could we expect the public to accept it?[6]

The Designs

In weighing the power of concept against formal execution in a final group of designs, the members of the *Findungskommission* unanimously agreed two proposals, one by Gesine Weinmiller and the other by Peter Eisenman/Richard Serra far transcended the others in their balance of brilliant concept and powerful execution. Though equally works of terrible beauty, complexity and deep intelligence, the proposals by Weinmiller and Eisenman/Serra derived their power from very different sources. The choice here was not between measures of brilliance in these two works but between two very different orders of memorial sensibilities: Weinmiller's was the genius of quietude, understatement, and almost magical allusiveness; the collaboration of Eisenman and Serra resulted in an audacious, surprising, and dangerously imagined form. One was by a young German woman of the generation now obligated to shoulder the memory and shame of events for which she was not to blame; the other was by two well-known Americans, architect and artist, one of whose Jewish family left Germany two generations ago. Together, we felt, these two designs would offer the public, government and organizers of the memorial an actual and stark choice. Their cases were equally strong, but in the end one would have to gather the force of consensus over the other.

In Gesine Weinmiller's three-sided plaza, visitors would descend into memory and wend their way through eighteen wall-segments composed of giant sandstone blocks scattered in a seemingly random pattern in the square. The walls surrounding the area on three sides created a rising horizon as one came further into their compass, slowly blocking out the surrounding buildings and traffic noise. This space would be both part of the city and removed from it. And only gradually would the significance of these forms and spaces begin to dawn on visitors: the 18 sections of stone wall recall *life* in Hebrew gematria (*chai*); the descent into memory space countered the possible exaltation of such memory and suggested a void carved out of the earth, a wound; the stacking of large stone blocks recalled the first monument in Genesis, a *Sa'adutha* or witness-pile of stones, a memorial cairn; the rough texture and cut of the stones visually echoed the stones of the Western Wall in Jerusalem, the ruin of the Temple's destruction; their rough fit would show the seams of their construction; the pebbles on which visitors tread would slow their pace and mark their visit in sound, as well as in the visible traces their steps would leave behind.

Then there was a striking, yet altogether subtle perspectival illusion created from the vantage point in one corner above the plaza: the seemingly random arrangement of scattered wall segments would suddenly compose themselves into a Star of David, and then fall apart as one moved beyond this point. The memory of Jews murdered would be constituted momentarily in the mind's eye before decomposing again, the lost Jews of Europe reconstituted only in the memorial activity of visitors here. Built into this design was also space for historical text on the great wall at the bottom of the decline into memory. Such a text would not presume to name all the victims of the crime but would name the crime itself. Built into this space was the capacity for a record of Holocaust history and for the changing face of its memory.

In its original conception, the proposal by Peter Eisenman and Richard Serra also suggested a startling alternative to the very idea of the Holocaust memorial. Like Weinmiller's, theirs was a pointedly anti-redemptory design: it found no compensation for the Holocaust in art or architecture. In its waving field of 4,000 pillars, it at once echoed a cemetery, even as it implied that such emblems of individual mourning were inadequate to the task of remembering mass murder. Toward this end, it took the vertical forms of its pillars—sized from ground level to five meters high, spaced ninety-two cm. apart—and turned their collected mass into a horizontal plane. Rather than pretending to answer Germany's memorial problem in a single, reassuring form, this design proposed multiple, collected forms arranged so that visitors have to find their own path to the memory of Europe's murdered Jews. As such, this memorial provided not an answer to memory but an ongoing process, a continuing question without a certain solution.

Part of what Eisenman called its *Unheimlichkeit*, or uncanniness, derived precisely from the sense of danger generated in such a field, the demand that we now find our own way into and out of such memory. And because the scale of this installation would be almost irreproducible on film shot from the ground, it demanded that visitors enter the memorial space and not try to know it vicariously through their snapshots. What would be remembered here are not photographic images but the visitors' actual experiences and what they remembered *in situ*. As might have been expected in a piece partly designed by Richard Serra, this design also implied a certain physical danger in such memory, a danger meant to remain implicit but so close to being actualized in its scale and forms as to suggest something more than a mere figure of threatening memory.

Before long, public consensus (though far from unanimous) gathered around the design by Peter Eisenman and Richard Serra. It was reported that Chancellor Kohl also strongly favored the design by Eisenman and Serra and even invited the team to Bonn to hear them personally explain their proposal. During their January 1998 visit with the chancellor, Eisenman and Serra were asked to consider a handful of design changes that would make the memorial acceptable to organizers. As an architect who saw accommodation to his clients' wishes as part of his job, Eisenman agreed to adapt the design to the needs of the project. As an artist, however, Richard Serra steadfastly refused to contemplate any changes in the design whatsoever. As a result, he withdrew from the project, suggesting that once changed, the project would in effect no longer be his.

While we were sorry to see the Richard Serra withdraw from the project, we could also fully understand the artist's prerogative to resist recommended changes in what he regarded as a finished work. Here, in fact, the artist's and the architect's modes of operation may always diverge: where the architect generally sees an accommodation to the clients' requests as part of his job, the artist is more apt to see suggested changes, however slight, as a threat to his work's internal logic and integrity. This conflict, too, is normal in the course of collaborations between artists and architects.

Despite our enthusiastic recommendation of Eisenman and Serra's design, in the sheer number of its pillars and its overall scale in proportion to the allotted space, the original design left less room for visitors and commemorative activities than we had wanted. Some of us also found a potential for more than figurative danger in the memorial site: at five meters high, the tallest pillars might have hidden some visitors from view, thereby creating the sense of a labyrinthine maze, an effect desired neither by designers nor commissioners. The potential for a purely visceral experience that might occlude a more contemplative memorial visit was greater than some of us would have preferred.

Therefore, among the modifications we requested of Peter Eisenman, now acting on his own, we asked for a slight downscaling of both the size of individual pillars and their number. In June 1998, I spent a day in Peter Eisenman's New York City studio to hear his rationale and to see the changes he had made, a day before he sent his newly designed model off to Berlin for safekeeping. Shortly after, I could report to the other commissioners that our suggestions had not only been expertly incorporated into the design by Peter Eisenman, but that they worked, in unexpected ways, to strengthen the entire formalization of the concept itself. Here I also found that I had, in effect, collapsed my roles as arbiter, critic, and advocate—all toward finding the language that the chancellor himself might use in justifying his decision to a still-skeptical public.

In Eisenman's revised design, I found that he had reduced both the number of pillars (from 4,200 to about 3,000) and their height, so that they would now range from half a meter tall to about three meters or so in one section of the field. Where the "monumental" has traditionally used its size to humiliate or cow viewers into submission, this memorial in its human-proportioned forms would put people on an even footing with memory. Visitors and the role they play as they wade knee-, or chest-, or shoulder-deep into this waving field of stones will not be diminished by the monumental but will be made integral parts of the memorial itself, now invited into a memorial dialogue of equals. Visitors would not be defeated by their memorial obligation here, nor dwarfed by the memory-forms themselves, but rather enjoined by them to come face to face with memory.

Able to see over and around these pillars, visitors will have to find their way through this field of stones, on the one hand, even as they are never actually lost in or overcome by the memorial act. In effect, they will make and choose their own individual spaces for memory, even as they do so collectively. The implied sense of motion in the gently undulating field also formalizes a kind of memory that is neither frozen in time, nor static in space. The sense of such instability will help visitors resist an impulse toward closure in the memorial act and heighten one's own role in anchoring memory in oneself.

In their multiple and variegated sizes, the pillars are both individuated and collected: the very idea of "collective memory" is broken down here and replaced with the collected memories of individuals murdered, the terrible meanings of their deaths now multiplied and not merely unified. The land sways and moves beneath these pillars so that each one is some three degrees off vertical: we are not reassured by such memory, not reconciled to the mass murder of millions but now disoriented by it.

In practical terms, the removal of some 1,200 pillars out of an originally proposed 4,200 or so has dramatically opened up the plaza for public commemorative activities. It has also made room for tourist buses to discharge visitors without threatening the sanctity of the pillars on the outer edges of the field. By raising the height of the lowest pillar-tops from nearly flush with the ground to approximately a half-meter tall, the new design also ensures that visitors will not step on the pillars or walk out over the tops of pillars. Since the pillars will tilt at the same degree and angle as the roll of the ground-level topography into which the pillars are set, this too will discourage climbing or clambering over. In fact, since these pillars are neither intended nor consecrated as tombstones, there would be no actual desecration of them were someone to step or sit on one of these pillars. But in Jewish tradition, it is also important to avoid the appearance of a desecration, so the minor change in the smallest pillars was still welcome.

In their warm, sandy tone, the concrete-form pillars will reflect the colors of the sun and sky on the one hand and remain suggestive of stone, even sandstone, on the other. The concrete will not have the rough lines of their pour forms but will be smooth, close to the texture of sidewalk. They can also be impregnated with an anti-graffiti solution to make them easy to clean. Over time, it will be important to remove graffiti as it appears, in order not to allow it to accumulate. The crushed-stone ground surface is also an excellent idea, in that it inhibits running, frolicking, or lying on the ground, even as it marks the visitors' own footsteps in both sound and space.

The architect prefers that the pillars, though stone-like, remain under-determined and open to many readings: they are alternately stones, pillars, blank tablets, walls, and segments. This said, in their abstract forms, they will nevertheless accommodate the references projected onto them by visitors, the most likely being the tombstone. This is not a bad thing and suggests the need to keep these pillars blank faced. With written text, they might begin to look very much like tombstones, in fact, and so might generate a dynamic demanding some sort of formal treatment as tombstones, even symbolic ones.

For this reason, I suggested that a permanent, written historical text be inscribed on a large tablet or tablets set either into the ground or onto the ground, tilted at a readable angle, separate from the field of waving pillars. Their angled position will bring visitors into respectful, even prayerful repose as they read the text, with heads slightly bowed in memory. These could be placed at the entrance or on the sides, under the trees lining the perimeter of the field, leaving the integrity of the field itself formally intact, while still denoting exactly what is to be remembered here. Thus placed, the memorial texts will not create a sense of beginning or end of the memorial field, leaving the site open to the multiple paths visitors take in their memorial quest. This, too, will respect the architect's attempt to foster a sense of incompleteness; it will not be a memorial with a narrative beginning, middle and end built into it.

On 25 June 1999, the German Bundestag took a series of votes on the matter of the memorial. It finally passed three principal motions: (1) The Federal Republic of Germany will erect in Berlin a "memorial for the murdered Jews of Europe"; (2) The design for this memorial will be the field of pillars proposed by Peter Eisenman, to which an information center will be added; and (3) A public foundation made up of the directors of other memorial institutions, as well as representatives from the organization of Jews in Germany, will be established by the Bundestag to oversee both the building of the memorial and its information center in the year 2000.

Now that Germany's "Memorial for the Murdered Jews of Europe" has been dedicated, is this the end of Germany's Holocaust memory-work, as I had initially feared? Obviously not. Debate and controversy continue unabated. Moreover, now that the parliament has decided to give Holocaust memory a central place in Berlin, an even more difficult job awaits the organizers: Defining exactly what it is to be remembered here in Peter Eisenman's waving field of pillars. What will Germany's national Holocaust narrative be? Who will write it and to whom will it be written? The question of historical content begins at precisely the moment the question of memorial design ends. Memory, which has followed history, will now be followed by still further historical debate.

On the dedication of the memorial in January 2000, fittingly fraught as always, the debate continued. Some, like Mayor Eberhard Diepken, stayed home like a petulant child who didn't get his way; others stayed home out of the deeply felt conviction that no memorial will ever be adequate to the task. Of those who came to the dedication, most came to remember, some to mourn, and some to share in the memorial's unflattering political limelight. Had I been able, I surely would have come—both to mourn and to watch with some satisfaction as Berlin continued to wrestle with its memorial demons.

From this American Jew's perspective, this last year has been a watershed for German memory and identity. No longer paralyzed by the memory of crimes perpetrated in its name, Germany is now acting on the basis of such memory: it participated boldly in NATO's 1999 intervention against a new genocide perpetrated by Milosevic's Serbia; it has begun to change citizenship laws from blood- to residency-based; and it has dedicated a permanent place in Berlin's cityscape to commemorate what happened the last time Germany was governed from Berlin. Endless debate and memorialization are no longer mere substitutes for actions against contemporary genocide but reasons for action. This is something new, not just for Germany but for the rest of us, as well.

For whether Germans like it or not, in addition to their nation's great accomplishments over the last several centuries, they will also always be identified as that nation which launched the deadliest genocide in human history, which started a world war that eventually killed some 50 million human beings, and which used this war to screen its deliberate mass murder of some 6 million European Jews. It is not a proud memory. But neither has any other nation attempted to make such a crime perpetrated in its name part of its national identity. For this space will always remind Germany and the world at large of the self-inflicted void at the heart of German culture and consciousness—a void that at once defines national identity, even as it threatens such identity with its own implosion.

Notes

1. This is adapted from James E. Young, *At Memory's Edge: After-Images of the Holocaust in Contemporary Art and Architecture* (New Haven, CT and London: Yale University Press, 2000).

2. For more on the debate surrounding the discovery of ruins on the Gestapo-Gelande and subsequent architectural competitions to memorialize this site, see James E. Young, *The Texture of Memory* (New Haven, CT and London: Yale University Press, 1993), pp. 81-90.

3. See *Denkmal fur die ermordeten Juden Europas: Kunstlierischer Wettbewerb: Kurzdokumentation* (Berlin: Senatsverwaltung fur Bau und Wohnungswesen, 1995).

4. From Peter Radunski's "Opening Remarks" to the First Colloquium on Berlin's Memorial to the Murdered Jews of Europe, 11 January 1997.

5. For articulate arguments against the memorial, see Reinhard Kosellek, "Wer das vergessen werden? Das Holocaust-Mahnmal hierarchisiert die Opfer," *Die Zeit*, no. 13 (19 March 1998); Gyorgy Konrad, "Abschied von der Chimare: Zum Streit um das Holocaust-Denkmal," *Frankfurter Allgemeine Zeitung* (26 November 1997): 41.

6. I raised many of these same issues, in slightly different form, in James E. Young, "Gegen Sprachlosigkeit hilft kein Kreischen und Lachen: Berlins Problem mit dem Holocaust-Denkmal—und meines," *Frankfurter Allgemeine Zeitung* (2 January 1998): 28.

Killing the Indian to Save the Child: The Near-Death of Spirituality

Tim Giago (Nanwica Kciji)

" We are two distinct races and must ever remain so. There is little in common between us. ...Your religion was written on tablets of stone by the iron finger of an angry God, lest you might forget it. The red man could never remember nor comprehend it. Our religion is the traditions of our ancestors, the dreams of our old men, given them by the Great Spirit and the visions of our sachems and is written in the hearts of our people."

—Chief Seattle, Suquamish (1786-1866)

There is a portrait of Robert F. Kennedy hanging on the wall just above my computer in my basement office. It is a large, framed (2 feet by 3 feet) picture of Kennedy walking down a lonely and empty asphalt road. There are small, snowcapped mountains in the background and tufts of sagebrush in the fields near the road. Senator Kennedy has his hands pushed deep into the pockets of his slacks and his hair and necktie are blowing in a chilly breeze. He is walking on the left side of the road and in front of him, trotting along in the middle of the road, is a speckled, black-and-white cocker spaniel. Kennedy is gazing at the dog with a look of tender love on his face. There is a sort of spirituality in this black and white picture.

I bought the poster in Boston at the Kennedy Museum and had it nicely framed. It reminded me of a day thirty-five years ago when Kennedy, then a candidate for president, stopped at Holy Rosary Indian Mission, my alma mater, on his way to campaign in California. My life was pretty aimless at the time, and while bumming around the country, I had stopped to visit the graves of my grandparents and my aunt in the Mission cemetery. I sat on the graveyard hill overlooking the Mission grounds and watched as RFK walked through the throngs of Lakota people. He stopped and reached down to pick up a small Indian girl. He brushed her hair from her face, whispered something in her ear, set her back on the ground and smiled.

The absolute admiration and love given to this man by the Lakota people gathered there that blustery day is something I never forgot. At a time when we (the Lakota and other Indian people) had lost nearly everything including hope; this man brought us hope. It was a sad day on the reservation when Robert F. Kennedy was assassinated a few weeks later. As I mentioned, he cast an aura that was almost *wakan* (spiritual) as he walked the Mission grounds where I grew up.

I point this out because in Lakota the word *wakan* means many things. It means a spirituality that is either received or transmitted. *Wakan* means that which is hard to understand because it is filled with such mystery. It means that spirituality is within us, all around us, or sent to us through a vision or through the love and passion of another. These things are all a part and parcel of that great mystery we call our spirituality.

Although Robert F. Kennedy was strong in his traditional Catholic beliefs, I felt that his spirituality came from somewhere beyond the Bible and the catechism. It is not possible to pound spirituality into someone's head from a pulpit; it must be inborn.

The Lakota and the other Indian tribes of the Western Hemisphere did not have what could be called a religion. Religion is something that is organized, dogmatic, and based on the written word. The Bible and Koran, for instance, are written documents that define the parameters to which the faithful in these religions must adhere in order to be saved and served.

Instead, the Indian tribes had a spiritual connection with the earth, wind, sky, water, fire, sun, moon, birds, fish and the animals that walked upon four legs. The first white settlers looked upon this spiritual connection with all natural things and labeled it paganism or heathenism. They never saw or experienced the pure natural beauty of the Indian spiritual ways.

How could they? They brought to this continent a religion based upon superstition and fear. Theirs was a religion that divided all things into good or evil. The white settlers could have easily come from another planet when they first landed on the shores of this Continent. The things they believed were totally alien to the beliefs of the indigenous people. And the things the Indian people believed were totally alien to the first settlers.

The irony of it was that many of the early settlers, such as the Pilgrims, came to this country in search of a place they could practice their religion freely and without fear. And yet, when faced with the very different spiritual beliefs of a people who took them to heart, cared for them, and taught them how to survive in a land alien to them, they dismissed the spirituality of the Indian people as childish, undignified, and far beneath their own dogmatic beliefs.

Many of the sacred ways of the Indian are based upon interpretation. The holy men and women have the latitude to interpret dreams and actions in a sacred way. This is truly a spiritual way simply because no two holy people interpret things in the same fashion. It is spirituality with freedom and independent thought at its foundation.

Lakota men often received their adult names because of a dream or a vision while doing a *hanbleyceya* (vision quest) and having that vision or dream interpreted by a holy man or woman. They could also be named for a great deed or misdeed. Crazy Horse, Tasunka Witko, received his name after a dream he had of horses dancing wildly, horses prancing on their back hooves and covered with hair curly from perspiration. In fact, his nickname, "Curly," was not given to him because he had curly hair as many non-Indians, including the author Mari Sandoz, claim, but because it tied in with his vision of horses dancing and sweating until their hair became curly.

Crazy Horse could have just as easily been named Dancing Horses or Wild Horses. In Lakota, *witko* can be translated to mean foolish or someone who pretends to be foolish, strange or maybe a little touched. It can also refer to the fool-maker who comes to a warrior in his dreams.

A young warrior goes out with a war party and returns to camp with a string of twenty horses captured from the U.S. Cavalry. He has returned to camp with honor and in his possession are horses taken from the American enemy. He is given a name for this great deed. He is named American Horse.

These are more than just names such as John or Bill. They are manifested in a physical and spiritual connection to things that are inside of and outside of the person receiving the name.

This is why it is so difficult for an Indian elder to answer when a non-Indian asks, "How do you say 'tree' in Lakota?" The elder will have in his or her mind a tree of pine, oak, willow or another. How do you say "tree" when the word itself is so non-descriptive? A tree must be described from the width of its trunk to the color of its leaves. A tree is a picture to be painted in words.

Is it a tree that played a role in this Lakota person's life? Is it a tree that was cut down to serve as the centerpiece of the sacred Sun Dance? Is it one of the trees used as poles to support the skins that covered the home, the tipi, of this Lakota person? Or is it a tree that one sat under as a child on a torrid summer day, wrapped in the coolness of its shade while dreaming the dreams of children? The tree then becomes more than just a tree. It becomes a physical and spiritual connection.

When a Lakota person died, the body was stretched out upon a scaffold and placed high in the branches of a tree. While the spirit made the journey to that place known to the Lakota as the Spirit World, the physical being was given back to nature to those who nourished it while it was alive. The body was given back to the birds, the insects and to the four-legged animals.

This burial ritual had been a part of the Lakota spirituality for thousands of years. It was an important thread woven into the spiritual fabric of what it means to be Lakota.

Can another culture rip out this thread without doing substantial damage? This is exactly what happened.

Western man did not care to learn about or understand the spirituality of the indigenous people. If a rite or ritual was not understandable to them or if it did not fit into the concepts so carefully crafted by the ministers of his particular faith, it did not belong. Therefore it was catalogued as pagan or heathen. Heathens and pagans were mentioned in the Bible with frequency. They were always the enemy fit only to be killed or converted. Because they were held in such low esteem, there was nothing spiritually they could teach that would benefit Western man.

Religious arrogance is nothing new to this planet. As history has failed to teach, it is religious arrogance that has been the cause of wars, torture, destruction, and death. And it is religious arrogance that caused man to find genocide not only acceptable, but also necessary. After all, weren't the Jews committed to the gas chambers because they practiced a religion the Nazis found incompatible and therefore unacceptable?

When the policymakers of the U.S. government finally determined that the genocide of the American Indian was no longer acceptable, they went back to the drawing boards. There was just too much land and natural and mineral resources that spoke of untold wealth still out there for the taking, and the indigenous people still stood in the way.

What were the options open to the white man? The first was an effort to make the Indian over in his own image. In order to save the child, one had to kill the Indian first. The Spaniards had shown some signs of success in Florida, California, and the Southwest. They established missions staffed with priests and began the process of de-Indianizing the Indian.

The Spaniards started by taking away the traditional names of the individual, just as they did in South and Central America; give the natives Spanish surnames and then obliterate the native language by replacing it with Spanish.

This was more easily accomplished by creating a condition of total dependency. They took away the means the natives used to feed and clothe themselves. They forbade them to practice their traditional, spiritual beliefs, supplanting them with Catholicism. The native people inhabiting the missions and the surrounding lands became virtual slaves to a new order. Men were separated from their wives, and the children were placed under the care of the missionaries. They were shorn of hair, clothed as the white children, beaten for speaking their native tongue, and schooled to believe that their ways were the wrong ways, and the process of de-Indianizing had begun in the Western Hemisphere.

There have been several scholarly books written on the subject of the impact of the Indian missions upon the natives of California and the Southwest. *The Natives of the Golden State: The California Indians* by Rupert and Jeanette Henry Costo is one of the best.

In the appropriate places I will suggest certain books for those who would do further research into a specific subject, but for the most part, the things I write about are those things that come from within. They relate to my personal inter-pretations of life and death based upon my own experiences.

For example, when I was a child reading the primers about Dick and Jane, the pictures in the books did not register in my mind as they would in that of an average white child. I saw the vividly green grass, the deep blue water and be-cause the scenery around my native community of Pejuta Haka (Medicine Root) on the Pine Ridge Indian Reservation is graced with similar beauty, this was something to which I could relate.

But the white, picket fences and the beautiful homes in the pictures did not register. They certainly did not look like the homes on the reservation. When I looked at a magazine and saw the wonders of refrigerators, electric stoves, and all of the modern appliances of that day, these also did not register. The pictures were from Fantasy Land to me. We still had kerosene lamps to light our homes, wood-burning stoves to cook on, wells from which to draw water, and out-houses for toilets. The same can be said of the stories I read and the pictures I saw in the Holy Bible. These also did not register with me. These were stories from another planet and from another time.

Did it matter to the white man that in his efforts to save the Indian child by killing the Indian he was also destroying the spirit? What is left when the spirit dies? Very little. I grew up with it. It was all around me on the reservation and in the towns that bordered it.

Many of us grew up listening to the words of the priest or minister, pretending to understand and going along with it simply because it was expected of us. We didn't know that our holy men and women were being systematically censored, imprisoned, and prevented from maintaining the ties to the children of the tribe that were so vital to the survival of spirituality.

The Indian reservations were divided into pies. Each slice was awarded to a different religious group to build schools and churches with one purpose in mind; kill the Indian in order to save the child. Not to be left out of the final solution of the Indian people, the U.S. government built massive boarding schools designed to serve as buffers between the children and their parents and grandparents.

The boarding schools were strategically situated. Children were rounded up and delivered by wagon, horse, auto, and train. They were issued mili-tary-type clothing; their heads shaved; and they were assigned to military style dormitories. They became numbers marching in step to all school and church functions.

If you ever get the opportunity, visit the grounds of the former Indian school at Carlisle, Pennsylvania. Visit the graveyard adjacent to the school and read the names on the tombstones of the many children that never made it home. The elders and the traditional Indians say they died of heartbreak. And who is to say they did not?

Visit the school grounds at Haskell Indian College in Lawrence, Kansas., and you will see more graves of children who died far from their homes and their families.

From the late 1800s to around 1960, for nearly seventy years, this systematic cultural genocide of the youth of the American Indian tribes was the law of the land. Never before and never again has the U. S. government and the church collaborated on such a massive scale. If the culture, traditions, attire, appearance, habits, language, and, above all, the spiritual beliefs of the Indian were destroyed, a new white Indian would emerge. In a few generations, America would have succeeded in creating a new citizen who, although still different in color and looks, was white in every other respect.

Justification can be found for any action against any race. If particular ethnic group is judged to be inferior, those considering themselves superior have every right to either destroy or acculturate, by any means, this minority. This is especially true if the self-procalimed superior group has God on its side. This was the basis for the edict of Manifest Destiny. A chosen people had every right to displace, convert or destroy those standing in the path of their vision of progress. The American Indian stood in the path of this nation's destiny. The assembly line intended to de-Indianize the Indian was set in motion.

I'm not talking about the mass production of ball bearings or ballpoint pens here. I am talking about a race of people. Three generations of Indian men and women were pushed through the doors of these factories of cultural and spiritual genocide.

What about these people? What about their descendants?

The aftermath of the boarding school experiment was not of significant importance to anyone except the victim. Consequently, little was written about this terrible time in the history of the American Indian except for small books dealing with the day-to-day experiences of the children. No one believed this experiment worthy of being included among the more sorry moments in U. S. history, and what is more, no one looked at the devastation it brought to several generations of Indian people. As a matter of fact, no one really cared. No one cared except the victim, that is. And the victim had no access to express those feelings in newspapers or books. The victim was a silent victim.

What were the lingering effects of the boarding school experiment upon the Indian people?

A television crew once visited the buildings and grounds of the old Stewart Indian School in Carson City, Nevada. They weren't there because of any commitment to the Indian people. They were there to do a show called "Sightings," a show about mysterious happenings, because so many stories had been floating around for years about the spiritual phenomenon at the now-defunct Indian boarding school.

Stewart, like the BIA boarding school in Phoenix, Arizona, or Holy Rosary, Marty, Stephan and St. Francis Indian missions in South Dakota, were just a few of the schools set up to de-Indianize the children. Stewart housed children from the Paiute, Washo, Shoshone, and Ute reservations. If fences had been built around these schools, they would have resembled prisons or reform schools.

Suzi Lisa, an Apache woman who is now the director of the Stewart Indian Cultural Center, an odd transformation for a site previously used to destroy cultures, believes that in order for the wounds of the terrible past to heal, the truth about the Indian boarding schools must be told.

Looking around at the buildings at Stewart, she said, "We have to know the truth. The truth is here. It may be buried, but it's not gone. It's in the foundations of this place.

It's in every rock that these children placed in these structures and in every cottonwood tree they planted. It's in the anonymous faces in our pictures."

Most of us old timers have seen the pictures of Indian children all dressed alike posing for the camera. There is something missing in the eyes of these children. It is as if some of them are already dead. The pictures were used by the different religious groups to solicit money for these schools. If the truth was known, much of that money went to support other functions of the church. Little of it was spent on the welfare of the children. I contend that the different religious orders charged with setting up Indian missions raised millions of dollars on the backs of the poor Indian children to build magnificent cathedrals elsewhere.

They spent millions of dollars brought in by their pathetic "Save the Indian Children" ads "begging for dollars letters" to buy rich farmland and other real estate to enrich themselves and their churches.

Near every boarding school there is usually a cemetery. So many of the children ripped from the loving arms of their parents and grandparents never saw their homes again. They died of the many diseases to which they had no immunity, or they died in mysterious ways that have been buried with them. And many of the children that survived these schools died in other ways.

Some died in a drunken stupor, and others, by overdosing on drugs. Others took years to destroy their bodies by abusing them with drugs and alcohol. But, sooner or later the end came. Many, filled with a hopelessness they could never understand, died by their own hand.

The violence in many Indian families was a thing that was never a part of their traditions. It was a violence that became a part of their everyday lives at the boarding schools. They stood as silent witnesses to the physical, mental, and emotional abuses that took place within the walls of buildings standing next to churches. Their keepers sexually abused thousands of children. When abusers became suspect, they were simply transferred to other Indian boarding schools to continue their evil destruction.

Most Indian cultures consider the children to be sacred, the future of the tribe. Corporal punishment was totally unknown to these children when they first were brought to the boarding schools. The first time I witnessed a young boy being beaten with a leather strap was an extremely traumatic time for me. Many times several of us were beaten with belts for the misdeeds of one. We did not understand why we were whipped when we had done nothing wrong.

How can anyone of intelligence expect that thousands of children could be housed in human factories, abused and violated, every thought pertaining to their parents and grandparents wiped from their minds, an alien religion forced upon them in their every waking hour, told that the old ways of their people were heathenish and ignorant and not expect that at least three generations of Indian children would be scarred for life?

What could we possibly learn about being a good parent in this environment? One of the biggest problems we, as Indian adults and parents, have had to overcome is our lack of parenting skills. Who did we have to emulate? The Jesuit priests and nuns? The bureaucratic overseers of the government boarding schools?

Parenting skills are learned at home. They are handed down from one generation to the next. This is true in all cultures. A Nez Perce man, a product of the boarding schools, said to me, "When they took the children away from their grandparents, they knew they had found the best way to destroy our language and our culture."

The grandparents were the traditional teachers. It was their responsibility to impart their wisdom to the young. How much did we (Indians) lose when this greatest source of our traditions, culture, and spirituality was denied us?

The tragic results of this hideous experiment are everywhere in Indian country. Children and even grandparents are often abused. Permanent relationships between a man and woman are uncommon. Children are abandoned by wandering fathers and left to be raised by single mothers. These things were absolutely unheard of two hundred years ago.

There are those who conformed. They embraced the new religion and became quite fanatical about practicing it. Some became nuns or even priests. Others became ministers in the churches attached to the particular missions they attended. Others became white for all intents and purposes. To a degree, the boarding school experiment did pay some dividends to a government that saw it as the final solution to the Indian problem.

And then there are those of us who saw this horrible experiment for what it was a way to destroy us as a people. When we started to speak out we were labeled as radicals and heretics. It was not popular thirty years ago to rock the boat so carefully crafted by the government or the church. I suppose it is like the old days when some Indians found work, liquor and semi-happiness living next to the fort. They were called "hang-around-the-fort Indians" by those who refused to surrender.

According to the BIA records, my great-grandmother was named Winyan Wakan. This translates as Holy Woman. A tribal Lakota elder who was also a medicine man, Pete Swift Bird, now deceased, told me she was given this name because she was a spiritual woman, a holy woman who conducted ceremonies and healed the sick, physically and spiritually.

This was not a profession. It was—and is—a hereditary way of life to the Lakota. For example, Rick Two Dogs, a highly respected holy man, can trace his spiritual advisors back five hundred years. When the children were separated from the grandparents and great-grandparents, the teachers, this cycle was nearly broken. But medicine men such as Rick Two Dogs survived. Their families took their spirituality underground in order to preserve it. And as this spirituality is revived, there are dramatic changes taking place in Indian country.

One serious problem caused by the boarding school experiment has been the important years of productivity lost to so many individual men and women. All of them knew they had a problem. They just could not put a finger on it. In the years when they should have been pursuing an education, whether in a school or at the feet of an elder, they were abusing themselves with alcohol and drugs. This has taken the very good years right out of the heart of the lives of these people. Many Indians, as a result, are late starters in life.

They have had to understand and then face the reasons they turned away from their own spirituality and embraced the destructive forces of alcohol and drugs. I know of many men and women who, although frightened to death to do it, turned their backs on the Christian teachings pounded into their heads at the boarding schools. I say they did it with fear because that is the way the Christian doctrine was taught. They sought out a traditional holy man or woman. In so doing, they returned to their roots, to their Native spirituality.

The changes in these individuals, if studied by a social worker or psychologist, would be considered astounding. But to those who broke the chains of the boarding schools, returning to their culture and to their ancient spirituality was not astounding. It was just the way it was meant to be. In their minds, once they turned back to the traditions of their ancestors, everything else that was good followed.

But this quiet revolution is just beginning.

In states with large Indian populations the percentage of men and women incarcerated in the state prisons is far higher than it should be. For instance, in South Dakota, where Indians make up about 10 percent of the total state population, their percentage in prison population is closer to 33 percent.

Many of the crimes committed by Indians happen while they are under the influence of drugs or alcohol. So many of these young people are descendants of the children who were victims of the government boarding schools and Indian missions. Having witnessed and been a victim to the many abuses that were a part of that system, they have returned home to become the abusers.

When a child grows up in a home where drunkenness, domestic violence, and child abuse are everyday happenings, these things become the norm. What other life does this child know? And when that child grows up, the cycle continues. The near destruction of Indian spirituality in the parent has come back to haunt the child. You cannot take several generations of children from their parents and grandparents, abuse them mentally and physically for most of their lives and expect them to live normal lives again.

Not only have you managed to destroy the normal life that child would have lived as an Indian, you have also destroyed that child's connection to normalcy in general.

The spirituality of the old-time Indian was so great that many created the music of their own death songs. The songs were not songs of sorrow or grief. They were songs about their lives. Songs that touched on deeds they had done, where they had been and what they had seen. They were songs to help guide their children on the right path.

Many tribal people thought of their lives as moving down a path or road. There was the dark or black road that was filled with hate, fear, and things that were evil. There was the good, red road that brought happiness, caring, sharing, and love. People made choices about which path they would follow. When one came to that fork in the road, it was all of the things one had learned from the elders and holy men and women that enabled them to choose the right road.

If they did not believe in or absorb or receive the benefits of these teachings, they would often take the wrong road. It was at these crossroads that so many victims of the boarding schools made the wrong decision because they did not have the knowledge of a traditional education or the spiritual strength to choose the right road.

The invisible tie that connected them to their past and to their spirituality through their elders had been cut. They were like the salmon of the Northwest trying to swim upstream and finding that dams had been placed in their path. They either found another way, or they died. Dying was not always a physical death. They sat in bars or in alleys drinking cheap wine in search of themselves. They were forced into the cities by the relocation programs of the 1950s and ended up in the ghettos never to find their way home. They died there as strangers in their own land.

Diseases that had never been connected to their people suddenly became epidemic. They died of tuberculosis, cirrhosis, and diabetes. Some tribes saw the diabetes epidemic claim 50 percent of their people. Sanitaria were built near Indian reservations to house those afflicted with tuberculosis. Indian men and women sat at the dinner tables with their children and parents while their complexions turned a sickly yellow.

Even their own neighbors and their own people turned from them in disgust as they staggered down the streets embracing a bottle of wine wrapped in a brown paper bag. They sat in alleys and shot dope. Modern diseases passed through dirty needles found their way into their veins. They began to die of AIDS and hepatitis. Just as surely as the smallpox epidemics of the sixteenth and seventeenth centuries decimated entire villages and entire tribes, the modern diseases of drugs and alcohol were nearly as destructive.

Those living in the cities returned to the reservations to die. They brought these diseases back home. Others died in the streets of the cities and ended up in paupers' graves.

Many children afflicted with the Fetal Alcohol Syndrome were born during these days and are still being born. They are children without a conscience. They are those children who are soon to become the worst predators this world has ever known. They now live on the Indian reservations and in the ghettos of America.

When the Indian people were blocked from their connection to their past, denied access to their holy people, stripped of their identity and beaten for speaking their own language, it didn't end on the playgrounds of the boarding schools. The children became adults. They left these schools filled with hate and anger, but they had no way to channel these dangerous forces. They turned much of that hate and anger inward. They took it out on themselves. And then sadly, they took it out on the people who loved them.

I recall lying in the upper bunk in the Holy Rosary Mission dormitory during the daylight hours because I had a fever. Several older boys were also ill and had dorm privileges that day. Tim Red Wolf and Willard Cuny were talking about a murder Red Wolf had witnessed on the reservation. They also talked about a woman I knew from Kyle who had been beaten up and raped.

I was thirteen years old, and their talk was frightening because it was coming from two guys I greatly admired. In fact, Tim had been named for my father. They were talking about people I had known and about terrible things happening in the village that was my home. This was my first introduction into the harsh realities of life on the Pine Ridge Reservation.

Tim Red Wolf was a tremendous athlete. He could have gone to college on an athletic scholarship anywhere, that is if Indians had been awarded such scholarships in those days, which they were not. He was handsome and intelligent. But he never made the connection to the spiritual side of his heritage. He tried Catholicism because it was expected of him, but the last time I talked to him, I realized he was a person lost. He never found his way back to his culture, and he never made it back to his spirituality, at least not in the Indian way. One day about two years ago, he walked away from his home, and he has not been seen since. If he were still alive, he would be about 70 years old.

Tim found his escape in the bottle. I believe he discovered much too late that it wasn't an escape he had found, but a prison. The bottle became his jailer. It denied him the very freedom from fear that he sought. When he was drinking, he was the warrior, the graceful athlete who could run faster than any man. But when he was sober, he was a man with little or no self-esteem; a man who had lost his spirit, his spirituality.

I believe Tim found what he was looking for when he walked away from life. He finally found the spirit that had been ripped from his heart at the Indian mission.

There have been, and there still are, thousands of Tim Red Wolfs in Indian country. Since the late 1880s when the boarding schools and the Indian missions were built to "Kill the Indian; save the child," these lost souls have been searching for a way back. It is through their tribal holy men and women that they are finding their way.

Denied this cultural and spiritual connection, many Indian children started to lose interest in schoolwork at about the eighth and ninth grade. They looked around at the physical structures of the mission and the boarding schools and saw no resemblance to their homes on the reservation. They looked at the white teachers and at the white priests and nuns and regarded them as foreigners, people who had nothing in common with them. They looked at the history books and recalled the phrases of "all men are created equal" and "liberty and justice for all," and they knew this to be a bunch of crap. They had visited the border towns and been called dirty Indians. They had been with their parents when they were refused service in restaurants or turned away from hotels because of the color of their skin.

If the schools taught them nothing but a pack of lies where could they turn to find the truth? Many could find no answer. They dropped out of school and started the cycle of alcohol and drug abuse. When they went to the cities looking for work they couldn't find jobs or a place to stay because they were Indian.

It was not uncommon for these lost souls to abandon religion entirely. Several former students of St. Mary's Mission on the Colville Reservation in Washington State said they had lost faith in a God completely; any kind of God. The most vivid memory they had of this mission boarding school was the infamous black belt that was used to beat them.

I am not generalizing here. Having traveled in the four directions of Indian country to speak at many high schools and colleges over the years, it has been brought home to me time and time again by the Indian people themselves — the pain, suffering, loss of faith, the sense of abandonment and despair and the final turn to alcohol and drugs in order to forget and to survive that I recall so vividly. Several times, as I talked about the boarding school experiment, older members of my audience burst into tears. They had pushed the painful memories so far back into their subconscious minds that it broke them apart to have these memories dredged up from the dark places they had been buried.

There are cultural entities in this world that have remained very much in touch with their ancient beliefs. I believe that man was much closer to things now considered to be supernatural hundreds and even thousands of years ago. Not just the natives of this hemisphere, but the ancient races of Europe, Asia and Africa, all were more in touch with their spiritual roots.

The American Indian didn't invent the wheel, but then the Indian never needed the wheel. In every culture there is a time and a place for all things. The evolution of the Indian was interrupted long before it was time. What would have happened to the people of the Western Hemisphere had the invasion not happened in 1492? We will never know the answer.

It has taken nearly five hundred years for a people pushed to the brink of cultural and spiritual destruction to find their way back. They accomplished this through themselves, and by and for themselves. No other race, religion or group could do it for us. This is something we had to do on our own. If it meant renouncing Christianity, that is what happened. If it meant proclaiming our land to be sovereign, that is what happened. And if it meant turning back to spirituality that survived only in our souls and minds, that is what happened.

There are thousands of Indian Christians in this world who will never know the absolute spiritual freedom of the true traditionalists. They will never know the mystery, scope or depth of the ancient ways of their own people because they have given themselves to the religion of a foreign country. They are the conquered ones because they sold their very souls to the religious beliefs of the invaders.

Not only did they sell their souls, but many of them joined the invaders in their efforts to destroy the spirituality of their own people. If it had not been for the strength, determination, courage and the deeply rooted spirituality of our holy men and women, we would have been destroyed because I believe that once the spirituality of a people is lost so then is the people. The government and the religious orders that built the boarding schools and the Indian missions knew this. And the experiment to implement it nearly succeeded.

Those opposed to the Indian's return to their own spirituality will defend themselves by saying there is only one God, and it doesn't matter where, when or how we worship Him. I wonder if the Muslim people would agree with this? If there is only one God the indigenous people of this continent should have been allowed to worship Him in their own way. But that was never meant to be.

The fanaticism of the Christian missionaries is that they fervently believed their religion was superior and it was the only true religion. Those who did not follow this line of thinking were heathens and had to be converted or condemned. Religious tolerance was not the strong suit of the early missionaries. In fact, it was these religious zealots who eventually persuaded the U.S. government to divide the Indian reservations up like slices of pie and allow them to build their churches and mission boarding schools on Indian lands. And like the Spanish invaders before them, the French and Anglo priests and ministers set out on their "God-given" mission of spiritual and cultural genocide.

Although it did not succeed, the combined experiment of church and state greatly contributed to the many problems that have plagued the Indian people for several generations. There is a direct line between the assault upon our spirituality and the near destruction of the Indian family and tribe through drugs, alcohol and the loss of faith and hope.

When the program "Kill the Indian; save the child" was finally halted, it had succeeded not only in killing many Indians, literally and figuratively, but it also nearly destroyed the future of all Indian nations—our children. It nearly destroyed the spirit, the soul and the mind of the child, that child believed to be sacred by all Indian tribes.

You can Neither Remember nor Forget what You do not Understand

Jordan B. Peterson and Maja Djikic

On June 28, 1914, a radical Serbian youth-group member, Gavrilo Princip, assassinated the Archduke Franz Ferdinand, heir to the Habsburg Empire, and plunged Europe into the First World War. Seventy-five years later to the day, the president of Serbia, Slobodan Milosevic, roused his people to combat in a speech before thousands of his supporters, gathered to commemorate the 600th anniversary of the Battle of Kosovo (1389) – an event that served as the focal point of a powerful collective Serbian sense of victimization and entitlement. "After six centuries," Milosevic told the enthusiastic crowd, "we are again engaged in battles and quarrels. They are not armed battles, but this cannot be excluded yet" (Malcom, 1996). The memory Milosovic invoked, mystified and distorted through the intermediary centuries of "unjust hardship" suffered by the Serb people, served to justify Serbian attempts to regain territory they felt unfairly deprived of. Milosevic proved exceedingly successful in exploiting this memory to rouse the aggressive defensiveness of his people, and in manipulating them into pundering and murdering in Bosnia and Croatia in the following years.

Memory is vulnerable, easily distorted to fit beliefs and modes of action that are more expedient than accurate. When the process of remembering becomes collective, such distortion may be greatly increased. Collective memories are acquired and transmitted in a social context, and are therefore the modifiable property of many people (De La Ronde and Swann, 1998; Hardin and Higgins, 1996; Rosenthal and Rubin, 1978; Snyder, 1974). The tendency towards social modification, which can serve positively to unite the members of a group, has a very negative, dangerous, underground aspect. Individuals appear somewhat constrained in their willingness to inflict destruction (or at least in the power to do so). Groups of individuals are not. The dangers of self-deception about past events, far from trivial in the personal case, are tremendously magnified in the social arena. The careless use of memory can lead directly to the grave abuse of people.

Group identity, like individual identity, is shaped by the past. Shared concepts, experiences, and memories bind individuals together, and provide them with an implicit, collective frame of reference (Pennebaker et al., 1997; Peterson, 1999a). Such collective frames of reference help group members understand their individual fates, communicate easily with other group members, and lay out collectively acceptable future plans. However, the memories upon which collective identity is based are prone to distortion, and groups, like individuals, frequently modify their memories, in the attempt to keep their self-images morally apposite and pristine (Baumeister and Hastings, 1997). Each of the several steps involved in the essentially reconstructive process of memory (Bartlett, 1932) can serve as an occasion or opportunity to alter the original event (Igartua and Perez, 1997) – often, in a self-serving manner. The record of the event is first inevitably condensed. Inopportune details may be omitted or suppressed, while those that show the group in a positive light are stressed. Then the story is elaborated. Events are incorporated into the account that may not have even been associated with the original story or sequence of events. Finally, and most importantly, the modified memory may be utilized or applied in a context that most particularly justifies present strongly motivated beliefs and actions of the group. Representations of presumed events far removed in time are particularly prone to these forms of distortion, as the effects of reconstruction accrue across generations.

The collectively constructed memory of the Battle of Kosovo, for example – used by Milosevic and other Serb nationalists to justify attempts to take over parts of their neighboring countries – accentuated the victimization of the Serbian people, while omitting all reference to the somewhat equivocal actual outcome of the Kosovo battle. Nationalist Serbian leaders agitating for war also consistently implied that the Serbs faced great threat, and proposed that such threat could be confronted pre-emptively in armed battle (Malcom, 1996). Appeal to past or present victimization to rationalize current atrocity appears a far from uncommon and impressively effective technique for rousing hatred (Staub, 1997). Recently, for example, Hutu journalist Leon Mugesera applied the rhetoric of past and potential victimization while delivering a speech at a rally in Northern Rwanda. He told his Hutu audience that the Tutsis with whom they had lived for generations originally descended from Ethiopia (a conjecture introduced by the nineteenth century English explorer Speke) to heighten out-group bias and to incite rage against them as intruders from another country (Off, 2000). Mugesera also warned of potential threat to justify current attacks of Hutus on their Tutsi neighbors. "Know that the person whose throat you do not cut now will be the one who will cut yours," said Mugesera (Off, 2000: 18). What he may have lacked in subtlety, Mugesera made up for in effectiveness. Within four years, 800,000 Tutsis were massacred.

Complete and accurate historical accounting might contribute to genuine reconciliation between individuals and groups previously or presently in conflict, at least in principle, and help to prevent outbreaks of future violence. But several obstacles, philosophical and practical, stand in the way of such completeness and accuracy. First, the only truly comprehensive representation of an event is the event itself. Any memory of an event must be, by contrast, incomplete, motivated and reconstructed. In consequence, there appears to be a fundamental conflict between the twin aims of coherence or comprehensibility of representation and correspondence with reality in memory construction. This conflict exists because of the necessarily paradoxical relationship that obtains between the tremendous complexity of remembered events, and the inevitably filtered and narrowed viewpoint of the limited individual observer. The very idea of historical truth has therefore has become subject to serious questioning. Furthermore, even if the existence of some transcendent and absolute historical truth is granted, provisionally, it is still very difficult, practically, to set up the circumstances so that the truth can be discovered – so that all the relevant participants in a given cultural or historical circumstance have the opportunity to tell their particular stories, and to have them incorporated into some coherent and accurate representation of the past.

It is, in consequence of these difficulties, a simple matter to deem all the participants in a given conflict as equally right, morally, equally pursuing their own valid historically determined visions of reality and justice. Since the Nuremberg trials, however, civilized societies have adopted the idea that certain modes of behavior are wrong – axiomatically wrong. This means that individuals and groups do not all necessarily stand equidistant from the truth, although they still retain some unspecified but implicit right to their own idiosyncratic views of a given event. So how might truth be conceptualized, in some manner useful to a discussion of truth and justice, given the troublesome problem of historical veridicality, the necessarily motivated stance of the observer, and the absolute impossibility of full "objective" representation?

The Frame and the Picture: Who Calls the Shots, and Why?

The presumption that the individual human mind operates like a videotape recorder, dispassionately observing the flow of ongoing events, and producing a permanent, objectively verifiable account of those events, appears natural, even self-evident. However, this intuitively appealing account – the "tape recorder fallacy" (Neisser, 1982) – is clearly inadequate, empirically and metaphorically. The sheer volume of information comprising any given sequence of events is so overwhelming that it cannot be comprehensively recorded, even in principle (Medin and Aguilar, 1999). The difficulty of coming to terms with such complexity is known, technically, as the frame problem. The frame problem, simply put, is this: how can a limited organism make realistic sense out of the unlimited information necessarily presented to it? Everything has to be simplified and modeled, without sacrificing "accuracy." But how? The frame problem has presented a virtually insurmountable obstacle to the development of machines that can operate with even a modicum of independence in any real-world environment (Brooks, 1991a, 1991b), and forced a complete reconsideration of the idea of representation. It constitutes an equally immense barrier to the understanding of human perception and memory.

Every account of any event inevitably utilizes only a tiny fraction of the information that originally comprised that event. Even a video camera must have an operator – must have a motivated, active director who calls the shots. Calling the shots, in a particular situation, means continual determination of what processes and objects will be included in the record, and what elements will be ignored. "What to ignore" is precisely the most complex of cognitive problems, in the real world, since almost everything has to be ignored. This problem of "relevant object" and "irrelevant background" – and the problem of the biases any solution necessarily introduces – could apparently be solved by random sampling of the environment that is to undergo representation. However, the immense database that comprises the real world is so vast that a sample of appropriate representativeness would still be far too large to be manageable. How do you sample appropriately from a population of infinite size? Practically, therefore, randomness is of less than no value. Anyone who has switched a video-tape recorder on accidentally during a family event, for example, soon learns that the snippets of unfocused scenery and fragmented dialog thus registered manage to be simultaneously uninformative, uninteresting, incomplete, and incoherent.

The human solution to the problem of sampling is motivation. We are always engaged with the environment – are always "being-in-the-world" – and are never dispassionate observers. We are always pursuing the limited goals we construe as valuable, from our particular idiosyncratic perspectives. We pay attention to, and remember, those events we construe as relevant, with regards to those goals. We do not and cannot strive for comprehensive, "objective" coverage. This process of motivated engagement allows us to extract out and remember a world of productive predictability from the ongoing complex chaos of being.

In his book *Searching for Memory* (1996), Daniel Schacter goes to great lengths to demolish the long-standing myth of memory as literal recoding of reality (echoing Bartlett [1932] and Jung [1959]). Schacter portrays memory as an essentially paleontological exercise. We reconstruct our memories from fragments of experience, using our broader understanding to guide us, just as dinosaurs are reconstructed from scattered bone fragments, in keeping with the broad knowledge of those doing the reconstruction (Schacter, 1996: 40). The events we remember were originally registered, in accordance with our motivations at the time, and are further revised, in the present, in accordance with what we now feel, want, and believe. We are bound to ignore, suppress, distort or even entirely fabricate fundamental aspects of the transpiring stream of events (ibid., p.102) if our current desires and beliefs compel us to do so.

Ziva Kunda (1990) has proposed, analogously, that individuals generally posit truths they find desirable – although they remain somewhat constrained by the necessity of mustering up evidence that supports those truths. This means at least that a balance must be struck between motivation and accuracy. People who wish to draw a particular conclusion attempt to be rational, at least *post-hoc*, and are therefore driven to construct a justification of their conclusion that might persuade a dispassionate observer. This means that people draw upon memories for facts and experiences that might support their desired conclusion, and that they creatively combine aspects of what they already know to develop new and supportive evidence, in favor of the views they currently espouse. She reviews evidence suggesting that this process is far from objective, as individuals fail to realize (1) that their conclusions are biased by their goals; (2) that a small and delimited subset of their personal knowledge is being pulled into play; (3) that alternative goals might draw out different aspects of memory; and (4) that completely different or even opposing conclusions might be accepted under alternative circumstances (see also Kruglanski, 1980; Pyszczynski and Greenberg, 1987; Pyszczynski, Greenberg, and Holt, 1985).

Such problems of motivated memory and reasoning become even more complex when the issue is not so much what physically happened in the past as *the meaning* of what happened. We can make tentative steps, after all, towards an objective accounting for certain events and processes. We can calculate to the second when a solar eclipse occurred a century ago, and we can specify to the meter where it could be observed. We cannot describe the psychological impact of the eclipse, however, with equal certainty. Consider, first, the immense difficulty of acceptably reconstructing an interpersonal event, such as a currently unresolved argument between two people. Then consider the difficulties in determining an acceptable account of something as complex as a war. Every individual battle must not only be noted, objectively – and portrayed in relationship to an ever-expanding net of relevant contextual information – as well as described in terms of its meaning, its implications for action and interpretation. It is no wonder that history is written by the victor.

Memory is not, therefore, and cannot be, an objective record of the past. There can be no memory without a subjective observer, and there is no subjective viewer who lacks a motivated viewpoint. All interpretations are therefore motivated, biased, if not by outright ideological concerns, then at least by a series of implicit decisions about where limited attentional resources might best be utilized. What does "best" mean, in such a context? How can memory be discriminated from fiction, since it is by necessity motivated and subjective? And is there anything that can halt the descent into pure post-modernism, or moral relativism, given such a position? If so, how do we distinguish between the claims of the Holocaust survivor to justice from the claims of the Holocaust perpetrator who maintains that his actions were justified (as his ideology presupposed)? Are we willing to presume that all positions are equally correct – which is tantamount to presuming they are all equally valueless (since value presupposes a hierarchy of accuracy, as to be "valuable" means to be *more* valuable). Such a position invalidates the whole notion of interpretation, or position, or opinion, or thought, and makes the search for historical accuracy seem entirely absurd. But there is a philosophically acceptable alternative to the determination of accuracy in the absence of objectivity – an alternative deeply rooted in pragmatism, a perspective that takes full account of necessary motivation, without abandoning in any manner the idea of or respect for the truth.

Representations of Motivated Actions: Principles and Pitfalls

We have proposed (Peterson, 1999a; Peterson, 1999b; Peterson and Flanders, in press) in keeping with several similar accounts (Adler, 1958, Oatley and Johnson-Laird, 1987), that perception, as well as action, is framed within a motivated narrative. This narrative, in its simplest form, specifies (1) a particular target of action; (2) a particular reference point against which that target is contrasted; and (3) a sequence of implementable behaviors that are designed to transform the reference point into the target (Peterson, 1999a, in press). The individual posits a desirable point "b," in accordance with his current state of motivation, contrasts that against point "a," his interpreted current position or state, and manifests a sequence of actions designed to eradicate the gap, or the value difference. The beginning and end points of this frame are abstracted interpretations (mental constructs), matched against the real world, which remain essentially axiomatic or invisible if correct. The actions are not abstractions, but the manner in which abstractions ground themselves in the world, through their implementation in behavior.

We construe the world in a linear manner, perpetually moving from a comparatively undesirable starting point to a comparatively desirable end point (and then, inevitably, producing a new motivated frame, and beginning the ascent again). Motivated frames that produce their desired end are deemed both sufficient and successful. Their accuracy or veridicality manifests itself to us in the motivational form of satisfaction, or satiation, and in the satisfied fading away of that frame of reference – a frame that, when successful, becomes a permanent part of our repertoire of useful frames. Motivated frames that fail, by contrast, are experienced as frustrating, disappointing, punishing, in need of revision or eradication.

This idea of motivated framing appears simple, in many regards, but it has several profound practical and theoretical consequences. First of these consequences is the possibility for more complete understanding of emotion, as well as perception, in relationship to thought and action. When we are operating within a motivated frame, all phenomena that aid our movement forward appear to us as positively valenced, as promising, as hope-inspiring. Phenomena that impede our movements, by contrast, appear as negatively valenced. Such valenced phenomena, positive or negative, are easily perceived as objects or events, at least when familiar. Non-valenced phenomena, however – neither helpful nor encumbering; neither friend nor foe; neither tool nor obstacle – are not perceived, are left latent, are invisible, are ground, rather than figure. This means, essentially, that we see what we need to see, rather than what is "there" – and, more profoundly, that the question of what is "there" cannot be answered in any comprehensible manner in the absence of a motivated viewpoint.

Second of these consequences is the necessity of coming to terms with the existence of value, as an emergent property of motivated narratives or perceptual frames. To act, in reference to a given target, is to presume, implicitly but necessarily, that the target is more valuable than the present position – and, more importantly, to presume that the utility or value of the current frame of reference may be judged by its success in attaining the goal. This means, equally implicitly and equally necessarily, that motivated reference frames that do not culminate in consummatory success must be regarded as ill posed, by definition (even if that definition has not been explicitly formulated). Frames that do not produce what they are specifically designed to produce have failed. One can say, therefore, that unsuccessful action-and-perception frames are inadequate, not so much from the impossible-to-attain objective viewpoint, as in accordance with the implicit value structure of the individual or individuals who constructed them. Unsuccessful frames are incorrect, error-ridden, wrong. And although this might not be a universally applicable definition of truth, it is at least a universally applicable definition of error, which is a good start.

Frames of reference that do not meet their stated ends are incorrect. Memories of past events constructed in accordance with such erroneous frames are insufficient. But reality does not speak for itself. It requires tremendous effort – and tremendous courage – to reconstrue a situation that has gone wrong. Delimited perception-and-action frames manifest their insufficiency in a manner that is frequently both complex and unspecifiable. This is because the subjective delimitation and narrowing that is a necessary part of pragmatic action-framing requires that most of the world be ignored – and ignored in an "invisible" and difficult-to-detect manner. The objects that make up goal-oriented perception, for example, are generally treated (perceived) as homogeneous units, in accordance not so much with their sensory features as with their function. A telephone may reasonably be viewed as a single thing, insofar as it is performing its duty and transmitting speech. As soon as it fails, however, its intrinsic complexity, ignored during its customary use, manifests itself, and "cries out" (Brown, 1986) to be perceived. Any of the myriad and complex subcomponents of the telephone might be at fault, with regards to any failure. The vast functional array that encapsulates an "object" – without which the "object" could not exist – recedes into invisibility, during the act of simple use. In the case of the telephone, this array includes the household wiring system to which it is attached, and the external exchange system that it is an integral part of. It should not be forgotten, either, that telephones might also fail – as they do, not infrequently, in third world countries – because of political or economic instability, rather than mechanical inadequacy. This means that the ignored part of a functioning telephone also consists of the stability of the broad social systems whose invisible and seamless operation constitutes part of the preconditions for its successful continued existence. The problem of "ignored ground," therefore, further complicates (or even constitutes) the complex situation of "emergent problem." Anything ignored for the purposes of current operations may reemerge without warning. Such reemergence reminds us that the world is much more complex – and much more threatening – than our conceptualizations generally allow.

Anything that interferes with an ongoing operation indicates the practical inadequacy of the concrete actions or the conceptual inadequacy of the values comprising that frame. Many such emergent obstacles are awkwardly complex and unspecified, rather than simple, obvious and self-evidently perceptible. We stated previously that a given frame might be considered insufficient or error-ridden, regardless of its specific content, if it does not achieve its specified goal when enacted – and that such consideration provided us with a universal definition of error. Because the reasons for error are frequently unclear, however, inadequacy of conceptualization can be rapidly compounded with regards to the severity of its consequences by failure to admit to or confront error, when it manifests itself. This additional failure might be regarded as a meta-error – an error in dealing with error. In our view, it is this meta-error that poses the most severe and often unrecognized danger to the establishment of universally acceptable historical truth.

Now, individuals aim at very different, and even opposing ends (so that very little may be said in principle about the absolute value of their goals). However, all individuals respond to disruption of their aims in an identical manner (or, at least, in a manner that can be defined as variation within specifiable parameters). Unexpected disruption of goal-directed behavior – emergence of novelty, or anomaly, or previously invisible complexity – invariably produces emotion. That emotion may be most simply considered a combination of *negative emotion*, or anxiety, or hurt, or disappointment, or frustration, which is immediate response to threat (the threat, in this case, is to the goal itself, as well as to the integrity of the goal-directed frame), and *positive emotion*, or hope, or promise, or curiosity, as disruption signifies the reemergence of ignored possibility (as unexpected failure at a hated job brings with it uncertainty, but also freedom).

Evidence of error, which is the reemergence of the ignored world, is meaningful, intrinsically, unavoidably and disturbingly meaningful – and that meaning is a complex and initially undifferentiated combination of anxiety and promise. This means that the world that reveals itself in error is meaning, before it is object or irrelevance. What determines the specific valence or meaning, negative or positive, of a given error? Equally importantly, what determines the magnitude of that valence? Some failures are trivial. Some provide desired freedom. Others are catastrophes. How can the meaning of mistakes be categorized, and considered? And what has such categorization or consideration to do with the relationship between memory and justice?

The question of categorization of the meaning of mistakes can best be addressed by considering a scheme proposed by Carver and Scheier (1998), after the control-systems engineer Powers (1973). Carver and Scheier point out that abstract philosophical concepts – ideals – can best be considered not so much as abstracted objects of perception, in the classical sense, as homogeneous groupings of behavioral schemes, simplified and treated as unitary classes, for the pragmatic purposes of abstract conceptualization. The principle "be thoughtful," for example, is not a disembodied attitude or value. It is instead a simplified representation of a non-contradictory grouping of predictable and consistent patterns of actions, concrete, mundane actions: make dinner for spouse, take garbage to curb, pick up children from school, give birthday card to secretary; do not bully subordinates, do not take undue personal credit for group accomplishments. These concrete patterns of actions themselves may be further decomposed into what are not so much whole behaviors as movements of muscles, and then into operations of the physiological control systems that underlie such muscle movements (and that are neither conscious, nor abstract, in any sense). This is a partial solution to the mind-body problem: abstractions are representations of behaviors, in large part, and remain valid only insofar as the behaviors that are thus represented actually exist, as patterns of actions. You are not thoughtful, despite your wishful abstract self-description as such, if you are frequently hostile (a sin of commission, from this particular value standpoint), or if you consistently forget your spouse's birthday (a sin of omission). The meaning of a mistake, then, is troublesome disruption of the frame system that produced the mistake (and the emergent necessity of facing the complexity ignored while that frame was in operation, and retooling conception in consequence).

The question of the relevance of such categorization (of the meaning of mistakes) to memory and justice can best be answered by considering this: an accurate representation or memory of a given emergent anomaly – particularly in the interpersonal or social domain (burning my spouse's dinner, for example, while fixing the sink) – means construction of a *socially acceptable account of the events*, as well as construction of a credible case that the likelihood of future similar errors will be decreased. The social acceptability of this account and the credibility of the case for improvement is most generally socially adjudicated or negotiated, before actual evidence or the lack thereof manifests itself in reality. Is the accurate memory of a disastrous meal, from the perspective of a necessarily interested observer, "my spouse is hostile and resentful about kitchen duties" or "my spouse made a simple error, when unfortunately involved in another beneficial activity?" Only time will tell. Repeated errors indicate insufficiently accurate representation – as does failure to put the event in the past, where it belongs. It certainly might be the case that either you or your spouse will be unable to forget the event (one, because "unjustly accused," the other, because provided with "inadequate excuses or explanations").

Such failure of representation, such failure of memory, such repetition of error, such inability to forget is partly a consequence of complexity – because emergent reality is genuinely difficult to frame, even when substantial effort is devoted towards such framing. Equally often, however – and much more controllable, at least in principle – is the contribution of motivated self-deception to the failure. It is easier to avoid than to confront, at least in the short term. Preexistent but erroneous conceptual systems at least have the advantage of their existence. New schemas have to be extracted from the unknown at a non-trivial cost. It is no simple manner to retool from whole cloth – and the lure of self-deception may appear irresistibly attractive by contrast. This process of self-deception – the meta-error referred to previously – is characterized not so much by some neo-Freudian act of repression as by much more passive refusal to face the emergent meaning-laden unknown courageously and then to think. Individuals confronted by anomaly frequently refuse to fully admit to such confrontation. They repeat the same counterproductive behaviors. They hold on to their inadequate frames of reference, despite their self-evident failures. They therefore leave the emergent domain of error unspecified and emotion laden. Such individuals – self-deceptive to the core – are afraid of having their basic life assumptions, their figure/ground distinctions, violated and overthrown, and of descending, in consequence, into unstructured, emotion-provoking, and once-ignored complexity and chaos. They refuse to believe in their own abilities, when confronted by what has not yet been understood. In consequence, they never generate a fully developed representation – a memory – of their mistakes. And although they might avoid suffering for their sins of omission, those they interact with will not be so lucky.

Self-Deception: Creating and Maintaining Distorted Memories of the Self/Other

Unwillingness to fully process anomaly – failure, threat, frustration, and disappointment – appears common, to the point of normalcy. Such unwillingness has been variously conceptualized, implicitly or as a matter of definition, as repression, self-deception or defense (Freud, reviewed in Westen, 1998) or, more recently – in a highly cited work of social psychology – as positive illusion (Taylor and Brown, 1988). Individuals characterized by "positive illusion," for example, manifest "overly positive self-evaluations, exaggerated perceptions of control or mastery, and unrealistic optimism" (Taylor and Brown, 1988: 193). It is of some interest to note that 95 percent of college students apparently fall into such a category (Taylor and Brown, 1994a). Taylor and Brown claim that positive illusions actually help maintain or even constitute mental health, rather than comprising a central feature of psychopathology (see also Taylor and Brown, 1994; Taylor, 1989). They draw evidence from three main lines of investigation.

First, the "normal" personality appears to hold cognitive biases that are both positive and pervasive. Second, measures of self-deception tend to correlate negatively with various indices of psychopathology, particularly self-report measures of anxiety and depression. Third, self-deception appears positively related to high self-esteem and to positive mood. Taylor and Brown claim, in consequence, that positive illusions "make each individual's world a warmer and more active and beneficent place in which to live" (p. 205). They argue, as well, that the distortions characterizing the self-deceiver (very much reminiscent of those outlined by Greenberg (1980), in his discussion of the "totalitarian ego") aid in the production and maintenance of traditional necessary and sufficient conditions for successful life adjustment: self-deceivers are happy, healthy and normal. Brown (1991; Brown and Dutton, 1995) maintains further that possible risks from these illusions (such as grandiosity) do not outweigh the benefits. Taylor, Collins, Skokan, and Aspinwall (1989) believe that those holding positive illusions (which are less reality distorting than classic defense mechanisms) are also sufficiently flexible to maintain responsiveness to corrective information. In keeping with this view, Taylor (1989) has written a layperson's book, recommending self-deceptive strategies as an aid to mental and physical health.

There exists, however, a body of work, interesting and at least as methodologically rigorous as the pro-positive illusion data, demonstrating (1) that the phenomenon of positive illusion is not necessarily ubiquitous and (2) that avoidance even of traumatic truths has consequences arguably classifiable as "bad." Myers and Brewin (1996) claim, for example, with regards to point (1), that the phenomenon of so-called ubiquitous positive illusion may actually be a consequence of the presence of "subgroups of overly positive individuals." They demonstrated that normal and nonanxious subjects showed no evidence of unrealistic optimism or overly positive self-evaluation, once the effect of a subgroup of "repressors" was taken into account. Paulhus' recent work (1998) speaks to the same point.

A veritable plethora of evidence exists pertaining to point (2). A recent meta-analysis has indicated, for example, that repressive-defensiveness is associated with *lack* of subjective well-being (life satisfaction, happiness and positive affect) and that the strength of this relationship outweighed that obtaining with all other measurable personality traits (DeNeve and Cooper, 1998). This potent relationship may exist, in part, because inaccurate and overly positive self-estimates tend to set the stage for failure. Robins and Beer (1996) study of self-enhancing freshmen speaks to this point. At the end of a single academic year, students whose self-reported academic performance was greater than their actual record reported significantly higher subjective well-being, compared with a group matched in level of ability that accurately reported their records, even though they had initially predicted greater academic success for themselves. However, they were 32 percent more likely to have dropped out of school. Martocchio and Judge (1997) similarly reported a negative association between self-deception and learning/skill-acquisition, which they attributed theoretically to the tendency for self-deceivers to make external attributions to protect their self-image, instead of engaging in the difficult process of actual learning. Shane and Peterson (submitted) have recently reported that self-deceivers voluntarily pay more attention to positive than negative contingent performance feedback when learning, and show dramatic decrements in performance, in consequence. Baumeister, Heatherton, and Tice (1993) found, finally, that individuals with high self-esteem tend to set unreachable goals. When faced with threat to these goals, they suffered larger drops in self-esteem than those who initially evaluated themselves in somewhat less positive terms. Baumeister, Smart, and Boden (1996) have tied such drops in self-esteem directly to the emergence of violence. These authors suggest that it is precisely those individuals with high but unstable self-esteem (unstable as a consequence of self-deception, or positive illusions) who are most frequently aggressive. These notions fit well with the detailed observations of the Scandinavian expert on bullying, Dan Olweus, who has studied tens of thousands of children, in an attempt to understand and control proto-fascist behavior. Bullies have a "relatively positive view of themselves," have "unusually little anxiety and insecurity (or [are] roughly average on such dimensions)," and do "not suffer from poor self-esteem" (Olweus, 1993: 34; see also Pulkkinen and Tremblay, 1982).

The potential pathway to hostile and aggressive self-esteem might be inferred from the results of two further studies: Garrison, Earls, and Kindlon (1983) found that six- and seven-year-old children whose self-ratings were higher than those derived from independent evaluators and teachers had more behavioral problems in school and were rated as more maladjusted by observers. Those children who rated themselves as less competent, by contrast (termed "diminishers") showed no pattern of difference from "normal" children in areas of adjustment. Johnson, Vincent and Ross (1997) have demonstrated that higher levels of denial are associated with worse post-failure problem solving, once the positive effects of self-esteem are controlled, and showed that greater self-deceptive enhancement predicted not only worse post-failure problem solving but increased levels of hostility. Why? Well, first, there is nothing like the belief in personal superiority to justify acts of psychological and physical violence. Second, there is nothing like refusal to change, when change is necessary, to insure that the world transforms itself over time into something so hostile that retaliatory or even pre-emptive aggressive action seems not only necessary, but justified (Peterson, 1999a, 1999b).

While self-deceivers claim decreased stress and increased health, their long-term health prospects nonetheless appear comparatively poor. Tomaka, Blascovich, and Kelsey (1992) found, for example, that self-deceivers made more generally benign appraisals of stressful tasks, in keeping with the pro-positive illusion expectation. Interestingly, however, high self-deceivers rated the totality of the laboratory experience as more stressful than the low self-deceivers, even though they initially appraised the specific stressful task they were completing in more benign terms. Jamner and Schwartz (1986) reported that the inattention to pain characteristic of high self-deceivers appears associated with poorer long term outcomes (delayed seeking of medical advice and consequent treatment for more advanced pathologies, premature discharge from hospitals, reduced monitoring in health-care facilities (Cohen, 1984), despite its apparent short-term "benefit" (reduced pre- and post-operative anxiety, reduced medication use, better response to medical treatment, faster and less complicated recovery from surgery (Cohen and Lazarus, 1973; Mullen and Suls, 1982; Suls and Fletcher, 1985). Finally, Shedler, Mayman and Manis (1993) provided evidence that individuals characterized by positive illusions heighten their stress reactivity, regardless of their self-reported calm. Very telling is the fact that self-deceivers' levels of reactivity exceeded those obtained from individuals who were manifestly distressed. Eysenck (1994) disagreed with many of the specific diagnostic/methodological statements of Shedler et al. (1993), but outlined a body of experimental evidence supporting one main line of their reasoning: "suppression of emotion can play a vital part" in increasing susceptibility to disease. Why? How? The classic answer is unconscious conflict (Freud, in Westen, 1998). But it is simpler to note the effect that habitual self-deception has on the world.

Imagine the self-hierarchy or self-narrative or self-description of a habitual self-deceiver – imagine his or her theory of the world. Every level of representation has been rendered increasingly inaccurate and insufficient by environmental or experiential change or alteration, followed by wilful failure to update conception in the face of error. Every goal-directed action, predicated on a no-longer valid conceptual hierarchy, is therefore increasingly likely to produce anomaly, and to result in frustration, disappointment and anxiety, as the "world" increasingly refuses to conform to no longer valid expectations or desires. The first two forms of negative affect (frustration, disappointment) are consequential to the "absence of expected rewards" (Gray, 1982); the latter, anxiety, a consequence of the emergence of once-controlled complexity (Davis and Whalen, 2001). "Frustration, disappointment and anxiety" sound a lot like "stress." We know that the limbically centered anomaly-detection and emotion generating systems are integrally involved in response to stress (Davis and Whalen, 2001; LeDoux, 1996), and that they help regulate the release of the stress hormone cortisol (Gray, 1987). We also know that cortisol hypersecretion contributes to hippocampal degeneration, memory deficits, obesity, cardiovascular disease, Alzheimer's disease, AIDS dementia, reduced central levels of serotonin, and depression (Raber, 1998; Stokes, 1995; Whitworth, Brown, Kelly and Williamson, 1995). This all implies that it is not so much "conflict" in the "unconscious" but the real-world consequences of categorical instability and failure to update habit that links self-deception to disease. Self-serving but pragmatically erroneous theories of self and world lead to failure of self and world. This might be regarded as the "whistling in the dark" hypothesis: self-deceivers allow themselves to remain blithely and blissfully unaware in an environment rendered increasingly dangerous by their inaction. The fact of this heightened danger, and not the repressed contents of the unconscious, is what makes life increasingly "stressful."

This theoretical perspective is in keeping with the findings of studies employing scales of socially desirable responding (a concept analogous to self-deception or repression). Such scales originated as "lie scales" – sets of questions designed to detect individuals who attempted to "fake good" while completing personality or psychopathology scales (Eysenck, 1994; Furnham, 1986; Paulhus, 1990; Ones, Viswesvaran and Reiss, 1996). The tendency to fake good, however, soon became conceptualized as a personality trait in its own right (Block, 1965; Sweetland and Quay, 1953). Development of the Marlowe Crowne Social Desirability Scale (MCSD, Crowne and Marlowe, 1960) therefore led rapidly to the development of a body of work on "need for social approval" (Crowne and Marlowe, 1964).

The relationship between self-deception and socially desirable responding can perhaps best be understood by analyzing the relationship between the self-hierarchy, as described previously, and the social milieu. People negotiate their "reality" (De La Ronde and Swann, 1998; Hardin and Higgins, 1996) – at least in part by using their impressions of others to guide their behavior (Rosenthal and Rubin, 1978; Snyder, 1974). This negotiated reality means establishment of shared, low-resolution assumptions, axioms and principles, which serve to foster cooperation among diverse individuals, and which add predictability to behavior and emotion in socially shared territories (Piaget, 1965; Peterson, 1999a).

From such a perspective, "identification with the group" means personal adoption of prevailing socially-constructed low-resolution axioms, and response to information supporting or endangering the integrity of those axioms, as if personally supported or endangered (Peterson, 1999a). Such "identification with the group" becomes self-deception when the presumption is made that individual behavior and desire is in concordance with societally established low-resolution axioms, despite ample evidence at the level of emotion (chronic frustration, anxiety, disappointment) that actual personal behavior and the societal ideal remain substantively at odds (either because of personal or social inadequacy) (Peterson, 1999a). Self-deceivers produce instability in their axiomatic low-resolution categories with the progression of time, for example, because of their voluntary failure to update skill and representation, when faced with anomaly. The instability of these categories means that the world increasingly becomes "hostile," as more and more anomaly is produced in the course of unstable category-predicated, goal-oriented activity (people are less predictable and friendly than expected, events in the world seldom turn out as desired, etc.). This increased hostility either motivates radical and painful self-reconstruction (unlikely, in the case of the habitual self-deceiver) or the adoption of an increasingly dangerous, vengeful, adversarial, totalitarian personality style (Peterson, 1999a; Peterson, 1999b).

A partisan of the most rigid orthodoxy... knows it all, he bows before the holy, truth is for him an ensemble of ceremonies, he talks about presenting himself before the throne of God, of how many times one must bow, he knows everything the same way as does the pupil who is able to demonstrate a mathematical proposition with the letters ABC, but not when they are changed to DEF. He is therefore in dread whenever he hears something not arranged in the same order. (Kierkegaard, in Becker [1973]: 71)

The authoritarian personality (Adorno, Frenkl-Brunswik, Levinson, and Sanford, 1950) was originally regarded as the prototypical fascist, and therefore by implication as someone necessarily right wing. This was a very convenient line of logic for the time, given the preponderance of left-wing thinking among twentieth-century Western academics. Shils (1954) proposed, however, that the emphasis on right-wing belief was misplaced; proposed that the extremists of the left might also be authoritarian. Both Eysenck (1954) and Rokeach (1956) presented data supporting this perspective, but were criticized extensively (Christie, 1956a, 1956b, Rokeach and Hanley 1956, Hanley and Rokeach, 1956, contra Eysenck; Stone, 1980, contra Rokeach). Altemeyer (1988) suggested reasonably enough in response to this argument that Western leftists and communists might not share the personality of communists in communist countries. He believed, instead, that "real" Eastern-bloc communists might be high in conventionalism, political conformity and authoritarianism, while those in the West, who apparently stood in opposition to current tradition, might be low in such attributes. Altemeyer's notion appears predicated on the idea that it is intense traditionalism and conservatism as such that characterize the totalitarian mind, rather than position on the spectrum of political belief. Vladimir Ageyev and his colleagues have since demonstrated that Soviet communists are in fact more authoritarian (McFarland, Ageyev, and Abalakina-Paap, 1992; McFarland, Ageyev, and Djintcharadze, 1996) than non-communists; demonstrated further that, "although the cultural authorities and enemies were opposite for the two cultures, support for the authorities and opposition to the enemies were components of authoritarianism in both cultures" (p. 1005, McFarland et al., 1992). In addition, Soviet authoritarians, like their western counterparts, typically oppose democrative ideals and civil liberties and are more ethnocentric (showing prejudice against Jews, national groups, women, dissidents, etc.). McFarland et al. (1992) therefore concluded: "authoritarianism is tied to conventionalism rather than to the specific conservative ideologies found in the West. Authoritarianism is not totally content free; if it were, the items would not cohere as a scale, and certainly, the same items could not cohere in such different cultures. Nonetheless, the same authoritarianism can be expressed as loyalty to different cultural norms, even opposite ones. In all cases, however, this intensified loyalty is coupled with hostility directed towards the culture's deviants, malcontents, and enemies and with support for the use of force against those who are perceived as threats to the accepted order" (p. 1008).

It appears to be voluntary rejection of individual capacity for exploration (and consequent failure to adaptively reconstruct of behavioral skill and cognitive category) that drives the authoritarian individual necessarily further and further into the arms of the state. This means that the authoritarian individual incorporates the state's presumptions into the self, but rejects any possibility that his or her individual efforts might add additional adaptive potency to or even transform the nature of that incorporated structure. Thus, the authoritarian's "protection from the unknown or anomalous" remains valid only in those circumstances where the state's perspective, expectations and desires dominate, and never in a situation where a truly individual response might be called for.

It is the creative capacity of the self, however, that comprises the *state's* only potential response to the manifestation of anomaly (in its environmental, personified, or ideological guises) (Peterson, 1999a; Peterson, 1999b). Tradition, by its very nature, can only deal with what has transpired previously. This means that the individual who has sacrificed his relationship with the creative capacity of the self, in an attempt to avoid anomaly-induced negative emotion, has no choice but to react to the emergence of anomaly with aggression, in the attempt to force it out of existence (so that tradition can once again provide all the answers). Indeed, empirical evidence exists to suggest that it is precisely under periods of threat that authoritarian identification increases (Doty, Peterson and Winter, 1991; Sales, 1973; Sales and Friend, 1973). The fact that authoritarians tend to be low in trait openness (Peterson, B.E., Smirles and Wentworth, 1997) (which is abstract exploratory behavior) also lends credence to such a suggestion, and offers the possibility of positing a causal model: Rejection of creative capacity, evidenced at least in part as self-deception, means increased authoritarianism under conditions of threat. By contrast, willingness to face threat forthrightly and creatively means adherence to the truth as process, rather than state, generation of new truth, in consequence, and constant individual and social redemption (although not considered in such terms by modern thinkers). In keeping with such a theory, there is a growing body of clinical evidence suggesting that not only do those who avoid the painful truth get worse, but that those who voluntarily expose themselves to the anxiety-provoking and depressing – even if extremely traumatic – get better.

Pennebaker and colleagues have demonstrated, for example, that normal individuals who detail their past traumatic experiences decrease their autonomic reactivity and their subjective experience of distress, stimulate productive behavioral change, enhance their immune function, and improve their physical health over time (Pennebaker, 1988, 1989, 1993; Pennebaker and Hoover, 1985; Pennebaker and Susman, 1988; Petrie, Booth, Pennebaker, Davison, and Thomas, 1995), while suppression of emotional thought, by contrast, decreases immune functioning Petrie, Booth and Pennebaker, 1998). Pennebaker is convinced, specifically, that the act of turning trauma into words is therapeutic (Pennebaker, Mayne, and Francis, 1997). If categories are regarded as functional (as means of goal-directed world-simplification, as means to obtaining desired ends) then the manner in which "verbal processing" might reduce stress is clear.

In the more explicitly clinical domain, Foa and colleagues have demonstrated that exposure techniques (which involve "reliving" a stressful event in imagination, over and over, in as much painful detail as possible) lead to long-term improvements for those suffering from post-traumatic stress disorder (e.g., rape victims), agoraphobics, and obsessive-compulsives (Foa, Feske, Murdock, Kozak, and McCarthy, 1991; Foa and Kozak, 1985; 1986). Conversely, female sexual assault survivors who attempt to suppress rape-related thoughts experience a significant rebound in the frequency of such thoughts (Shipherd and Beck, 1999). It should be noted that the magnitude of exposure-related improvement appears positively related to the stress induced as a consequence of the imaginal replaying. Participants characterized by higher levels of treatment-induced state physiological reactivity are also those who improve most significantly as a consequence of treatment. In their extensive review, Foa and Kozak (1986) note that exposure to feared situations constitutes a core element of theoretically diverse yet successful psychological treatments for anxiety. Perhaps this core element exists for two related reasons: first, exploration, categorization and update of habit truly eradicates dangerous anomaly; second, belief in the fundamental utility of such voluntary exploration constitutes veridical, necessary and generalizable "self-efficacy" (Williams, Kinney, and Falbo, 1989; Williams, Kinney, Harap, and Liebmann, 1997) or even genuinely useful self-esteem. These studies and reviews strongly suggest that those who force themselves to come to terms with the categorical significance of anxiety-provoking and painful events are those who come through such events with their integrity restored.

We are now in a position, therefore, where we can understand, in detail, the processes that underlie self-deception and the distortion of memory, and the manner in which those processes virtually ensure the emergence of personal and social psychopathology. Individuals operate within a goal-oriented structure, with a hierarchical nature (Carver and Scheier, 1998; Peterson, 1999a). Ongoing experience is evaluated with regards to its implications for that structure. Events that indicate goal-attainment are positive; those that indicate failure or other disruption, negative (Gray, 1982; 1987; Oatley and Johnson-Laird, 1987). Events in the latter class are always undesired and frequently unexpected. The unexpected is not understood, although it is nonetheless immediately evidence that current plans and goals are insufficient. This insufficiency must be rectified, for desired progress to continue; such rectification can only take place once the unexpected and undesired has been explored.

"Explored" means evaluated with regards to the other goal-oriented schemas that make up the self-hierarchy; means, further, reconstruction of those schemas at the conceptual and skill levels, at whatever level appears most appropriate, so that similar future operations do not produce anomaly. Voluntary refusal to engage in this process, and then action as if the world has nonetheless been stabilized, constitutes self-deception. This is action as if the error message is irrelevant (when it in fact emerged as a consequence of plans and conceptualizations already acted upon as valid by the individual in question), or is insufficient reconceptualization, in the service of the shortest-term, immediate and most narrow goals. Such voluntary refusal inevitably produces a deterioration of skill and concept, particularly at the higher levels of conceptualization, and increasingly destructive mismatch between expectation, desire and reality. This continual but self-induced punishment breeds hostility, resentment and hatred (as well as evermore stubborn refusal to "face the facts," even when defined subjectively) (Peterson, 1999a; 1999b).

So what does this all mean? It means that most of the time we operate within the confines of our normal stories, which allow us to parse the world up into comprehensible, functional categories, evaluate ongoing occurrences, and attain those things we deem desirable. It means that now and then, because of our own ignorance, because of the stasis of our schemes of categorization, or as a consequence of unrealized change in the nature of the previously unmanifest world (and those three phenomena are not really distinguishable) things do not unfold according to our plans. We are made aware of our failures as a consequence of our innate default emotional response to the emergence of anomaly. We then avoid, and stubbornly maintain the structure of what we now know, by our own definitions, to be invalid, or we approach the terrible unknown cautiously, explore, and update in some normal or even revolutionary sense our goal-directed structures of conceptualization and behavioral routine.

Anthony Greenwald (1980), in his classic social-psychological paper on the totalitarian ego, compared the information-control strategies of the typical individual to that of authoritarian states, noting that such strategies were designed to "preserve organization in cognitive structures." It is certainly the case that the organization of cognitive structures must be maintained (Kelly, 1955). Otherwise, everything degenerates into chaos, and chaos is not affectively irrelevant. It is, by contrast, terrifying; is in fact the essence of terrifying. Yet the other side of terror, so to speak, is pathological order, just as dangerous and frightening. It is a tricky business to negotiate between Scylla and Charybdis, but recourse to self-deception in the service of stability merely ensures that reality conspires to flood the sinful world (Eliade, 1978). Greenwald shrank from drawing the most painful conclusions from his observations. He states: "the use of terror as a device for social control is a fundamental part of [Hannah] Arendt's conception of totalitarianism, yet it obviously has no analog in the functioning of ego" (footnote: 609). This absence of ego-analog is something far from obvious. The positing of such a lack of identity appears more as a dangerous form of naivety, and also constitutes an implicit presupposition of whole lines of current theoretical and experimental endeavor in social psychology (as detailed previously).

The eminent Protestant theologian Reinhold Niebuhr (1944) has observed something most pertinent and instructive in this regard: "It must be understood that the children of light are foolish not merely because the underestimate the power of self-interest among the children of darkness. They underestimate this power among themselves" (p. 11). It is certainly possible, and appears more than likely to be the case, that totalitarian states are not so much oppressive political structures forced upon innocent and otherwise benevolent subordinate individuals, as they are indubitable expressions of the general self-deceptive philosophy of the majority of the individuals comprising those states. The "totalitarian ego" is certainly capable of oppression and aggression. The self-deceptive individual is, likewise, perfectly willing to sacrifice the best in him or herself to the conveniences of the moment and, if the situation arises and the horrible act can be appropriately rationalized, to sacrifice the dangerous and irritating other to the rigid god of static belief. This is a depressing and frightening notion, but seems to be the lesson put forth in the strongest terms by Orwell (1965), Arendt (1994), Frankl (1971), Solzhenitsyn (1975) and, more recently, Goldhagen (1996) and Chang (1998). Active and, more importantly, passive processes of self-deception that feed collective memory distortion may well serve the short-term and narrowly defined purposes of the individual and the state. It appears likely, however, that the sins of the self-deceptive accumulate, and find their expression in long-term terror and catastrophe. And so one might posit that states that refuse to include the voices of the victimized, and that refuse to tell the truth about past arrogance and error, are also precisely those states that tend towards continual aggression, as well as continual self-destruction. And a true skeptic might notice that such an end might actually constitute such a state's true desire.

Violating Fundamental Beliefs: The Nature of Traumatic Memories

"Positive illusion" and individual self-deception constitute distortions in viewpoint that are frequently subtle enough to pass unnoticed, despite their potential for generating pathology. Self-deceptive individuals and those who surround them can therefore continue to "whistle in the dark," as long as the feedback that they receive from the environment is not powerful enough to force them to become genuinely conscious of and reexamine their implicit frames of reference. Even catastrophic failure of action or belief may remain unprocessed. However, such failure has its emotional costs and consequences (as necessary desire remains unfulfilled; as protection from the complex world disappears), despite stubborn refusal or absolute inability to investigate the causes of pragmatic insufficiency. It is perfectly possible to suffer from failure, after all, without coming to any real understanding (indeed, any real representation) of the world events that produced such failure.

Cultures, like individuals, have a value hierarchy. That hierarchy is complex. Much of it is implicit, coded in patterned behavior, and not necessarily fully represented in an explicit abstract manner. Individuals nest their personal and somewhat idiosyncratic value hierarchies within the confines of an overarching hierarchy, provided by the cultures they are part of. In this manner, the differing values and behaviors of plumbers, prison guards and shepherds may be brought into the twin domains of social desirability and predictability, so that the entire culture may benefit from the diverse activities of varying individuals, without being unduly threatened by that diversity. The cultural value hierarchy – the corpus of laws, both written and unwritten, that governs that culture – might be regarded as the embodiment of the social contract, whose existence is most particularly revealed in the behaviors manifested by the individuals who compose that culture (rather than in the abstract representations purporting to encapsulate that culture). The existence of a given social contract gives rise to expectations, on the part of individuals, with regards to likely rewards and punishments (and with regards to what might be reasonably ignored, in a given situation). Culture, like memory, can therefore be said to be functioning properly, if its continued operation meets the expectations of its participants, in sufficient measure ("sufficient" meaning: dreams of alternatives do not become sufficiently motivating to impel social revolution).

What if expectations are violated? What if the rules of the game are broken? Well, it depends on the magnitude of the rule. Violated expectations, or emergence of anomaly, at the level of action, are likely to threaten only the most timid of cultural participants, while providing the majority with an optimal dose of novelty. Most people enjoy minor transformations of low level behaviors or concepts, as long as those alterations are potentially productive or aesthetically pleasing. But disruptions higher up the abstraction hierarchy become increasingly threatening, increasingly traumatic. It may be somewhat pleasing if you discover that your spouse is assembling the new furniture incorrectly, despite his or her general mechanical competence. It is anything but pleasing if you find out that he or she is having an affair. In the latter case, more large-scale theoretical frame conceptualizations, invisible, stabilizing axioms vanish. More of the previously ignored complex world reemerges. A sense of betrayal and personal incompetence rises, in precise proportion to the perceived magnitude of the error ("magnitude": area of territory, space and time, past, present and future, now rendered both unpredictable and non-productive in consequence of the error). Such violation of fundamental presupposition constitutes trauma. Trauma is sudden negative emotion and confusion, at axiomatic levels of belief. Trauma is indicative of major error in conceptualization. Trauma is simultaneously unforgettable, because of its emotional intensity, and incomprehensible, because of its complexity.

Individual memories of traumatic events are particularly relevant to the current discussion. Cultures differ most dramatically with regards to their interpretation of past traumas. And it is of great interest to note that the terrible and incomprehensible things that an individual does are even more likely to produce psychopathologies of trauma than the terrible things that befall an individual. In the former case (an individual doing an incomprehensible act) the traumatized individual has encountered a situation that exceeds his understanding. He has done something that supersedes his own model of himself. He has revealed himself to himself, for example, as a force for great evil. Because this revelation shakes his understanding of the world to the core, he does not precisely remember. To remember is to tell a coherent story, detailing causality in behavior, and no such story can be easily told about the great individual capacity for evil. To remember is to tell a story imbued with meaning. Where there is no specified meaning, the story suffers, in consequence. The same problem of coherence obtains for the victim. The child who is a target of vicious sexual assault, to take an extreme case, might not precisely remember (although he may also be unable to forget). How is a four year old to make coherent, representable sense of an event simultaneously so violent and shocking? So shrouded in secrecy? So much a violation of the trust that is a precondition for the child's dependence on adult care and protection?

Van der Kolk and Fisler (1995) have taken great pains to detail the paradoxical nature of traumatic memory. Trauma is the emergence of the unknown, in doses large enough to shatter long-standing presuppositions of predictability and stability. Tim O'Brien's autobiographical description of the reaction of soldiers to the absolute undesirability of the actual combat situation serves as dramatic illustration of the potential consequences of such shattering:

> For the most part, they carried themselves with poise. Now and then, however, there were times of panic, when they squealed or wanted to squeal but couldn't, when they twitched and made moaning sounds and covered their heads and said Dear Jesus and flopped around on the earth and fired their weapons and

cringed and sobbed and begged for the noise to stop and went wild and made stupid promises to themselves and to God and to their mothers and fathers, hoping not to die. In different ways, it happened to all of them. Afterward, when the firing ended, they would blink and peek up. They would touch their bodies, feeling shame, then quickly hiding it. They would force themselves to stand. As if in slow motion, frame by frame, the world would take on the old logic – absolute silence, then the wind, then sunlight, then voices. It was the burden of being alive. (1990: 18-19)

The unknown is not represented, and cannot be, just as the nature of the parent who perpetrates a violent assault on a child is a phenomenon beyond comprehension, beyond mapping. But the event still occurred. So what is remembered, what cannot be forgotten? Traumatic memories are highly emotion-laden and fragmentary. They consist of great fear, and flashes of sensory images. The neurophysiological work of Joseph LeDoux (1996), given a twist to account for unpredictability as primary motivation for fear (Davis and Whalen, 2001), explains exactly why.

Reaction to the unknown is a multi-stage process. When something unexplored (incomprehensible, dangerous, unpredictable) first manifests itself, it is not an object. It is instead something to motivate action (freezing, running away), before thinking, and perhaps even before emotion. The brain circuits that motivate such immediate action are phylogenetically ancient, very fast, with regards to sheer processing time, and very low resolution, imprecise. Why? Because life is in danger, when the unexpected emerges. Failure of plan, of behavior, of conceptualizations means, in an instant, that anything could happen. One of the potential consequences of "anything" is harm. Freeze! Run! The unknown is, therefore, most immediately, "that which compels immediate paralysis," or, "that which impels me to run in the opposite direction." That is categorization too, behavioral categorization, before emotion and certainly before object or name. Only after behavioral categorization is there emotion. Pain, frustration, disappointment, rage and anxiety (integrally linked negative emotions) surface in a confused jumble. All behavioral response systems are simultaneously set at alert, so that appropriate action (aggression, screaming, crying, flight) can be instituted on less than a moment's notice.

In the absence of further danger, curiosity emerges. Additional exploration takes place, and the gathering of additional information. Only then will object recognition, naming, ensue (a process that in many very complex situations can take minutes, days or months and not the tenths of seconds we normally associate with immediate, familiar object perception). How should betrayal by a lover, or a belief – a collapsed ideology – be construed? What are the objects, in a world of betrayal? How should experience be construed, in the absence of the relationship, or the cognitive structure? This is not a question that finds its immediate resolution. Very old brain circuits mediate our initial behavioral, then emotional, responses to the unknown. Then the newer, linguistically sophisticated but slower circuits take over, if they are allowed to, if we are willing to face the threat and complete the work. What is that cannot be remembered, in the case of true trauma? Anything about the event that was not understood (which means almost all of it): the causal sequences leading to the violent assault, for example, the nature of any behavioral patterns characteristic of the abused child that were temporally proximal to the event or increased its probability (however inadvertently and innocently) and, most importantly, how the child's conceptualizations and actions might be altered in the aftermath of the assault, so that its future probability will decrease. This and only this can be considered a sufficiently "accurate" representation.

If the linguistically sophisticated classification circuits cannot come up with a coherent account of the event (which is "what happened, pragmatically, but not necessarily objectively" and which is "correct" only in the case where a causal account has been generated in sufficient detail so that the account is socially transmissible and where repetition of the error is unlikely) then the emotional circuits, with their low resolution high action-motivation classification system, retain control over the memory. The memory is, at that point, only that low-resolution, high-action motivation classification, and nothing else (no "accurate video-tape recording" somehow repressed into the unconscious, in complete form). The emotional classification makes the event both incomprehensible and unforgettable. The ancient emotional systems say, over and over again, in the form of recurrent traumatic images, "Here is a threat which has been insufficiently processed. Process it. Your life is in danger. Process it. Your life is in danger." And since they are automated systems, in large part, and since their job is only threat identification and communication, they are perfectly willing to say the same thing *ad infinitum*, and to ensure that the traumatized individual is unable to get on with his or her life until the terrible event has been made inclusive, coherent, communicable, and unlikely to repeat. An accurate historical memory therefore has precisely those properties – and is most difficult to generate in precisely those cases that originally generated the most negative emotion, confusion, and chaos.

If my account of an event, say, as perpetrator, does not take into consideration your account, as victim (which means that it does not provide a story or encapsulation that is coherent, to you, and communicable, to you, and further, if it fails to convince you that it will not ever happen again), then your inability to forget and get on with your life is evidence for the insufficiency of my account. Understanding is the barrier to repetition. Understanding the past makes it go away. And "go away" means that it does not rear its ugly head in the present, in the form or recurrent "memory," or in the future, in the form of replication of the original trauma. Germans who are still Nazis neither remember nor forget. Russians who are still Stalinists neither remember nor forget. They still embody the past, are still the past. The stories of their victims have not been incorporated into their historical narratives. They have not taken into account those they turned both literally and metaphorically into ground, when pursuing their own too-narrow interests. And these interests are defined as "too narrow" not merely by the fact of vicious aggression, terrible as that was, but by the absolute abject failure of those interests and the presuppositions they were founded upon to produce anything but constant painful evidence of their own conceptual inadequacy. The Nazi ideology failed by its own express standards – as well as by the standards applied by their enemies. The Stalinists failed, too, to make the future better, in any way, than the past, including those ways defined as better by Stalinists.

Aleksandr Solzhenitsyn (1975) made a brilliant, but terrifying supportive point in his *Gulag Archipelago II*. He was particularly interested in the case of communist ideologues, swallowed up despite their orthodoxy by the terrible waves of Stalinist persecution in the 1940s and 1950s in the Soviet Union. He considered them to be extremes of a more general case: "How could it be anything but hard! It was more than the human heart could bear: to fall beneath the beloved axe – then to have to justify its wisdom" (p. 326). To be so convinced that the world was a particular way, and then to be faced with such hard evidence that it was not? And what was the choice of these self-betrayed individuals? To fall into a terrible pit, to admit that everything one had believed in was wrong (including memories, since they are beliefs too), or to deny one's own suffering, to make one's own motivations and emotions heretical? Imprisoned ideologues therefore not only suffered rejection and imprisonment, but rejection and imprisonment amplified by the fact that every complaint uttered in protest was heretical, was evidence for the insufficiency of the belief that both provided protection and gave hope? How could such a terrible trauma be remembered? Not without complete painful difficult dissolution of the current value system. Not without the incorporation into any new system of all the claims of the oppressed and rejected – including the now heretical self.

> Ye have heard that it hath been said, Thou shalt love thy neighbour, and hate thine enemy.
> But I say unto you, Love your enemies, bless them that curse you, do good to them that hate you, and pray for them which despitefully use you, and persecute you;
> That ye may be the children of your Father which is in heaven: for he maketh his sun to rise on the evil and on the good, and sendeth rain on the just and on the unjust.
> For if ye love them which love you, what reward have ye? do not even the publicans the same?
> And if ye salute your brethren only, what do ye more [than others]? do not even the publicans so?
> Be ye therefore perfect, even as your Father which is in heaven is perfect. (Matthew 5:43-48)

Acknowledgment of Suffering as a Form of Justice

"Fundamental to all forms of justice is official acknowledgment of what happened, whether by criminal process or by truth commission," according to Judge Richard Goldstone, former UN Chief Prosecutor in the war crimes trial in former Yugoslavia, and investigator of past political violence in South Africa. Setting the historical record straight by investigating grave human rights abuses, for example, might be regarded in theory as likely to aggravate already tense situations in countries recovering from genocide (such as Bosnia or Rwanda). But such a theory appears incorrect, socially – as it appears incorrect on the individual level, with regards to individual trauma. On the contrary, failing to attempt such historical confrontation, adjustment and adjudication creates several dangers (or leaves those already in place lurking, and liable to reemerge).

If the perpetrating group does not acknowledge and take responsibility for past violence, the victimized group cannot reasonably re-establish any relationship of trust (a necessary precondition for any civilized reconciliation), since the motivations, theoretical positions and causal action sequences underlying the original violence may well still be in place. Furthermore, if international court tribunals or similar institutions do not punish or at least identify the perpetrators of the crimes, the victims are likely to take responsibility for punishment in their own hands, continuing the cycle of violence. The problem of what Nico Frijda (1997) calls "unfinished business" will continue to manifest itself, if the perpetrators refuse, for example, to disclose the locations of victims' bodies or mass graves or any other information necessary to victims' families. The survivors are faced with moral obligations to their departed loved ones, and with the necessity of understanding their final fate, in order to grieve them properly – in order to bury the past. Both the living and the dead can reasonably claim not to be denied the suffering they endured. Suffering is, after all, injustice speaking for itself. And for the survivors, acknowledgment and condemnation of horrors endured becomes in itself a form of justice. In consequence, establishing a truthful, inclusive, complete and coherent historical record of violent conflicts will help decrease the likelihood of repetitive cycles of violence, and help foster genuine reconciliation.

The "taking into account" of that which is excluded makes society much stronger. The exclusion of the suffering from full membership in society means that the social group no longer has access to the full range of creative human possibility that the excluded potentially represent. Furthermore, continual conflict between victimizer and victim in any culture saps the strength of that culture. The perpetrators become increasingly totalitarian, cruel and rigid. The victims become increasingly resentful, hostile and nihilistic. Northrop Frye (1982, 1990) portrayed the entire Old Testament as a series of stories about the catastrophic consequences of emergent totalitarianism and cruelty among cultures who continually denied the weaker members of society their full rights as citizens. The philosopher of religion Huston Smith (1991) draws a pertinent example from the Bible, to illustrating this point. Naboth, the story's protagonist, refused to grant his family vineyard to the grasping King Ahab. In consequence, he was framed on false charges of subversion and blasphemy, and then stoned. Since blasphemy was a capital crime, his property was confiscated by the state. When news of this conspiracy reached the prophet Elijah, the Word of the Lord descended up on him, saying:

"Arise, go down to meet Ahab king of Israel, who is in Sama'ria; behold, he is in the vineyard of Naboth, where he has gone to take possession.

And you shall say to him, 'Thus says the LORD, "Have you killed, and also taken possession?"' and you shall say to him, 'Thus says the LORD: "In the place where dogs licked up the blood of Naboth shall dogs lick your own blood."' (1 Kings 21:18:19 RSV)

Smith states: "The story carries revolutionary significance for human history, for it is the story of how someone without official position took the side of a wronged man and denounced a king to his face on grounds of injustice. One will search the annals of history in vain for its parallel. Elijah was not a priest. He had no formal authority for the terrible judgment he delivered. The normal pattern of the day would have called for him to be struck down by bodyguards on the spot. But the fact that he was 'speaking for' an authority not his own was so transparent that the king accepted Elijah's pronouncement as just" (p. 289). Smith points out that the surprising point in this account is not what the king does, for he was "merely exercising the universally accepted prerogatives of royalty in [his] day. The revolutionary and unprecedented fact is the way the prophet challenged [his] actions"(p. 290). Smith describes the philosophical axiom underlying this challenge the "Prophetic Principle," and concludes, "stated abstractly, the Prophetic Principle can be put as follows: The prerequisite of political stability is social justice, for it is in the nature of things that injustice will not endure. Stated theologically, this point reads: God has high standards. Divinity will not put up forever with exploitation, corruption and mediocrity" (p. 292).

Societies predicated on the idea that even the weak, vilified and downtrodden are worthy of respect thrive and last. Societies that exploit, or forget the weak, risk – from the mythological perspective – the "eternal vengeance of God" (Peterson, 1999a):

Thus says the LORD: "For three transgressions of Israel, and for four, I will not revoke the punishment; because they sell the righteous for silver, and the needy for a pair of shoes –
they that trample the head of the poor into the dust of the earth, and turn aside the way of the afflicted; a man and his father go in to the same maiden, so that my holy name is profaned;
they lay themselves down beside every altar upon garments taken in pledge; and in the house of their God they drink the wine of those who have been fined.
(Amos 2:1-16 RSV)

Conclusion

Memories, individual and collective, are shaped by our motivations, past and present. This shaping is inevitable, because the world is complex beyond comprehension. But such inevitable shaping is transformed into distortion by our arrogant and fear-predicated reluctance to abandon or modify cherished beliefs in the face of disconfirming evidence (even when that disconfirmation is personally defined). The individual and collective rigidity engendered by such reluctance produces increasing suffering, on our part, as well as that of others, as the world moves away from our conception, and desires and need both remain unfulfilled.

The historical, psychological, and mythological record makes the story quite clear: individuals and societies that tip the balance too far away from correspondence and completeness of representation towards simple authoritarian coherence risk degrading their relationship with complexity. Such degradation carries with it its own inevitable and severe punishment, as the ignored world takes its revenge. This means that there are intrinsic albeit complex and subtle moral limits on what constitutes accurate memory, despite its difference from complete objective representation. Memory has to make sense. It is, after all, a model of the past, simplified so it can be represented and communication. Memory has to meet the emotional and motivational needs of those who carry it, because it is a construct of emotional and motivated beings. But memory also has to remain flexible enough, to allow for update, as new and relevant facts come to light. It also has to account for past trauma – perpetrated, as well as suffered – and decrease the likelihood of such trauma in the present and future. It must account, acceptably, for the experience of all those whose being made up the past – must encompass and acceptably represent suffering in the past, on the part of those whose devalued being made up that suffering, and who can therefore neither remember nor forget the past, in the present.

References

Adler, A. (1958). *What Life Should Mean to You*. New York: Capricorn Books.

Adorno, T. W., Frenkel-Brunswick, E., Livinson, D. J., and Sanford, R. N. (1950). *The Authoritarian Personality*. New York: Harper.

Allaman, J.D., Joyce, C.S. and Crandall, V.C. "The Antecedents of Social Desirability Response Tendencies of Children and Young adults." *Child Development, 43*, 1135-1160.

Altemeyer, B. (1988). *Enemies of Freedom: Understanding Right-Wing authoritarianism*. San Francisco, CA: Jossey-Bass Publishers.

Apsler, R. (1975). Effects of Embarrassment on Behavior Toward Others. *Journal of Personality and Social Psychology, 32*, 145-153.

Arendt, H. (1994). *Eichmann in Jerusalem : A Report on the Banality of Evil*. New York: Penguin.

Bartlett, F.C. (1932). *Remembering: A Study in Experimental and Social Psychology*. Cambridge: Cambridge University Press.

Bauer, M.E., Vedhara, K., Perks, P., Wilcomck, G.K., Lightman, S.L. and Shanks, N. (2000). Chronic Stress in Caregivers of Dementia Patients is Associated with Reduced Lymphocyte Sensitivity to Glucocorticoids. *Journal of Neuroimmunology, 103*, 84-92.

Baumeister, R. F., Heatherton, T. F., and Tice, D. M. (1993). When Ego Threats Lead to Self-Regulation Failure: Negative Consequences of High Self-esteem. *Journal of Personality and Social Psychology, 64*, 141-156.

Baumeister, R. F., Smart, L., and Boden, J. M. (1996). Relation of Threatened Egotism to violence and Aggression: The Dark Side of High Self-esteem. *Psychological Bulletin, 103*, 5-33.

Baumeister, R.F. and Hastings, S (1997). Distortions of Collective Memory: How Groups Flatter and Deceive Themselves. In Pennebaker et al (Ed.). Collective *Memory of Political Events: Social Psychological Perspective*. New Jersey: Lawrence Erlbaum Associates, Inc.

Becker, E. (1973). *The Denial of Death*. New York: The Free Press.

Block, J. (1965). *The Challenge of Response Sets: Unconfounding Meaning, Acquiescence, and Social Desirability in the MMPI*. New York: Appleton-Century-Crofts.

Brewer, M. B., and Schneider, S. (1990). Social Identity and Social Dilemmas: A Double-edged Sword. In D. Abrams and M. Hogg (Eds.), *Social Identity Theory: Constructive and Critical Advances*. London: Harvester-Wheatsheaf

Brooks, A. (1991a). Intelligence without Reason. MIT Artificial Intelligence Laboratory: *Artificial Intelligence Memo 1293*.

Brooks, A. (1991b). Intelligence without Representation. *Artificial Intelligence, 47, 139-159*.

Brown, J. D., and Dutton, K. A. (1995). Truth and Consequences: The Costs and Benefits of accurate Self-knowledge. *Personality and Social Psychology Bulletin, 21, 12, 1288-1296*.

Brown, J. D., (1991). Accuracy and Bias in Self-knowledge. In C.R. Snyder and Dr. R. Forsyth (Eds.), *Handbook of Social and Clinical Psychology*. (pp. 158-178). New York: Pergamon

Brown, L. L., Tomarken, A. J., Orth, D.N., Loosen, P.T., Kalin, N.H. and Davidson, R.J. (1996). Individual Differences in Repressive-defensiveness Predict Basal Salivary Cortisol Levels. *Journal of Personality and Social Psychology, 70, 2, 362-371*.

Brown, R. (1986). *Social Psychology* (2nd Ed.). New York: Free Press.

Byrne, D. and Bounds, C. (1964). The Reversal of F Scale Items. *Psychological Reports, 14, 216*.

Carver, C. S., and Scheier, M. F. (1998). *On the Self-regulation of Behavior*. New York, NY: Cambridge University Press.

Chang, I. (1998). *The Rape of Nanking: The Forgotten Holocaust of World War II*. New York: Penguin.

Christie, R. (1956b). Some abuses of Psychology. *Psychological Bulletin, 53, 439-451*.

Christie,R. (1956a). Eysenck's Treatment of the Personality of Communists. *Psychological Bulletin, 53, 411-430*.

Cohen, F. and Lazarus, R. S. (1973). Active Coping Processes, Coping Dispositions, and Recovery from Surgery. *Psychosomatic Medicine, 35, 375-389*.

Cohen, F. (1984). Coping. In J. D. Matarazzo, S. M. Weiss, J. A. Herd, N. E. Miller, S. M. Weiss (Eds.). *Behavioral Health: A Handbook of Health Enhancement and Disease Prevention* (pp. 261-274). New York: Wiley.*

Crocker, J., and Luhtanen, R. (1990). Collective Self-esteem and Ingroup Bias. *Journal of Personality and Social Psychology, 58, 60-67*.

Crowne, D. P., and Marlowe, D. (1960). A New Scale of Social Desirability Independent of Psychopathology. *Journal of Consulting Psychology, 24, 349-354*.

Crowne, D. P., and Marlowe, D. (1964). *The approval Motive*. New York: Wiley.

Davis, M. and Whalen, P.J. (2001). The amygdala: vigilance and Emotion. Molecular Psychiatry, 6, 13-34.

Davis, P.J. (1987). Repression and the Inaccessibility of affective Memories. *Journal of Personality and Social Psychology, 53, 585-593*.

De La Ronde, C., and Swann, W. B., Jr. (1998). Partner verification: Restoring Shattered Images of our Intimates. *Journal of Personality and Social Psychology, 75, 374-382*.

DeNeve, K. and Cooper, H. (1998). The Happy Personality: A Meta-analysis of 137 Personality Traits and Subjective well-being. *Psychological Bulletin, 124, 197-229*.

Derry and MacDonald, 1983 (I can't locate this reference);

Doty, R. M., Peterson, B. E., and Winter, D. G. (1991). Threat and authoritarianism in the United States, 1978-1987. *Journal of Personality and Social Psychology, 61, 629-640*.

Edwards, A. L. (1953). The Relationship between the Judged Desirability of a Trait and the Probability that the Trait will be Endorsed. *Journal of Applied Psychology, 37, 90-99*.

Edwards, A. L. (1957). *The Social Desirability variable in Personality assessment and Research*. New York: Dryden.

Eliade, M. (1978). *A History of Religious Ideas. Vol. 1. From the Stone age to the Eleusinian Mysteries*. Chicago: Chicago University Press.

Esterling, B. A., Antoni, M. H., Kumar, M. and Schneiderman, N. (1990). Emotional Depression, Stress Disclosure Responses, and Epstein-Barr viral Capsid antigen Titers. *Psychosomatic Medicine, 52*, 397—410.

Esterling, B. A., Antoni, M. H., Kumar, M. and Schneiderman, N. (1993). Defensiveness, Trait anxiety, and Epstein-Barr viral Capsid antigen antibody Titers in Healthy College Students. *Health Psychology, 12*, 132-139.,

Eysenck, H. J. (1954). *The Psychology of Politics*. New York, NY: Praeger.

Eysenck, H.J. (1994). Neuroticism and the Illusion of Mental Health. *American Psychologist, 49*, 971-972.

Eysenck, S. B., Eysenck, H. J., and Barrett, P. (1985). A Revised version of the Psychoticism Scale. *Personality and Individual Differences, 6*, 121-129.

Foa, E. B., and Kozak, M. J. (1985). Treatment of anxiety Disorders: Implications for Psychopathology. In A. H. Tuma and J. D. Maser (Eds.), *Anxiety and the anxiety Disorders* (pp. 451-452). Hillsdale, NJ: Erlbaum.

Foa, E. B., and Kozak, M. J. (1986). Emotional Processing of Fear: Exposure to Corrective Information. *Psychological Bulletin, 99*, 20-35.

Foa, E. B., Feske, U., Murdock, T. B., Kozak, M. J., and McCarthy, P. R. (1991). Processing of Threat-related Information in Rape victims. *Journal of Abnormal Psychology, 100*, 156-162.

Frankl, V. (1971). *Man's Search for Meaning: An Introduction to Logotherapy*. New York: Pocket Books.

Frijda, Nico, H (1997). Commemorating. In Pennebaker et al (Ed.). Collective *Memory of Political Events: Social Psychological Perspective*. New Jersey: Lawrence Erlbaum Associates, Inc.

Frye, N. (1982). *The Great Code: The Bible and Literature*. London: Harcourt Brace Jovanovitch.

Frye, N. (1990). *Words with Power: Being a Second Study of the Bible and Literature*. London: Harcourt Brace Jovanovitch.

Furnham, A. (1986). Response Bias, Social Desirability and Dissimulation. *Personality and Individual Differences, 7*, 385-400.

Garrison, W., Earls, F., and Kindlon, D. (1983). An application of the Pictorial Scale of Perceived Competence and acceptance within an Epidemiological Survey. *Journal of Abnormal Child Psychology, 11*, 367-377.

Goldhagen, D.J. (1996). *Hitler's willing Executioners: ordinary Germans and the Holocaust*. New York: Alfred Knopf.

Gray, J. A. (1982). *The Neuropsychology of anxiety: An Enquiry into the Functions of the Septo-hippocampal System*. Oxford: Oxford University Press.

Gray, J. A. (1987). *The Psychology of Fear and Stress* (2nd ed.). Cambridge: Cambridge University Press

Greenberg, J., and Pyszczynski, T. (1985). Compensatory Self-inflation: A Response to the Threat to Self-Regard of Public Failure. *Journal of Personality and Social Psychology, 49*, 273-280.

Greenwald, A. G. (1980). The Totalitarian Ego: Fabrication and Revision of Personal History. *American Psychologist, 7*, 603-618.

Hanley,C. and Rokeach, M. (1956). Care and Carelessness in Psychology. *Psychological Bulletin, 53*, 183-186

Hardin, C.D. and Higgins, E.T. (1996). Shared Reality: How Social verification Makes the Subjective objective. In R.M. Sorrentino, E.T. Higgins et al. *Handbook of Motivation and Cognition* (Vol. 3, pp. 28-84). New York: Guilford Press.

Harland, D (1998). *Report of the Secretary-General Pursuant to General Assembly Resolution 53/35 (1998).: Srebrenica Report.*

Igartua, J.and Perez, D (1997). : Art and Remembering Traumatic Collective Events; the Case of the Spanish Civil War. In Pennebaker et al (Ed.). *Collective Memory of Political Events: Social Psychological Perspective.* New Jersey: Lawrence Erlbaum Associates, Inc.

Jamner, L. D., and Schwartz, G. E. (1986). Self-deception Predicts Self-report and Endurance of Pain. *Psychosomatic Medicine, 48,* 211-223.

Jamner, L. D., Schwartz, G. E. and Leigh, H. (1988). The Relationship between Repressive and Defensive Coping Styles and Monocyte, Eosinophile, and Serum Glucose Levels: Support for the opioid Peptide Hypothesis of Repression. *Psychosomatic Medicine, 50,* 567—575.

Johnson, E.A., Vincent, N. and Ross, L. (1997). Self-deception versus Self-esteem in Buffering the Negative Effects of Failure. *Journal of Research in Personality, 31,* 385-405.

Jung, C.G. (1959). Archetypes of the Collective unconscious. R.F.C. Hull (Trans.). *The Collected works of C.G. Jung* (Vol. 9(1)). Bollingen Series XX. Princeton: Princeton University Press.

Kelly, G. (1955). *The Psychology of Personal Constructs.* New York: Norton.

Kruglanski,A. W. (1980). Lay Epistemology Process and Contents. *Psychological Review, 87,* 70-87

Kuiper, N.A., Derry, P.A., and MacDonald, M.R. (1983). Self-reference and Person Perception in Depression: A Social Cognition Perspective. In G. Weary and H. Mirels (Eds.), *Integrations of Clinical and Social Psychology* (pp. 79-103). New York: Oxford University Press.

Kunda, Z. (1990). The Case for Motivated Reasoning. *Psychological Bulletin, 108,* 480-90.

Lane, R. D., Merikangas, K. R., Schwartz, G. E., Huang, S. S., and Prusoff, B. A. (1990). Inverse Relationship between Defensiveness and Life Time Prevalence of Psychiatric Disorder. *American Journal of Psychiatry, 147,* 573-578

LeDoux, J. (1996). *The Emotional Brain: The Mysterious underpinnings of Emotional Life.* New York: Simon and Schuster.

Levy, S. M., Herberman, R. B., Maluish, A. M., Schlien, B. and Lippman, M. (1985). Prognostic Risk assessment in Primary Breast Cancer by Behavioral and Immunological Parameters. *Health Psychology, 4,* 99—113.

Lorig, T.S., Singer, J.L., Bonnano, G.A., Davis, P et al. (1994-1995). Repressor Personality Styles and EEG Patterns associated with affective Memory and Thought Suppression. *Imagination, Cognition and Personality, 14,* 203-210.

Malcom, N. (1996). *Bosnia: A Short History.* London: Papermac.

Marks, G. (1984). Thinking one's abilities are unique and one's opinions are Common. *Personality and Social Psychology Bulletin, 10,* 203-208.

Martocchio, J.J. and Judge, T.A. (1997). Relationship between Conscientiousness and Learning in Employee Training: Mediating Influence of Self-deception and Self-efficacy. *Journal of Applied Psychology, 82,* 764-773.

McFarland, S.G., Ageyev, V.S. and Djintcharadze, N. (1996). Russian authoritarianism Two years after Communism. *Personality and Social Psychology Bulletin, 22,* 210-217.

McFarland, S.G., Ageyev, V.S. and Abalakina-Papp, M.A. (1992). Authoritarianism in the Former Soviet Union. *Journal of Personality and Social Psychology, 63,* 1004-1010.

Medin, D.L. and Aguilar, C.M. (1999). Categorization. In R.A. Wilson and F. Keil (Eds.) *MIT Encyclopedia of Cognitive Sciences.* Cambridge, MA: MIT Press.

Millar, K. U., and Tesser, A. (1987). Deceptive Behavior in Social Relationships: A Consequence of violated Expectations. *The Journal of Psychology, 122,* 263-273

Mullen, B., and Suls, J. (1982). The Effectiveness of attention and Rejection as Coping Styles: A Meta-analysis of Temporal Differences. *Journal of Psychosomatic Research, 26,* 43-49.

Myers, L. B., and Brewin, C. R. (1995). Repressive Coping and the Recall of Emotional Material. *Cognition and Emotion, 9,* 637-642.

Neisser, U. (1982). *Memory Observed: Remembering in Natural Contexts*. San Francisco: Freeman.

Niebuhr, R. (1944). *The Children of Light and the Children of Darkness*. New York: Charles Scribner's Sons

O'Brien, T. (1990). The Things They Carried. New York: *Broadway* Books.

Oatley, K. and Johnson-Laird, P.N. (1987) Towards a Cognitive Theory of Emotion. *Cognition and Emotion, 1*, 29-50.

Off, C. (2000). *The Lion, the Fox and the Eagle*. Random House Canada

Olweus, D. (1993). *Bullying at School: What we Know and what we Can Do*. Cambridge: Blackwell.

Ones, D.S., Viswesvaran, C. and Reiss, A.D. (1996). Role of Social Desirability in Personality Testing for Personnel Selection: The Red Herring. *Journal of Applied Psychology, 81*, 660-679.

Orwell, G. (1965). *Nineteen Eighty-four*. London, England: Heinemann Educational Books Ltd.

Paulhus, D. L. (1990). Measurement and Control of Response Bias. In J. P. Robinson, P. R. Shaver, and L. Wrightsman (Eds.), *Measures of Personality and Social-psychological attitudes* (pp. 17-59). San Diego, CA: Academic Press.

Paulhus, D.L. (1998). Interpersonal and Intrapsychic adaptiveness or Trait Self-enhancement: A Mixed Blessing? *Journal of Personality and Social Psychology, 74*, 1197-1208.

Pennebaker, J. W. (1988). Confiding Traumatic Experiences and Health. In S. Fisher and J.Reason (Eds.), *Handbook of Life Stress, Cognition and Health*. (pp. 669-682). New York: Wiley.

Pennebaker, J. W. (1989). Confession, Inhibition, and Disease. In L. Berkowitz (Ed.), *Advances in Experimental Social Psychology* (Vol. 22, pp. 211-244). New York: Academic Press.

Pennebaker, J. W. (1993). Social Mechanisms of Constraint.(In D. M. Wegner and J. W. Pennebaker (Eds.), *Handbook of Mental Control* (pp. 200-219). Englewood Cliffs, NJ: Prentice Hall.

Pennebaker, J. W., and Hoover, C. W. (1985). Inhibition and Cognition: Toward an understanding of Trauma and Disease. In R. J. Davidson, G. E. Schwartz, and D. Shapiro (Eds.), *Consciousness and Self-regulation* (Vol. 4, pp. 107-136). New York: Plenum.

Pennebaker, J. W., and Susman, J. R. (1988). Disclosure of Traumas and Psychosomatic Processes. *Social Science and Medicine, 26*, 327-332.

Pennebaker, J.W (1997). *Collective Memory of Political Events: Social Psychological Perspective*. New Jersey: Lawrence Erlbaum Associates, Inc.

Pennebaker, J.W., Mayne, T.J. and Francis, M.E. (1997). Linguistic Predictors of adaptive Bereavement. *Journal of Personality and Social Psychology, 72*, 863-871.

Perloff, L. S., and Fetzer, B. K. (1986). Self-other Judgements and Perceived vulnerability to victimization. *Journal of Personality, 50*, 502-510.

Peterson, B.E., Smirles, K.A., Wentworth, and Phyllis A. (1997). Generativity and authoritarianism: Implications for Personality, Political Involvement, and Parenting. *Journal of Personality and Social Psychology, 72*, 1202-

Peterson, J.B. (1999a). *Maps of Meaning: The architecture of Belief*. New York: Routledge.

Peterson, J.B. (1999b). Neuropsychology and Mythology of Motivation for Group aggression. In Kurtz, L. (Ed.). *Encyclopedia of violence, Peace and Conflict* (pp. 529-545). San Diego: Academic Press.

Peterson, J.B. (in press). The Meaning of Meaning. In Wong, P. *Selected Proceedings on Searching for Meaning in the New Millennium*. INPM Press.

Peterson, J.B. and Flanders, J. (in press). Complexity Management Theory: Motivation for Ideological Rigidity and Social Conflict. Cortex, XX, XX-XX.

Petrie, K. J., Booth, R. J., Pennebaker, J. W., Davison, K.P. and Thomas, M.G. (1995). Disclosure of Trauma and Immune Response to a Hepatitis B vaccination Program. *Journal of Consulting and Clinical Psychology, 63*, 787-79.

Piaget, J. (1965). *The Moral Judgement of the Child.* New York: The Free Press.

Powers, W. T. (1973). *Behavior: The Perception of Control.* Chicago: Aldine Publishing Company.

Pulkkinen, L., and Tremblay, R.E. (1992). Patterns of Boys' Social adjustment in Two Cultures and at Different ages: A Longitudinal Perspective. *International Journal of Behavioral Development, 15*, 527-553.

Pyszczynski, T. and Greenberg, J. (1987). Toward and Integration of Cognitive and Motivational Perspectives on Social Inference: A Biased Hypothesis-testing Model. In L. Berkowitz (Ed.), *Advances in Experimental Social Psychology* (Vol. 20, pp. 297-340). New York: Academic Press.

Pyszczynski,T., Greenberg,J. and Holt,K. (1985). Maintaining Consistency between Self-serving Beliefs and available Data: A Bias in Information Evaluation. *Personality and Social Psychology Bulletin, 11*, 179-190.

Raber, J. (1998). Detrimental Effects of Chronic Hypothalamic-pituitary-adrenal axis activation. From obesity to Memory Deficits. *Molecular Neurobiology, 18*, 1-22.

Robins, R. W., and Beer, J. S. (1996). *A Longitudinal Study of the adaptive and Maladaptive Consequences of Positive Illusions about the Self.* Unpublished Manuscript, University of California, Berkeley.

Rokeach, M. and Hanley,C. (1956). Eysenck's Tender-Minded Dimension: A Critique. *Psychological Bulletin, 53*, 169-176.

Rokeach, M. (1956). Political and Religious Dogmatism: An alternative to the authoritarian Personality. *Psychological Monographs, 70*, (Whole No. 425)-18.

Rosenberg, M. (1979). *Conceiving the Self.* New York: Basic Books.

Rosenthal, R. and Rubin, D. B. (1978). Interpersonal Expectancy Effects: The First 345 Studies. *Behavioral and Brain Sciences, 3*, 377-386.

Sackeim, H. A. (1983). Self-deception, Self-esteem, and Depression: The adaptive value of Lying to oneself. In J. Masling (Ed.), *Empirical Studies of Psychoanalytical Theories* (pp. 107-157). Hillsdale, NJ: Analytic Press.

Sackeim, H. A., and Gur, R. C. (1979). Self-deception, other Deception, and Self-reported Psychopathology. *Journal of Consulting and Clinical Psychology, 47*, 213-215.

Sales, S.M. and Friend, K.E. (1973). Success and Failure as Determinants of Level of authoritarianism. *Behavioral Science, 18*, 163-172.

Sales, S.M. (1973). Threat as a Factor in authoritarianism: an analysis of archival Data. *Journal of Personality and Social Psychology, 28*, 44-57.

Sapolsky, R. M. (1996). The Price of Propriety. *The Sciences, 36*, 14-16

Schacter, D.L (1995). *Searching for Memory: The Brain, the Mind, and the Past.* New York: Basic Books.

Shea, J.D., Burton, R. and Girgis, A. (1993). Negative affect, absorption and Immunity. *Physiological Behavior, 3*, 449-457.

Shedler, J., Mayman, M., and Manis, M. (1993). The Illusion of Mental Health. *American Psychologist, 48*, 1117-1131.

Shils, E. A. (1954). Authoritarianism: "Right" and "left". In R. Christie and M. Jahoda (Eds.), *Studies in the Scope and Method of "The Authoritarian Personality."* New York: Free Press of Glencoe

Shipherd, J.C. and Beck, J.G. (1999). The Effects of Suppressing Trauma-related Thoughts on women with Rape-related Posttraumatic Stress Disorder. *Behavior Therapy and Research, 37*, 99-112

Sieber, W.J., Rodin, J., Larson, L., Ortega, S., Cummings, N., Levy, S., Whitesdie, T., Herberman, R. (1992). Modulation of Human Natural Killer Cell activity by Exposure to uncontrollable Stress. *Brain and Behavioral Immunology, 6*, 141-156.

Smith, H. (1991). The world's Religions. San Francisco: Harper.

Snyder, M. (1974). Self-monitoring of Expressive Behavior. *Journal of Personality and Social Psychology, 30*, 158-164.

Solzhenitsyn, A.I. (1975). *The Gulag archipelago, 1918-1956: An Experiment in Literary Investigation* (T.P. Whitney, Trans.) (Vol. 2). New York: Harper and Row.

Staub, E. (1989/1997). *The Roots of Evil: The origins of Genocide and other Group violence.* Cambridge: Cambridge University Press.

Steele, C. M. (1988). The Psychology of Self-affirmation: Sustaining the Integrity of Self. *Advances in Experimental Social Psychology, 21,* 261-302.

Stokes, P.E. (1995). The Potential Role of Excessive Cortisol Induced by HPA Hyperfunction in the Pathogenesis of Depression. *European Neuropsychopharmacology, 5* (Supplement), 77-82.

Stone, W. F. (1980). The Myth of Left-wing authoritarianism. *Political Psychology, 2* 3-19.

Suls, J., and Fletcher, B. (1985). The Relative Efficacy of avoidant and Non-avoidant Coping Strategies: A Meta-analysis. *Health Psychology, 4,* 249-288.

Swann, W. B., Stein-Seroussi, A., and McNulty, S. E. (1992). Outcasts in a white-lie Society: The Enigmatic worlds of People with Negative Self-conceptions. *Journal of Personality and Social Psychology, 62,* 618-624.

Swann, W. B., Wenzlaff, R. M., Krull, D. S., Pelham, B. W. (1992). Allure of Negative Feedback: Self-verification Strivings among Depressed Persons. *Journal of Abnormal Psychology, 101,* 293-306.

Sweetland, A. and Quay, H. (1953). A Note on the K Scale of the MMPI. Journal of *Consulting Psychology, 17,* 314-316.

Taylor, S. E. (1989). *Positive Illusions: Creative Self-deception and the Healthy Mind.* New York: Basic Books.

Taylor, S. E., and Brown, J. (1988). Illusion and well-being: A Social Psychological Perspective on Mental Health. *Psychological Bulletin, 103,* 193-210.

Taylor, S. E., and Brown, J. D. (1994). Positive Illusions and well-being Revisited: Separating Fact from Fiction. *Psychological Bulletin, 116,* 21-27.

Taylor, S. E., Collins, R. L., Skokan, L. A., and Aspinwall, L. G. (1989). Maintaining Positive Illusions in the Face of Negative Information: Getting the Facts without Letting Them Get to you. *Journal of Social and Clinical Psychology, 8,* 114-129.

Tesser, A. and Moore, J. (1990). Independent Threats and Self-evaluation Maintenance Processes. *Journal of Social Psychology, 130,* 677-691.

Tesser, A., and Campbell, J. (1982). Self-evaluation Maintenance and the Perception of Friends and Strangers. *Journal of Personality, 50,* 261-279.

Tesser, A., and Smith, J. (1980). Some Effects of Friendship and Task Relevance on Helping: Your Don't always Help the one you Like. *Journal of Experimental Social Psychology, 16,* 582-590.

Tomaka, J., Blascovich, J. and Kelsey, R.M. (1992). Effects of Self-deception, Social Desirability and Repressive Coping on Psychophysiological Reactivity to Stress. *Personality and Social Psychology Bulletin, 18,* 616-624.

Tomarken, A. J., and Davidson, R. J. (1994). Frontal Brain activation in Repressors and Nonrepressors. *Journal of Abnormal Psychology, 103,* 339-349.

van der Kolk, B.A. and Fisler, R. (1995). Dissociation and the Fragmentary Nature of Traumatic Memories: Overview and Exploratory Study. *Journal of Traumatic Stress, 8,* 505-525.

Weinberger, D. A., and Gomes, M. E. (1989). *Sensitized, Self-assured, and Repressive attributional Styles: A New Look at Non-depressive Bias.* Unpublished manuscript.

Weinberger, D. A., Schwartz, G. E., and Davidson, R.J. (1979). Low anxious, High anxious, and Repressive Coping Styles: Psychometric Patterns and Behavioral and Physiological Responses to Stress. *Journal of Abnormal Psychology, 88,* 369-380.

Westen, D. (1998). The Scientific Legacy of Sigmund Freud: Toward a Psychodynamically Informed Psychological Science. *Psychological Bulletin, 124,* 333-371.

Whitworth, J.A., Brown, M.A., Kelly, J.J. and Williamson, P.M. (1995). Mechanisms of Cortisol-induced Hypertension in Humans. *Steroids, 60,* 76-80.

Williams, S.L., Kinney, P.J. and Falbo, J. (1989). Generalization of Therapeutic Changes in agoraphobia: the Role of Perceived Self-efficacy. *Journal of Consulting and Clinical Psychology, 57*, 436-442.
Williams, S.L., Kinney, P.J. Harap, S.T. and Liebmann, M. (1997). Thoughts of agoraphobic People during Scary Tasks. *Journal of Abnormal Psychology, 106*, 511-52.

Where Religion Confuses Yet Faith Gives Hope: Conflict Resolution in Northern Ireland

Derek Wilson

I wish to examine the dynamics of living in a contested place where people and groups are not culturally prepared to walk towards one another, to meet and include, but are prepared for distance from the other, tending to move apart and remaining at least distrustful.

My central theme is: "How, when so much of ones life prepares you for separation and distance, can people be prepared to walk together, taking risks in relationships and building new and inclusive working practices and organizational cultures?"

"I am therefore I think" is my starting point but if I am culturally and religiously prepared for separation how can I think and act my way into a new way of being with those others I am "wise to" but not "wise about"?

In the first section, I wish to assist you understand the context of Northern Ireland by

1. Taking you into the fascination of the ethnic frontier[1] and the ways all institutions and relationships are shaped by the dynamics of such a place;

2. Introducing the patterns of communal deterrence we have lived within;

3. Examine how yesterday's violence cannot remain secret but will corrupt today's relationships when they are unacknowledged

4. Introduce you to the ways of avoidance and politeness being preferred rather than meeting and dealing with issues.

Conflict resolution in an ethnic frontier has to acknowledge the initially peripheral nature of reconciliation work and yet through our work and the work of others we see this understanding deepen- and become more central to institutional life and public policy. *Reconciliation is in all our interests.*

Understanding the Context

Through living in a contested society I have become acutely aware of how people's feet, including my own, are prepared to walk towards those I am told I am like and away from those I am told I am different to.

When people and the organizations we participate in are so easily able to learn separation and cement partisanship there are huge societal costs. One such cost is the erosion of any models of relationship and common activity that models trust between diverse peoples and traditions.

In my own experience a turning point in life was being with one individual in 1965, the now 85-year-old founder of the Corrymeela Community, Ray Davey, who had been a prisoner of war for more than three years in Italy and then, finally, in Dresden when it was bombed. Ray challenged us with a vision of community and the ecumenical view of the world; he gave us possibilities to move beyond the excluding and separate ways of living which so many of us were prepared for in Northern Ireland as we grew up.

It is people taking steps forward that changes the directions of organizations; how is it that we so easily lose faith in our possibilities to effect change by taking such simple steps?

1. The Ethnic Frontier

The dynamics of life in Northern Ireland are, for me, best understood in interpreting where I live as an ethnic frontier, a term proposed by Frank Wright (Wright, 1992).

Here you cannot just be a citizen, you are either a member of the "loyal" group or the "disloyal" group; the national identity or not.

Individual identity is always linked to some communal belonging because strangers are people who do not fit in and are therefore to be distrusted.

> A group meeting between teachers and community activists were sharing experiences of living and working here. Story after story is told. In one a woman from the Catholic tradition speaks about nursing a dying member of the security forces while neighbours around her call her names, saying "he is not worth it." In the telling of the story the protestant people in the group listen deeply, it is the experience of this woman that moves them all, some to tears.

The security forces are seen to belong to the Crown and Protestants are loyal to that crown. The assumptions of Protestants are both reinforced and shattered in this experience. Which way will people choose? The story of the crowd fits their stereotypes whereas the challenge comes from listening to the woman's anguish and struggle to put humanity above politics?

In such spaces the need for meeting can free people who are otherwise hostage to the communal fears and communal common sense.

In the Frontier All Aspects of Life Become Hostage to It

The divisions in our society are not just felt on the margins but experienced, and often avoided, in the centre of institutional and organizational life be that the sporting, cultural, voluntary, religious or community activities people pursue or in the openness to moving about town centres and the workplaces.

Cultural religions, masquerading as faith, have played a major part in this disabling process. In such religious expressions the other is absent and unacknowledged. Initiatives where a different quality of community relations work and ecumenical activity is occurring also exist but they remain still on the margins, often outside mainstream institutional support.

2. The Dynamics of Communal Deterrence

The cultural reality in such a place is that "all actions of the others" are unacceptable and "all actions by us" are understandable. My actions are always only because of their provocation and therefore necessary. In such circles many people are only brought up to see the other as devious and always threatening.

Such a society has the capacity to turn "even the benign into dust" (Barclay).

When polarization forces us to look pessimistically at the worst things coming from their side, that which is redeeming often disappears from our attention. (P 512 Wright)

It is so difficult to enable new reconciling actions in the midst of such communal deterrence. The *overwhelming reality has been of societies and cultures* perpetuating themselves in this fearful climate.

3. Cultural Common Sense— Separation, Avoidance, and Politeness

In a contested society the cultural common sense becomes one of learning to be polite whilst wishing that such issues could be avoided if one has to be with the other. Real common sense prefers that of separation, wishing that such meetings were not necessary.

"In our town everyone knows about everyone else, on all sides…There have been incidents in the town between the traditions but there is a silence about who did it, even though, within each group, people know who did the different actions on behalf of their group."

Here the communal politeness ritualises the tension and makes it manageable. However the other cannot be got rid of and all remains an uneasy peace.

4. Meeting Together is Diminished

So, in a contested place the very need for relationships of trust to be established is diminished by people being culturally prepared for separation, avoidance or politeness. In such encounters the tools and expertise to be at ease and confident with the other are blunted further and states of polite concealed aggression are settled for.

5. Stability and Secrets no More

In the ethnic frontier of Northern Ireland one learns the essential truth that is hidden within the structures of stable societies. That is that states, nations and religions have violent edges and that, in their formation, violence has been a very present reality.

In such a contested place churches are "institutions in bad conscience." They behave as if they are in the centre of stable nations. The reality of the frontier confronts them with their connivance with one tradition, their ambivalence about violence and their alliances with different cultural traditions. In these actions they diminish the gospel text which invites "men and women, slave and free, Greek and Jew" to enter a new, inclusive and transcending identity in the shelter of the gospel. In such a place Christianity becomes a religion not a faith, in such a place the space for meeting is diminished.

The task of reconciliation is still peripheral

This space for meeting is the very space needed for some reconciliation experiences to take place. Such work has often been dependent on brave and courageous people and groups, often silently taking risks.

When people do meet it is possible, at least, to understand the dynamics we all are caught up in and that very action and knowledge breaks the mechanisms' hold a little.

What we need are ways in which individual experiences of change are held and carried by groups, and organizations.

Eventually this will need to be assisted by a public policy climate that establishes trust building as a core strategic objective.

In reality reconciliation work even within the voluntary sector has been a peripheral interest. The *hard work* of relationship building and modelling new organizational forms of working, which are inclusive of others, has often been laid to the side. The real work of developing models of relationship building and organizational practice which resolves conflicts and mediate new relationships between people, traditions and cultures here has often been devalued.

The cumulative reality of growing up in an ethnic frontier then is:

1. That we are more at ease with those who are similar to us and less prepared to and prepared for meeting those who are different to us.

2. Such a lack of relationships and structures between people across the traditional divide who are at ease with one another bedevils any processes moving forward.

3. When the base of the populations has so little inter-connection then politicians merely reflect this lack of trust and understanding and, being public representatives, have difficulty giving any reconciling lead.

4. When religious enmity and political fears resonate together the space for meeting, the possibilities of the unexpected and the opportunities for healing are severely limited.

Discerning Useful Ways to Understanding Conflict

In this section I wish to:

1. Understand the places where people learn the old ways of separation and cultural blindness

2. Seek new places and relationships where understanding grows.

Where do People Learn These Old Ways?

Ethnic frontiers are contested areas at the borders of historically rivalrous states. In such a place fear predominates. The fear is often denied politely in the public spaces where people meet and ignored in the groups people voluntarily choose to belong to, which are often mono-cultural.

We have identified three organizational cultures through which these issues are ignored, coped with or addressed. Two have costs in terms of relationships and investments of time to maintain them; and the third has benefits and potential savings which, if embraced would be a step forward in a conflict resolution process.

A *Culture of Partisanship* is characterised by the fact that the main stakeholders belong predominantly to one group or tradition. If others do belong they submerge their differences, fit in or leave.

A *Culture of Neutrality* where all issues are monitored numerically. It will in fact be rare for such places to be neutral, as the organization will take its lead from the particular identities of those at the top. In times of unrest this legally required structure would emphasise harmony and similarity in the workplace in order to get beyond the difficulties outside.

A *Culture of Diversity* is where the nascent needs to be more openly diverse for the wider society and for business is acknowledged. Here such a culture models ways forward beyond a divided society.

Looking at these models:

On the pessimistic side of the equation we have a lack of institutional commitment to addressing the needs of an increasingly diverse society coming out of conflict.

This means an unwillingness to see reconciliation in practical steps in the daily negotiations between people in leisure, sporting, workplace, faith and community life.

The ways people are trained to walk culturally are deeper than the ways, which need to be learned. Yet it is these ways that must be built.

What has to be learned in order to move in this direction will only be learned "on the way."

Church Community and Reconciliation

For those concerned with church life it is a salutary lesson to explore how partisan such church organizations are in a conflict. This is not to argue that churches all have to become diverse and, in belief terms, diluted. Rather it is to ask how such partisan organizations can acknowledge the other in some manner within their life, structures and programmes so that their belief is not being secured in the denial of the other's existence.

The reality of many opposed to reconciliation in church circles is they have preyed upon rather than prayed with those who were different to them.

While acknowledging the vast work that some people have undertaken from within a church base the reality is that this work has been carried by individuals and small groups more often than by institutional proclamation. Those initiating such activity have a history of being ridiculed by their co-religionists.

A dominant influence in the churches in Northern Ireland has been an implicit theology of separation. This has dominated all churches. This has meant that that the religious institutions have been unable to model ways of living inclusively; the organizations associated with them in everything from youth clubs, uniformed organizations and adult education groups have been separating institutions more than mediating, integrating or facilitating ones. (Of course these have been and are beacons such as the ISE, ICC Peace Education Project, Corrymeela and others yet these remain sustained by the committed individuals more that the energetic denominations.)

The recent growth of Church Fora in local areas has been a most welcome development. However it is important to note that often "doctrine" or an "ecclesiastical shepherd" did not lead their development; rather it was a response to an invitation by trusted third parties or laypeople or the local Council Chief executive.

These initiatives are important because they are invitational and inclusive in their character; permanently open to those who have not yet responded that they may eventually do so.

The focus of activity is often commonly agreed important civic work. Here the churches can develop a Civic Leadership function around civic events and themes.

Here the language of ecumenical action is about social and community issues, not doctrine and belief. Here the clergy are involved in reflection. Regret for past actions and inactivity are stated. These are signs of an internal reflective process.

Such examples are welcome signs of people moving away from taking the opportunity to avoid responsibility and scapegoat someone else.

It is significant that the working together of the churches is being rekindled by the interest of secular authorities and individual lay people.

Conflict Resolution—Doing Whatever You Can?

What we need is an understanding of peace and reconciliation work which:

Empowers individuals and small groups in their educational work or work on community issues. This is work with people within the traditions and groups who now see the importance of working outside and around those old habits and ways that continually trap us—finding ways forward together.

Supports translators and interpreters—middle level people and groups who understand the needs on the ground and are able to link those issues and themes with the political, institutional and policy needs at the apex. This creates people whom Lederach calls "insider partials" (Lederach,1997).

Engages and enables champions of approaches that can be incorporated within the political, public, private and voluntary sectors.

Reflections

Such work is, in my experience, relatively "happenstance." Institutions and organizations are notoriously resistant to change, especially organizations that consider they have held the conflict at bay and created oases of calm in the midst of the conflict.

Moving out of conflict there needs to be a critical mass of people working on similar issues or sharing similar approaches but promoting these in very different and varied manners.

This body of unexpected people is where the energy flows come from. They are in public, private, political, religious, community and voluntary life. They are members of groups and just individuals responding positively to the invitation of a new and inclusive future.

Conflict Resolution Approaches

So a Conflict Resolution approach needs to be diverse in its reach, focussed on personal, group and organizational opportunities and informed by a political awareness of the ethnic frontier.

It needs to:

- work in good faith, be open to possibilities, which evolve, rather than to take on the need to change the world oneself;

- be modest about the contribution conflict resolvers make

- be open to all those others who are unexpected allies working within that same location gives the best possibilities for movement.

This means that people in each sector need to acknowledge people of good-will in others; this means being open to people working out of faith perspectives, differing political perspectives, community activists, trade unionists.

Conflict resolution should not feed rivalries further. Attempts by peace loving people to build a counter culture against which more people rail and fight often populate the battlefields of peace work and defuse energy.

It is important to commit oneself for the long haul, with or without political solution in view, knowing that these processes are essential for civil society.

Conflict resolution work must build practices and models, which contrast with what, exists and invites people into an agreed society.

Conflict resolution has to be in a state of invitation, essentially open to all because of a belief in the power of relationships in which real and lasting changes can occur.

What are the possibilities and costs of learning anew, of being confident to move with one's feet towards the other, being more understanding and wise about the other?

> New histories will only take root…if they grow out of new relationships which give them meaning. If we explore our histories together with people whose experience is of the opposite side of the deterrence relationships, then new history may eventually flourish. (Wright, 1990, p. 30)

What I wish to do now is explore some examples of work in these different areas.

The Search for Relationships

I will introduce you to:

- some models of interpersonal meeting and dialogue to understand rivalry and conflict;

- examine how these understandings inform models of inclusive organizational change and development;

- ·examine the role of peace building in terms of establishing and supporting "models of contrast."

A Culture of Learning

A contested society gives little space for people to meet anew; many such spaces are colonised by the communal fears or are owned by the competing traditions.

The churches, as many other organizations, have often narrowed the space for meeting together, shaped by the conflict in part. Many institutions have not had the character of a learning organization.

A learning organization is one where the relationships between the different strands within the organization and with others outside are being continually critiqued, examined and transformed within a learning structure and policy framework.

As an educationalist I know that people, in safe and supportive structures, can make life-changing decisions or steps. Such a supportive structure is dependent on the nature of our relationships together.

1. Assisting People in Groups Understand Present Realities

In our work we seek to undergird diverse people who, in their own places and organizations are part of a process of conflict resolution, even though their job titles do not indicate this.

We stand alongside people as diverse as "youths at risk," youth workers, community groups, community mediators, criminal justice system staff, teachers, church people and people of faith, trade unionists, managers, chief executives and local politicians. Often these diverse people meet in mixed tradition groups.

Learning in Relationships

We learn in relationships, whether those relationships are with people close to us or in institutions and organizations.

One educational approach is to assist people examine the relationships they are involved with, starting with their issues and concerns. We offer a number of visual models, a set of lenses that give people space to explore their relationships and make connections to other areas of life. The lenses are ways of understanding basic relationships and some basic models are as follows.

Model-Obstacles

Struggling to achieve what is unachievable is a model-obstacle. Perfection is one such example. Doctrines, dogmas and ideologies are in this category too, especially in an ethnic frontier. Nationalism, Loyalism and Ethnicities, in my situation, also come into this category because they promote ideal types, which can never be achieved in an increasingly mobile and interdependent world.

Some of the time we, and people we belong with, consume our lives in such model-obstacle behaviours. In all these dynamics attaining the impossible is the dominant quest. In that pursuit relationships with the other are increasingly broken and empty. Nothing changes and we become obsessed in trying and depressed in failing.

Learning in relationships of rivalry where all that matters is winning or holding your own can leave a legacy of highs and lows or of continual anxiety and uncertainty. If there are no brakes on the rivalry then the rivals use all their time in the rivalry and whatever point there was in the relationship has disappeared from view. In rivalry all differences are used in the fight, people use their energy in the equilibrium of a power play or in chaos.

In some groups working for peace there has been a climate of scapegoating the middle class participant, calling them irrelevant or the working class member, calling them violent. Such simplifications and rivalries destroy possibilities for new understandings to grow.

In a conflict experiences of peace and structure are essential if some vision of order is to be worked for. When there are differences of condition and mood and experience in a group, and all members are given equal value and regard these very differences of experience can give participants more structure than they had before.

While the mass of fears can be greatest in working class areas, fear threatens everybody and everyone threatens everyone else; people are interdependent.

Model -Model Relationships

Being in a relationship with a person, a group or human reality with which I do not rival and where I learn from the other, remaining distinct and different is to experience being in a model-model relationship. It is the dream of every parent and the wish of every child, especially in late adolescence!

In such a relationship each person learns without fear or threat. This is the basic relationship in which trust and freedom grow, in which change and growth occurs.

Example:
Parent Child or Teacher Pupil
To walk through life when children are young and be a model parent or teacher even for some minutes gives space and freedom to the child.

To face this child growing up physically and emotionally to become an adult sometimes means there is little space and freedom.

There only is freedom when each allows the other their place and identity; when eventually the parent dies as parent and is open to be a new kind of parent, even that most cherished of parental ambitions—that of an adult friend.

To always be in the process of becoming and never to get stuck in this relationship is the gift parents and children can give to each other at adulthood.

Scapegoats
A major reality when people get out of relationships is the experience of chaos and indifferentiation—at such periods the search for order is often secured in the experience of finding the scapegoat.

In our conflict the dead are our scapegoats; the intimidated people and families are others.

They are all people sacrificed out of our inability to find relationships together and political structures that mediate those relationships.

They are victims because our rivalries and fights have been so intense that we failed to see them as people like us.

Example:

Maura spoke on the eve of the twenty-fifth anniversary of her son's murder by paramilitary gunmen. Earlier in the evening, over a meal, she had spoken with present day members of the group that had been associated with her son's death all those years ago for which no one has ever been convicted.

When she spoke, she indicated that she would rather be the mother of someone who had been killed than of someone who had killed. She hoped that the killers had made new choices in life.

In that moment some people associated with that paramilitary group now group, although young at the time, recalled the atmosphere in their street at the death of Maura's son and remembered the cheers that went up. These men, hearing Maura went out of the room, sick with that past memory being recalled when meeting and hearing Maura. Some hours later they expressed their deep sorrow.

Here the scapegoat of their group returned and stood before them.

In an ethnic frontier your scapegoats cannot be got rid of forever, within a frontier area everyone is cheek by jowl. When the scapegoat stands before you can either try to push them away or deal with the feelings that come up and find some new way forward together.

Thank goodness there are victims and survivors and former paramilitaries that are open to that process, wishing no more hatred and killing.

The Application of These Models

We have examined themes and issues that have concerned people on topics as wide apart as Nationalism and Loyalism, Threats and Intimidation, Law and Order, religious beliefs to child-parent conflicts, sexuality and female-male relationships. The space people gain within the exploration of one issue travels with them into other areas.

In a conflict people are readily made objects in the fight. In such an educational approach people take their place, no longer only the objects of the wider communal dynamics but, in some degree, they and we become subjects again.

2. Tackling the Workplace

In the midst of trying to assist cross-cutting groups form in the midst of such a separating and comfortably segregating society the work of Rene Girard on the scapegoat, and of Roel Kaptein on these models of relationships, has been fundamental.

The dynamic of separating and denial are but first steps on the path to scapegoating, that ultimate experience of having no name or identity but that of victim. These rivalrous behaviours are all about uncoupling our relationships, denying our interdependence.

The driving out of one in the midst of so many apparently agreeing others is the often subtle, and deeply hidden, mechanism we all have to confront.

This is the experience and deep knowledge that people from minorities know much about. Many of us from majorities such as male, white, well to do, successful, educated, non-disabled and non-minority ethnic communities know li ttle about this, yet protest much when criticised.

Learning Anew

The scapegoating process is deeply hidden within successful societies. Girard spoke of "human beings must become reconciled without the aid of sacrificial intermediaries or resign themselves to the imminent extinction of humanity...

> ...(The definitive renunciation of violence, without any second thoughts, will become the sine qua non for the survival of humanity itself and for each of us" (Girard, 1987, pp. 136 -137).

Wider European Parallels

The dynamics of ethnic frontiers are increasingly part of wider European realities and perhaps often approximated to within large areas of some of our metropolitan cities everywhere in Europe and North America. In such places the workplace may well become a new boundary of ethnic frontier politics.

The prosperity and stability of regions are deeply linked with their ability to harness the talents and social interchanges, the social capital, between diverse peoples, traditions and skills.

Our current pre-occupation in these islands with regional and national identities whilst issues of asylum seekers and refugees rise up the political priority lists sit uneasily.

Are the stable regions of these islands and the nationalisms associated with them open to real diversity?

Are the metropolitan centres of Britain and Ireland able to embrace the other, whether that is the "old others of these islands" along with the "new others-the new arrivals"?

The Workplace as a Crucible or a Platform for New Relationships?

A second raft of conflict resolution approaches is being developed. We are taking the theme of trust building learned in the voluntary, faith and community sectors into the workplace. The workplace is one of the only places in Northern Ireland, apart from civic buildings, public spaces and Higher Education, where people have to move in mixed environments.

The medium was through one of those unexpected meetings in 1991 when we were invited to test out our approach with trade unionists working on dangerous shop floor incidents of intimidation by Counteract, an anti-intimidation unit of the Trade Union movement.

The culture of that time was that such workplace incidents were understood to be isolated events rather than a product of the ways we had settled to live. In an attempt to challenge that perception we continued to assist one another from then on.

Work on diversity in the workplace is central to the creation of a diverse and inclusive community, socially and economically; it is central to establishing hope for that broader direction.

We have now taken this work on earlier intimidation incidents and developed it into a pilot Equity, Diversity and Interdependence Framework (Eyben, Morrow, Robinson, and Wilson) with public, private and voluntary organizations as a tool of conflict resolution.

The earlier discussion models, the space to visualise and meet together at a deep level and the practice of assisting people have difficult discussions in mixed tradition groups feeds and nurture this process.

Conflict Resolution now gives a deliberate impetus to support the establishment of models of multi-cultural working.

This approach asserts that the workplace in a contested place can be turned to build models of peace and trust.

Work on establishing diversity in the workplace is about:

- constructing procedures and practices for dealing with difference;

- giving working people the opportunity to gain some transcending perspectives together;

The Equity, Diversity, and Interdependence Framework

The Equity, Diversity, Interdependence (EDI) Framework is a quality tool designed to support organizations in Northern Ireland address the challenges of mainstreaming the principles of fairness, diversity and mutuality.

It is an attempt to meet the new learning needs of a society trying to reshape its relationships.

It moves beyond the existing standards of silence and avoidance to recognizing that to be different is to be human and that exploring our differences with one another enhances our productivity as individuals, as organizations and ultimately as a society.

The Framework is based on three inextricably linked principles that we believe form a negotiated process for peace building at a policy and practice level.

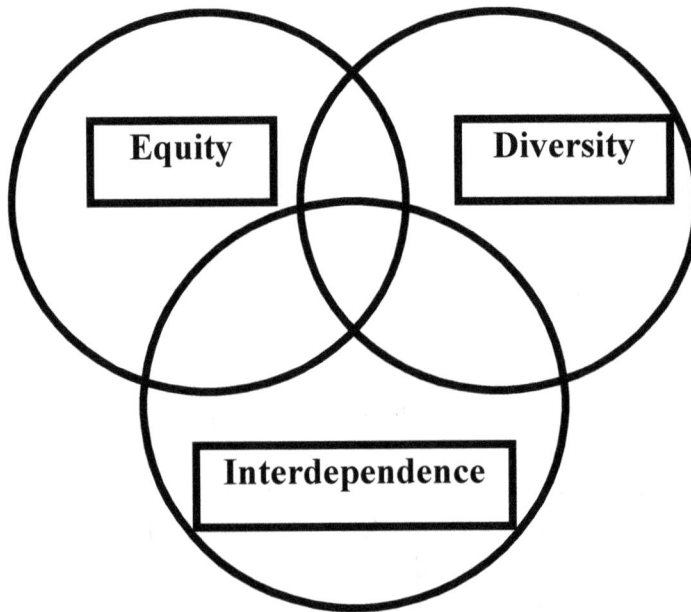

The search for equity or fairness is the underpinning of any democratic society.

At the same time, we are different and a recognition and valuing of our differences as individuals and as members of different ethnic, political or religious groups is the mark of a civil society.

However, equity approaches are likely to fail, and the affirmation of diversity likely to ghettoize, *unless our interdependence with one another is acknowledged*: we are shaped by our relationships and our potential as human beings and as a society is dependent on the breadth and depth of these relationships and networks.

The bedrock of effective learning relationships is trust. In a society where common sense teaches you to trust "only your own" caution rather than entrepreneurialism shapes development opportunities.

Fostering a culture of mutuality and cooperation that crosses sectarian divisions is not only a moral imperative but also a key development objective for the North of Ireland.

Why work on multiculturalism?

People from Black and Minority Ethnic traditions, whose numbers are so small relative to the dominant traditions, have remained relatively private, often keeping to their own cultural communities in Northern Ireland. In the past they have suffered victimization and scapegoating and there is recent evidence of these attacks escalating.

Valuing diversity means that people from all groups and traditions are able to become included and work in a new and common direction. Such work challenges the partisan and neutral cultures spoken of earlier.

The fear of difference is universal. This fear is sharpened, exposed in a place like Northern Ireland, where the costs of ignoring division and separation have been all too apparent.

Conflict resolution now needs to integrate all work associated with fear and "dis-ease" and so we now locate work on sectarianism into all other "dis-eases" people experience.

The experience of being uneasy comes first; then comes the attempt to project those feelings on to some available, usually more vulnerable, person or group.

The same dynamics are at the core of all "dis-ease" about difference.

How do we work?

The leadership task across the business, public and not-for-profit sectors is to have the courage to learn in broader relationships, to be seen to do so, and in so doing challenging the dynamics of fear and exclusion.

We have spent several years working with several public bodies whose workforce was not representative of the wider population. One organization had a predominantly British ethos and one an implicit Irish ethos. The majority tradition in each was of the order of 85% plus.

The Critical Dialogue Process

In both cases we sought to establish a "critical dialogue process" with the organization.

Elements of this approach were:

The organization was asked to put up a small and diverse group of people who would be their project team internally on the theme of equity, diversity and interdependence.

Because of the dominant conflict in our society we asked for people from minority traditions in the organization to make at least one third of the group. Because both organizations had very few women in senior positions we insisted that at least one third were women. Being public bodies we requested that the trade unions were represented.

Outcomes of the Critical Dialogue Approach with Two Public Agencies:

The Internal Work

In each case the organization initially offered a team that did not take account of the diversity theme they were seeking to address.

The "critical dialogue approach" meant that the project did not commence until such a group, jointly agreed by the organization and the external change group, was established.

People from the top or deputy chief position down to the lowest grade of permanent employee were involved, thus modelling new relationships.

The groups began to model a new dynamic around majorities and minorities that was a contrast to the dominant organizational ethos.

People from minorities increasingly took the opportunity to speak up about their experiences.

Senior managers experienced a quality of discussion in this diverse group that contrasted with previously held organizational realities.

In Conclusion

Social capital is an essential strand to a society's wealth (Putnam,1993).

In a divided society, people organise themselves fundamentally along identity lines thus limiting the range of possible relationships and limiting economic and social goals.

Building trust now becomes a pragmatic necessity and public bodies now have to give a priority to being responsive to the needs of the diversity of citizens and customers linked to it.

Here the ground breaking work of people and groups in the voluntary, community and faith sectors, openly exploring their fears and hurts in earlier years has contributed to models of understanding and learning about fears in my society.

Here communal scapegoating dynamics in community life are linked to the need to challenge bullying and intimidation practices in the workplace, assisting those places become places where new relationships between diverse peoples might be modelled.

3. Assisting Contrasts Evolve

Often peace work has been rivalrous in character, moral in tone and condemnatory. Often those accused have felt unable to move forward. For me now conflict resolution has to be more invitational, showing a belief in others and believing that they and we can change.

Peace work has to have more the character of inclusion and invitation. *In a word, it needs to develop the character of "contrast."*

Let me bring you into a weekend meeting of people with different experiences of violence at the Corrymeela Reconciliation Centre, an ecumenical community formed in 1965 and inspired by the work of Iona.

On the panel discussion is the woman I spoke of earlier, with her is a member of a former paramilitary group now committed to peace making, a disabled police officer and the father of a boy killed in one of the most recent bombs by another paramilitary group.

In the conference are also relatives of victims of killing, survivors of serious injury associated with the actions of people from paramilitaries, the security services and police and other civilian actions.

That audience is not a one-night event but a learning community for a weekend, a community carefully prepared in advance and in agreement with the wider agenda of becoming other-wise. Since that event group members have committed themselves to continue learning together and meeting.

I want to convey the quality of the relationships engaged in through such meetings, (what Oughourlion calls interdividual psychology).

It is in that space of relationships that we are all moved and defined; it is in that space we are offered new insights, experiences and understandings that we might choose to act on, choosing new ways to live.

It is in such spaces of differences between peoples; in life's harshness and in its bounty; in its beauty and its pain that we have possibilities to make a difference.

In such relationships unexpected understandings evolve, unexpected sharing occurs and is acknowledged.

Such unexpected outcomes are seeds of new relationships and possibilities of crossing the line of separation.

Such experiences and such fragile groups, as they meet, are contrasts to all around them. They are invitations into a new life beyond the conflict, not forgetting but also not being so dominated by the hurts that future lives are condemned also.

4. What Has This to do with the Ecumenical Task?

Finally I wish to examine what this practice means for those in the voluntary, community and faith sectors and consider whether this forwards any new understanding about the ecumenical spirit and the place of faith in this situation. And acknowledge that the very peripheral nature of reconciliation work, especially in the voluntary, community and faith sectors is its very possibility to act.

I have taken you into the fascination of the ethnic frontier (as long as you do not live in it!) and the ways all institutions and relationships are shaped by that dynamic.

I have introduced you to the patterns of communal deterrence we have lived within and examined how yesterday's violence cannot remain secret but will corrupt today's relationships when it is unacknowledged.

I have introduced you to the ways of avoidance and politeness being preferred rather than meeting and dealing with issues.

Ethnic frontiers are bereft of many solid and meaningful relationships across the lines of difference.

Conflict resolution in an ethnic frontier has to acknowledge the initially peripheral nature of reconciliation work and yet reconciliation is in all our interests.

The steps on the way are solid meetings between people and groups where each begins to recognize the difficulties of the other and respects their mandate and uncertainties.

The ecumenical witness knows that we have something to do on this earth "thy will be done on earth as it is in heaven" does not write off the earthly chance we have to make a difference.

God's will is about the promoting of *justice and right relationships between people and within and between institutions if we are to make the earth a different place.*

It is an understanding that there is no place for an individual faith unless that same faith propels one into taking that theme of finding right relationships into all aspects of life.

This witness is world centred and involves the interpersonal, social, economic, justice and environmental aspects.

It carries within it a deep assertion that we are all interdependent as a contrast to a world obsessed with individual independence.

Working with other institutions and seeking to bring these perspectives into their daily practice is where the business of the faith community must be, not in exhortation or trumpeting, but in the silent commitments of many relationships, words and actions, in creating the spaces where people are respected and valued and where differences are not hidden.

This Jesus we say we follow lived in a form of ethnic frontier. He enjoyed, in my understanding, a model-model relationship not a rivalling relationship with his disciples, even allowing them to doubt or betray him.

Many of those he met came into the atmosphere of new beginnings with him yet were allowed to choose otherwise, still mimetic with the culture and attitudes and fears of those they depended on.

Jesus railed against religious people who put ideology or belief before relationships and meeting, turning them into obstacles. He continually pointed out how people's rivalries were drawing them into losing the wider picture and consuming their lives, drawing on the stories and incidents of brothers and sisters fighting from Cain and Abel, Joseph and his brothers and Martha and Mary.

He also was the ultimate scapegoat, urging people to see how the mob was driving the scapegoat process and able to discern that they had lost their reason. To the end he still wished them to be healed and turned in a new direction, "they know not what they do."

For me many foundation insights in my work come from the Gospels and come to life when applied to everyday relationships and institutions.

Communities of Faith

The challenge for churches and people with a faith perspective in Northern Ireland then is to carry these understandings of the gospel into all the social spaces we are formed within.

While it is fine to define the church as being within the voluntary sector category it is not enough for us to confine our actions and comments to these areas of life.

I am arguing that we turn our attention to challenging practices in the social life and workplaces people move within.

The church, in theory, is one institution where all conditions of people belong together. How much can it be a community of contrast or is it so deeply mimetic with the wider social structures, incapable of remaining as a question mark, a sign and an instrument that diverse peoples can be together?

The increasing separation from those who have different experiences, educationally and socially, means there is less knowledge and experience of difference within us.

When people lose connecting points with those who are different to them, this is a disabling reality. It has implications for our future social cohesion and for attempts to build a more inclusive society.

Scapegoating and the Gospel Texts

The scapegoat theme and unveiling the danger of escalating mimetic rivalry was for Girard and his close friend who worked with us, Roel Kaptein, the central theme being revealed in Jesus' life.

In the moments before the Crucifixion we are confronted with the ways in which people and groups often resolve difficulties, preferring their own to others; being prepared to scapegoat those who are no more responsible than we are.

The Girardian view of the Gospels is of a text continually seeking to unveil and unmask these rivalrous and scapegoating ways of securing ourselves through the denial and victimising of others. To unveil these mechanisms has become a dominant task in our educational work with people and groups.

These insights give new possibilities for ecumenical action. To be centrally engaged in unlocking this knowledge and the manners in which people and groups are trapped in repeating (being mimetic with) rivalries, obstacles and scapegoating rather than being open to new models of meeting and organizational practice is an educational task for churches.

It is salutary that, in my experience, groups seeking to do this work with such vigour come primarily from outside the church community.

There really has to be a new ecumenical journey of people interested in unlocking the power of fear and violence in conflicts. In our work, particularly associated with the ecumenical community of Corrymeela and now the Future Ways Programme, in the University of Ulster, it has informed the practice of several of us, shaped our analyses and given connections between the academic and the practical.

It is liberating to practically connect Gospel insights to those spaces and practices where people and organizations do their work of freeing people for growth and development. It only makes sense when expressed in concrete themes, language and practice. It is rightly rejected when clothed in religious language.

In connection with taking this work into the difficult area of church education and practice we now face a crossroads, an invitation into new relationships with those we are estranged from. This needs those of us within the churches to imbibe and commit ourselves to a relational theology.

What does a Relational Theology Mean?

From a theoretical and practical perspective we know that scapegoating, once revealed, loses its power, and at best work uneasily.

Are we condemned to remain just like the people of Gerasa, secure in our living as long as an identified scapegoat, Mad Mob, remained in the graveyard? Is it so difficult to choose to live with one another in a new manner? Are we so wedded to this mechanism that we know of no other way to live?

Peace like social inclusion is a challenge to the status quo. When the status quo has suited the traditional Unionist superiority of rivalry and winning and so much of what Republicans wish in an "Ireland Free" could turn out to be a model obstacle-an improbable dream; we need relationship building and engagement to take us out of these forms of rivalry.

The reality of life within an ethnic frontier is that we are brought up to see the other as a wolf; every sheep is a wolf in disguise. This means that we are less prepared to meet the other- we are never willing to meet them as they are before us, they are always that wolf.

The tragedy is that we are still unwilling to acknowledge our predicament. As a society we are all too quick to identify with Abel, the victim, and none too ready to say we belong to Cain. (Morrow) And yet we are closer to Cain than

Abel, *more than three thousand people have been killed and many more have been injured* and traumatized –these were not by natural causes but through the actions of people like you and I.

Cain was the modern man, the person wedded to the new tools and the new economy; the man prepared to kill and deny that action in order to get his way. We are too readily wedded to victims than acknowledge the link to the victimizer.

Our predicament is that all, by our silence and inactivity have made it more possible that guns; violence and killing have been used over the years. We all wish to move forward as though we are all "innocents" and yet each of us is guilty of, at least, neglect and avoidance.

Being relational, living out the ecumenical reality means that we:

- belong together;

- maintain a faithful stance that deals with facts not myths,

- are located in the midst of rivalrous pressures without being completely overwhelmed by them;

- seek to be a contrast to those pressures that demand resolute belonging to at least one conflicting tradition;

- live in a manner where the past is acknowledged but a future of new relationships is anticipated and lived out;

- follow a God of the Future, a god of the Exodus in the midst of traditions that honour a god of the past.

In the experiences of the disciples and followers of Jesus I read of men and women who sometimes understood little of what this Jesus was about and yet moved with him.

They were continually frustrated by his openness to others; they were shocked by his challenges to pompous religious outlooks and they were continually invited to see God being with those who were the outcasts; the marginal and peripheral of this world.

I also read in John of those who do "Gods will" being given the doctrine to support their work. These are the tasks of Relational Theology.

One of the ways to follow "Gods will" is to commit to relationships and practices which seek to include those different to us. It is, in some cases, to make real steps forward in bringing practices and safeguards in workplaces and social spaces. Deep down it is to know that each of our places will only be secure when we secure the place of the other first-that too is a Gospel understanding.

The ethnic frontier of Northern Ireland gives an opportunity to seize gospel insights on rivalry, scapegoating and trust building and apply them to educational work, institutional structures and cross-community meetings. It may have been a harsh location but it has released insights.

When our feet get used to walking with and towards others then we will become very wise; wise enough to continually work to ensure that our interdependence, one with another, remains at the forefront of communal life.

We need to step out on that journey, feet first towards one another; we need the wisdom that only comes as people meet together and walk with one another.

References

Eyben, K., Keys, L., Morrow, D., Wilson, D. (2002). "Learning Beyond Fear: New Events Seeking New Habits." In *Reflection, The SoL Journal on Knowledge, Learning and Change*, Vol. 3, No. 4: Cambridge MA: MIT Press.

Eyben, K., Morrow, D., and Wilson D. (2002). *The Equity Diversity and Interdependence Framework-A Framework for Organizational Learning and Change*, Coleraine: University of Ulster.

Eyben, K., Morrow, D., Wilson D. (1997). *A Worthwhile Venture – Practically Investing in Equity, Diversity and Interdependence in Northern Ireland*, Research Report supported by the Central Community Relations Unit and the University of Ulster.

Fay, Morrissey, Smith., *The Cost of the Troubles Study* : final report / INCORE. - (Londonderry) : (INCORE), 1999

Girard, R. (1977, 1979). *Violence and the Sacred* , Baltimore, MD: John Hopkins University Press.

Hamber,B (1998) *Past Imperfect, Dealing with the Past in Northern Ireland and Societies in Transition*, United Nations University.

Kaptein, R. with Morrow, D. J. (1993). *On the Way of Freedom*, Dublin: Columba Press.

Lederach, J.P. (1997). *Building Peace and Sustainable Reconciliation Across Divided Societies* , USIP Press

Morrow, D., and Aughey, A., eds. (1996). *Northern Ireland Politics* , Harlow: Longman.

Morrow, D., and Wilson D. (1996). *Ways out of Conflict- - Resources for Community Relations Work* , Belfast: Corrymeela Press.

Morrow, D. (1991a). "Teaching and Learning with Adults in Northern Ireland" in Poggeler, F., and Yaron, K., eds. *Adult Education in Crisis Situations*, Jerusalem: Magnes Press.

Putnam R. (1993). *Making Democracy Work — Civic Traditions in Modern Italy*, Princeton, NJ: Princeton University Press.

Wright, F. (1992). *Northern Ireland - A Comparative Analysis*, Gill and Macmillan Ltd.

Wright, F. (1996). *Two Lands on One Soil*, Dublin: Gill and Macmillan Ltd. and The Understanding Conflict Trust.

Justice Perfected:
Cinematic Exemplifications

Leonard V. Kaplan and Vincent R. Rinella

Poetic justice as a concept suggests the notion that there is a gap between justice, an inchoate ideal, and legal practice. The notion also promises, perhaps with an ironic twist, that justice, unmodified, is achievable, "naturally." Where poetic justice is operative those who experience the denouement feel a sense of satisfaction , a completion that the human world can provide meaningful resolution to unfairly caused human suffering, and that sometimes when bad things happen to good people the transgression will be punished, if not for the good of the victim, then for the rest of us. Poetic justice, in experience, can redeem theological truths where it acts as a corrective to the transgressive despite human institutional imperfection or outright corruption.

Literary and cinematic representations present scenes of instruction for identifying many of the terms that make for a sense of resolution of justice needs within and external to institutional arrangements. They define the gap between poetic justice, justice without ironic turn, and institutional possibility. This chapter will analyze two movies that provide the sense of justice and therefore psychological closure that can be classified as exemplary of poetic justice. Where justice is so notoriously difficult to define philosophically, artistic commentary and analysis can point toward specification of necessary elements of any such definition. Exemplifying justice has been of classical importance, certainly central to Plato and Aristotle. For Aristotle, the way to understand the good or the just depended upon pointing to individual cases and not essential definitions as exemplary.

This analysis continues in a tradition of calling on art to complement and sometimes exceed the limits of philosophy's current position on human reason, initiated by the Greeks, notably, Plato, Aristotle, and to a lesser extent Aristophanes and seriously willed to us by the philosophers of the German Enlightenment from Kant, Schelling, Hegel, Hölderlin through Nietzsche, Heidegger, and Benjamin.[1] More recently, legal scholarship has, in the name of law and literature, or law and humanities, rediscovered the relevance of art to jurisprudence. Aristotle not only posited the power of tragedy to delimit the boundaries of philosophic or rational conceptualization, but also recognized the relationship of tragic representation to legal rhetoric as tied together for Athens and epistemology. Eden persuasively argues that Aristotle's rhetoric analysis complements his poetics, and that law and tragedy are similarly implicated in the evidentiary process of fictionally adducing truth for audience and jury in like manner.[2] So law and tragedy are connected at the origin of the Western classical tradition. Eden mentions Sidney's continuation of the Aristotlean tradition of arguing in his defense of poetry that poetry and law through fiction capture a truth that eludes philosophy, Plato's attack on the poets notwithstanding. Freud had a similar insight when he made clear that Shakespeare and Dostoevski had more to teach about human psychology than professional psychologists.

One finding from this canon is that postmodern and poststructural analyses, whatever their merit, do not negate canonical understanding and reason. A corollary finding is that the quest for originality often obscures the continued relevance of past analyses. Aristotle's position of tragedy, for example, still instructs and does not diminish the experience of the tragic. Nor does it necessarily help us avoid the ontic experience that tragedy represents. This chapter seeks to allow the artwork to speak for itself with respect to any illumination of the justice question. Postmodern sensibility cannot, of course, maintain the innocence of interpretive transparency. All commentary is suffused with ideological and theoretical presumption. Perhaps that is why the simple power of profound narrative is such a relief. Experience, itself clarifies and moves us where concepts remain abstract and contested.

Intellectual solution does not generally lead to existential repair. Hegel's solution of the question of the political and ethical definition of the modern state still has not and no longer can achieve the actuality he expected from it.[3] More recently, despite the claim that Freud's discovery of the Oedipus complex has been exceeded by changing material conditions, the so-called waning of the Oedipus complex described with clinical and theoretical sophistication by Loewald has not diminished the Oedipal heuristic in a significant set of instances.[4] Simply put, Aristotle and Freud remain relevant for this and other contemporary studies whether explicitly noted or not. Dialectical synthesis remains idealized. Aristotle's views on tragedy still unlock some of the mystery of audience reception of the work. Freud's analysis of the parricide, reduced to bourgeois Vienna still resonates in the mimesis of Jean de Florette of Provence in early twentieth-century life. The merit of the artwork is that it cannot be reduced to Aristotle or Freudian analytics. It exemplifies their insights and continues to evoke a sense of the tragic and an exemplification of the justice that poetry can beautifully represent.

Experiencing justice, even in a limited fictive case goes beyond the gesturing toward justice that the Aristotelean tradition dictates. Students in the contemporary legal academy can go through a major part of the curriculum without the mention of justice as a significant aspect of analysis. Law has long since broken away from justice as a necessary, even a sometimes violent ordering to assure adequate conflict resolution and some commonality about the rules of the road.[5] For legal positivists, law can be wrong, perhaps even evil and still law. Only natural lawyers, generally, but not only in the Thomist tradition, claim that law that is evil is not law at all. Sarat lists some positions on justice in relationship to legal analysis that identifies many of the various positions in today's legal academy. He quotes the postmodernists, Douzinas and Warrington, for example, "Justice has the characteristic of a promissory statement. A promise states now something to be performed in the future....This promise, like all promises, does not have a present time, a time when you can say 'there it is, justice is this or that.'"[6] Clarence Morris, a more traditional jurisprudential theorist claims, as Sarat points out, that "though there can be law without justice , justice is realized only through good law."[7] Sarat's quote from Derrida, which declares justice to be an unattainable aspiration, has an unsurprisingly Biblical ring. Resonant with Moses who gets to see but not enter the Promised Land, Derrida captures the longing and frustration for justice seekers, "[J]ustice would be the experience that we are not able to experience."[8] But *Jean de Florette* and *Manon of the Springs* do not merely promise or intimate the possibility of justice, they together provide the experience of justice satisfied and that is the only justice that there is. In this time of postcritical realism, where the United States Supreme Court in *Bush v. Gore* interceded against the ideological predicates of its five-person majority, where corporate theft is often legal indeed, exemplifications of justice can prove therapeutic and worthy of commentary. In the short run, the population of the United States has forgotten *Bush v. Gore*. Memory ties to justice, whether it be the forgotten killing of a king of Thebes or twentieth-century genocides or the disappearances of citizens of twentieth-century South American states through state criminality or the forgetting of corporate scams. These events are not of the same scale but distorted or repressed memory of ethical or criminal transgression can constitute a pollutant on the communal body that when not uncovered can continue to poison beyond the point where signification can even be registered. *Jean de Florette* and *Manon of the Springs* evoke the issues that engage present-day psychology and politics in a seemingly more innocent venue. The pollution that becomes remembered by the community at a time of hardship is caused by human agency mirroring Oedipus the Usurper. And like Oedipus, community generativity and father against son criminality is tested. But unlike Oedipus, the tragic is both marked, experienced, and transcended in a redemptive or just moment.

The movies that we will analyze are located in a pastoral setting, early twentieth-century peasant Provençe, no less. The setting, more particularly, a village with its surrounding agricultural life, not only frame the narrative but act as a natural character within it. More specifically, the place of water, representing God and nature provide both backdrop and explicit figure for the narrative impulse. The "springs" of the second film's title figure as replenishment, deprivation, and the place where individual and village memory are located. The rate and location of rain complement the springs as the agent of God or chance to individual and communal flourishing, mere survival, or disaster. Communal and personal memory of the location of the "hidden" springs and of the rate and location of rainfall provide the condition for the combined work's refection on individual and communal responsibility.

Without memory, there can be no responsiveness, no transgression, guilt, punishment expiation and responsibility. There can be suffering, but suffering without memory can seem arbitrary and meaningless. Memory provides the possibility of meaning and human agency. Memory is also collective in that beyond individual agency communal obligation can be assessed, repressed, or confirmed. But memory is itself contested, revised, distorted, manipulated, and, ironically, occasionally the basis for a renewed affirmation of human significance.

Jean de Florette, and *Manon of the Springs* form an "epic" binding three generations, tests the Bible's ontological claim that the sins of the fathers' will be visited on the children of the third and fourth generation.[9] Each of the two films presents classic justice issues, a grammar of concepts that inhere in defining justice and responsibility— love, character, intention, betrayal, transgression, suffering, narcissism, paranoia, punishment, vengeance, retribution, isolation, and community.

Each film organizes its justice terms to deal with suffering, death, sacrifice, recognition, resolution, and a degree of redemption. Each narrative escapes kitsch, or melodrama and provides a sense of depth of resolution. Each also presents a narrative structure that calls into question the relationship between form and audience reception that bears on the aesthetic, but more importantly on the ethical and jurisprudential conceptualization of justice.

The chapter will argue that despite the trope of irony that inheres in poetic justice as well as in postmodern consciousness, the elements that satisfy audience need for a just outcome have a recognizable structure that is rooted in the Western canon, the problematic collective distillation of Jerusalem, Athens, and Rome. The analysis will suggest that the canon has always reflected certain knowable aspects of what must be included in important judgments on justice, postmodern skepticism notwithstanding. After the fact we can identify a just resolution; before the fact we can reason that certain elements must be weighed to reach just approximation.

Jean de Florette, a story of betrayal and tragedy concludes in *Manon of the Springs*, a narrative of vengeance, retribution, and transcendence. The story grounds itself in a French peasant community and exemplifies the life, character, and motivations of a village and its surrounding community. It reflects its communal stability, memory, and vulnerability to the world outside its everyday frame of experience. The complete narrative, itself, has been characterized as saga, epic, and "rousing tale of retribution."[10] Like any worthy art, it absorbs consciousness and creates a world that demands emotional response and after the fact, critical judgment. And it provides a satisfaction that heals any rift between the either/ or of the putative division of the ethical and the aesthetic. In short, it connects and suggests beyond the didactic and the conceptual.

Despite the announcement of the death of tragedy (like the death of God) from Nietzsche through George Steiner[11] with the inchoate hope of a contemporary restoration, tragedy, prematurely pronounced dead, still figures in contemporary art. If the tragic represented a literary form reaching a concrete literary reality in the Greek poets, it did so because it exemplified the possibility of a certain deepening of human character in the face of an impossible fate, a certain stance against suffering, a certain meaning that may be called freedom but of a very limited nature, a freedom of dignity despite the impossibility of the triumph of the will and/or wisdom against fate. Without the fact of tragedy as central to the narrative of these films there would be no moment of justice, poetic or otherwise. The conditions of the fictive Thebes might be lacking but Marcel Pagnol, the author of the novels on which the pictures are faithfully based and Claude Berri the films' director make twentieth-century village life in Provençe the site of human betrayal, pathos, suffering, bitterness, despair, dignity, reversal central to Aristotle's notation on tragedy as a requisite for the redemption, the poetic justice intimating the possibility of Christian grace.

Where left and right descried the mass society of what Marcuse called the one dimensional consciousness of a bureaucratic twentieth-century governess, Berri juxtaposes a French peasant mendacity and humanity that still moves late twentieth-century consciousness, that still speaks to the viewer. We further, even after the genocides of the twentieth century, can identify with the suffering of a good, flawed man, pity and credit the suffering as meaningful and perhaps ironically deserved. The loss of tragedy as possibility has been echoed in less severe form by the loss of the Oedipus complex and, for the same reasons, the narcissistic intellectual distaste for the seeming lack of depth of contemporary human consciousness.

Several moments of the tragic are central to the working through of the possibility of justice evidenced in the culmination of the films under analysis. The tragic as theme and form, indeed, mark the possibility of a just outcome given the bad faith and betrayal that propel the narrative action.

The story in the first film centers on a struggle for land between a hunchback and city-dwelling accountant Jean Caderot (Gerard Depardieu) and a greedy, wealthy peasant, Cesar Soubeyran, (Yves Montand) who covets the land for his nephew, a somewhat strange, awkward, and apparently not very bright or ambitious peasant, Ugolin (Daniel Auteuil) who returns from military service with a dream of growing and marketing carnations. Ugolin, at first secretive about his dream of growing carnations, clearly is in love with the flower and fantasizes about fields of carnations—his Eden. Cesar is impressed when Galinette (his affectionate nickname for Ugolin) takes produces a crop that brings in decent money. It's not the flowers but the profit that impresses the canny old man. Papet (the affectionate name Galinette calls Cesar) is, one suspects, proud of his nephew's first and seemingly only ambition. He makes clear that Galinette is his only heir and must carry on the Soubeyran line, a supreme source of pride and obligation for Cesar.

Cesar, crafty and manipulative though he is, cares for his anti-social, disheveled nephew. He does not nag him into a marriage which despite his physical lack would be possible because of his name and probable inheritance. He tries but is rebuffed when Ugolin, makes it clear he has no need or desire for a wife. He can sew his own socks; he lives shabbily and does not need or want a housekeeper, the function he sees for a wife. He takes care of his sexual needs by visiting prostitutes routinely, he informs his uncle. He wants his dream of fields of carnations. And his Papet finds meaning in helping him to actualize his dream. What they must get is a water supply that is secure. Water is a resource comparable to gold for the valley and its inhabitants.

There is land, the land that Jean inherits that Cesar knows has a spring that will fulfill Ugolin's needs. Old Man Camoins owns the land but has let it go to seed. This old peasant is particularly cantankerous and anti-social. He dislikes Cesar and all the Soubeyran clan and provokes Cesar to anger and to battle in which his family name is disparaged. In a scene of almost Shakespearean comedy, he yanks the blasphemer from a branch of the tree he is tending and swings him around. The comedy is interrupted when Camoins falls and hits his head on a rock. Cesar and Ugolin quickly leave the scene without checking on Camoins' well being. In fact, Ugolin has to stop Cesar from going back to finish Camoins off so as to more readily buy the land from the heir.

Neither Cesar nor Ugolin express a modicum of guilt when it turns out the old man has died. Nor at his burial, attended by the whole community, does anyone express any concern or care for the old man who apparently was both disliked and feared. In a slapstick manner that permeates and relieves the cruelty and sorrow of the film, the villagers comply with their understanding of what the old peasant would have desired. They bury his loaded rifle with him and follow behind the casket until someone points out the gun is loaded and has a hair trigger. The procession comically parts into two lines outside the likely line of fire. Camoins will not be missed or mourned. The viewer feels little outrage at what is at least manslaughter. (The very least decency would have dictated the Soubeyrans' enlisting help for Camoins.) The loss of this life is of little concern.

Cesar's plan to purchase the property is frustrated, however, when it turns out that Florette, a former town resident, lives long enough to inherit and in her turn die. The land passes to her hunchback son Jean who by the village's usage is dubbed Jean de Florette rather than Cadoret, his surname, Florette's son. So the hunchback Jean inherits the coveted land from his mother Florette. who was born and raised in the village but left it and never returned though she moved to a nearby village. *Manon of the Springs* will provide an explanation for Florette's abandonment of the village and a more complete understanding of the conditions that motivated the players in *Jean de Florette*.

Jean has abandoned his city job as tax collector, not a sympathetic job in the minds of the villagers who become aware of it as they are aware of much else. He has a dream for himself, wife and daughter, the young Manon, for an idyllic life on this ancestral land. Jean's view of the house and farm are rooted in a childhood Edenic vision. Nor is his view so distorted. The Provençal setting, rugged, rolling, mountainous is beautiful. Its beauty and hardness is integral to the story. In the recent past, the valley *was* an Eden with orchards of apricots, almonds and more that the market no longer supports. The very hard-nosed Cesar, himself has harbored the fantasy of restoring the glory and beauty of his ancestral family orchards that he abandons for Galinette's carnation dream.

Jean, to the dismay of the Soubeyrans, has come to settle the land not to merely vacation or admire his inheritance. Jean, too, has a practical vision, what seems a harebrained scheme to breed and raise rabbits. Though Jean comes from peasant stock, he is a city man, one with no knowledge of farming. He has a marvelous, innocent, and ultimately painful enthusiasm. He sees himself as a modern man and naively believes in the theoretical, more specifically, the applied science and statistics of manuals. He has a scientific manual for all contingencies and a well-developed plan of action. His scheme encompasses the growing of a crop to feed his family and care for the rabbits. He has planned assiduously. Nor is he greedy. He has made allowances and to his mind his expectations are quite reasonable, at least theoretically.

Jean represents modernity against the folkloric peasant wisdom of Cesar, the epitome of the hard-won mixture of experience and superstition. He has never married, has sufficient money and so his energy is spent on actualizing Galinette's dream. His family name and fortune is focused on this nephew, his sole heir. Peasant family pride, patience, and cunning shrewdness are marshaled against an unsuspecting Jean.

Jean has devised a method to allow the rabbits to reproduce in an open field. He has brought with him a set of heavy pipes whose use neither the peasant who helps him haul his furniture and tools, nor the Soubeyrans can fathom. He has devised an ingenious plan; the pipes properly dug, augmented by a properly crafted fence will allow movement by the rabbits and protection from fox and other predators in the open. They will grow healthy and will care for themselves naturally. Science, method, and routine provide Jean's enabling map. All this is relayed to Cesar, who scoffs to Ugolin at the stupidity of the city dweller's singular silliness.

Cesar has as a stamina, patience, thoughtfulness, and assurance that in the older man mirror attributes unleavened in the exuberant younger Jean. With Ugolin, he prepares a strategic opening in a chess game against the innocent Jean to gain the land for Gallinette and the carnations. Carnations against rabbits, the duplicitous battle lines are drawn. He instructs Ugolin whose property adjoins Jean's to befriend Jean both to spy and hasten the failure of his enterprise. He assures Ugolin of Jean's ultimate downfall as his nephew reports each endeavor in gardening and the buying of the first rabbits. He also spies on the family without their knowledge. We watch him mock the ideas and very difficult work that the family puts forth. At times he seems almost sympathetic to what he sees as misguided and futile effort. Papet's coaching involves Ugolin in the everyday life of his neighbors and unsuspecting adversaries.

This inspires a marvelous performance by Daniel Auteuil as Ugolin. This secretive, anti-social, seemingly stupid peasant develops into a character of tragic dimensions. We watch him attach himself to the family, share water from his supply, provide a general helping hand. In short, as a spy he performs what seems to provide the only communal support and friendship that the Florette family receives. Only the young Manon, named after the heroine of Massenet's opera her radiant mother had triumphantly performed, rejects Ugolin. She finds him repugnant. Jean, doting and attentive parent admonishes her for this rejection which he attributes to Ugolin's physical mien. Ugolin learns to care for the family.

With childlike enthusiasm, Jean shows Ugolin four valuable seeds from Australia that his theoretical calculations show will provide an abundance of squash, more than enough for his needs. Everything is thought through. He has enough capital from his inheritance to last three years, ensuring sufficient time for ultimate security. Jean can establish a successful, yet modest niche in the marketplace and a rich and harmonious life for himself and family. He and his wife restore the abandoned farmhouse and he sets about implementing his rabbit-growing scheme before Jean even arrives. (Ugolin had damaged the house, particularly breaking roof tiles before Jean even arrives with the hope of discouraging any beneficiaries.) Jean's meticulous planning seems, at first, naive and flawed in its exclusively theoretical foundation. The community ridicules his theoretical practice and his wasted struggle, but his theory and labor initially yield results. Cesar who has shaken his head at Jean's stupidity in planting his vegetables, is chagrined when the initial crop not only produces but produces sooner and better that his own. The audience can only enjoy this reversal of expectation and delight as Galinette presents a basket of the crop to his uncle, a gift to Ugolin for his support. Cesar's deaf woman servant holds two large potatoes thrusting them with pleasure at the angry and scornful Cesar. But the pleasure of well-earned triumph is short lived.

Jean's scheme does not lack intelligence, hard work, commitment, care. He *has* proved thoughtful, even brilliant, in fact, inspired. Water, however, will be his downfall. He knows that water is a difficult commodity in the valley. He has calculated the average rainfall for each month of the growing season. He knows that there is a well on his land. But a drought hits the valley and he finds that the well that he thinks will save him is distant from his crop. At first Ugolin volunteers water from his supply. Father, wife, and the child Manon carry water and pile their mule with water from Ugolin's up a very steep and rocky path. And we watch the abundant crop die in the heat despite a superhuman effort from Jean. Water is a problem through two years of extraordinary effort. We watch, aware of the painful futility of the family's effort. The peasants, themselves working against the water deficit, show no compassion. They watch him hauling the water up the path and one remarks with no dissent that he feels for the mule. But Jean never gives up, not when Ugolin refuses the rental of his mule which could save the crop with the claim that use of the mule is promised to others according to past practice and not when he breaks down the fencing to allow the rabbits freedom so they can fend for themselves in finding water he cannot provide. He becomes feverishly ill but is saved by a Piedmontese woman with her home remedy. Still he goes on with agonizing obsessiveness.

Jean breaks down and asks his wife to pawn an emerald given to her by an admirer from her opera days. But, resonant with Maupassant's story, she has already pawned the gift which turned out to be fake. Nevertheless, Jean persists. We think that he will finally give up when Cesar makes his move. Cesar instructs Ugolin to offer to buy the property at what seems a fair price which is by Ugolin's own account, half of the land's worth if it had a secure water source. Jean shocks his wife and Manon when he inquires about the price from Ugolin. Surely this is the end. In Ugolin's idiom, Jean is from the city, unsuited for farming and should go back and become a teacher. But no. Jean has a final inspiration. He will mortgage the farm, buy another mule, get some dynamite, dig a cistern to store water, and finally attempt to divine a spring. Of course, the audience knows and the villagers know that the spring is at hand but has been plugged and hidden by the Soubeyrans.

So we watch as Jean breaks his back and taxes his spirit digging deep against hard resistant rock for the hidden spring. Finally his equanimity is exhausted. His anguish and sense of outrage at the fundamental unfairness of human existence echoes Lear and Job. It is bad enough to be a hunchback but why would God further punish him. Still, he does not yield until he is hit on the head by the fallout of his dynamite for the water he seeks. And who has given him his mortgage to pay for the dynamite and for the second mule? Cesar, of course. He reasons, to an admiring Ugolin's, he will either make money on the interest or be able to seize the farm at a bargain rate on default.

We watch in horror and identify, but surely our own hubris would not turn into such disastrous foolishness. The fault is in Jean and in the meanness of the conspirators and the indifferent community. The Soubeyrans watch and the villagers watch the destruction of the son of Florette, one of their own but a tax collector, one who does not buy their bread. The villagers perform as chorus but a chorus with its own complicity. They know there is a spring. It is just not their business.

The penultimate scene in the film presents the passing of title to the land to Cesar at what the banker says is a remarkably fair price. Though he does allow it would be worth twice as much if it had a water source. To the viewer's horror, Cesar and Ugolin do not even wait for Manon and her mother to leave the scene before they uncork the spring. Like helpless voyeurs, we watch the child Manon watch the unveiling of the water's source. And she cries, to Cesar's ears the cry of a rabbit seized by a bird of prey. In an unholy joy, Cesar baptizes Galinette in the name of the father, the son and the Holy Ghost, the king of the carnations.

Jean's struggle, his intelligence, his equanimity, courage, and righteousness evoke Jobean rage and audience pity as his massive efforts are defeated by God and man. Jean's death rings of tragedy. The Soubeyran's perfidy approaches Shakespearean ambition, narcissism, and deceit. Where *Jean de Florette* intimates tragedy resonant of Greek poetry and Shakespearean depth, *Manon of the Springs* resolves into vengeance, retribution, and transcendence, beyond the pagan into the possibility of Christian redemption in this life.

Manon, who stays behind to become a wild goat herder isolated from the village comes to recognize the cause of her beloved father's defeat and demise. Her mother has left, saddened to return to her career in opera to salvage her life. Manon refuses to leave the land and initially stays on with an elderly couple Jean had allowed to settle on his land. The second film narrates the shift from Manon's personal vengeance to a "natural" retribution and finally to communal healing and redemption.

Jean de Florette is a cinematic contribution to tragic representation. Jean's demise is not that of Oedipus, nor Antigone, or that of the Oresteia but tragedy nevertheless. Inexorably, with pride and determination, the righteous Jean has destroyed himself and thus his family's future. Jean played his freedom out against a destiny as fated as that of Oedipus at the crossroads. He gave everything but did not free the valley from pollution. Rather the reverse is true. His death brings a pollution to the village.

Jean's sacrifice is for naught. He represented only his personal dream not a communal concern. But his anguish has more nobility, less mendacity than what has been left to Miller's dying salesman. Jean achieves a certain mythic stature by the sheer madness of his unrelenting effort. We experience the identification

with the fallen hero, the fear and pity that Aristotle identifies as hallmark to tragedy—poetry's response to philosophic (conceptual) limit. But we feel no cathar-
sis only the seeming inevitability of horror and injustice to a good man. The
intensity of audience rage against the injustice, the felt need for retribution set the
stage and provide the requisite predicate for justice, a response that will restore
harmony after the outrage we have participated in, even as viewers. The intensity of outrage becomes an identifiable element in what the film teaches as a
factor in the weighing of, in this case, the poetry of justice. Our outrage is further
enhanced because we do take illicit pleasure in Cesar's plotting. He, after all, is
merely an analogue to our own sharp business practices and no more grasping
that the instrumental greed of contemporary, corrupt chief operation officers of
Enron inter alia. Marcel Pagnol, the author of the novels that Claude Berri brings
remarkably to life, does not end with the tragic.

The Judeo- and particularly the Christian moment cement the satisfaction of
redemption and therefore justice played out in the revenge story that *Jean de
Florette* demands. *Manon of the Springs* produces just satisfaction and thereby
fulfills a satisfaction that can be identified as justice actualized. The truth of justice is not in the concept but in the lived experience of the two works. Experience, the lived internalization and felt necessity of what could be but was not
contingent is spelled out in these artworks. Naming the concepts, identification,
fear or pity is hollow if not specified by the experience of the work itself. We can
know the Aristotelean terms. We can know we fear for Jean and we can know
we pity him. We can even know that pity contains at the psychoanalytic level a
certain smug contempt. But with all this knowledge the experience remains un-
diluted. The post-Freudian psychological man with due reflection can abstract
the self out of lived response but at the cost of experience itself and perhaps at the
cost of recognizing the failure of justice which the art of *Jean de Florette* makes
palpable.

Manon of the Springs brings the relief and satisfaction we identify as exemplary of poetic justice. With *Manon*, we can be more specific and add to specu-
lative thought about a poetry of justice, already started in the Bible, and Greek
tragedy, notably Aeschylus' *Oresteia*. Pagnol, the novelist and Berri, the director
give us a work that includes tragedy in various forms, that of Jean and that of
Cesar and with variation that of Ugolin. But it also alters the terms of possibility,
leaving a deep melancholy but also reconciliation and redemption. In other words,
the work honors tragedy but frames it in a narrative of Christian resolution. And
even in this postmodern world, the films work.

In fact, we claim that the two films act as necessary reminder that tragedy may
be fundamental to human experience but that hope exists beyond the respective
tragedies of three of the significant characters. The experience of Jean and Manon
still can remind us of hope, possibility, the simplicity of individual tragedy, revenge and satisfaction. Brechtean narrative did not redeem. Not with all its bril-

liance did people take to the streets. We know now that we consume art more than we allow art to capture and seize us toward any transcendence or redemption, words in a theological grammar Nietzsche taught us we must outgrow. We should move toward the assumption of human responsibility. But Jean de Florette and Manon have not been transcended. In their simple, but brutal Provençal setting they speak of a vision that still can instruct, with narrative form made no less powerful despite postmodern vitriol with which with which we can too easily identify. Tragedy and theology can still animate jurisprudence. Amos and Aristotle must make a comeback beyond the academic.

The two films, from an Aristotelean perspective, must be viewed from the action of the drama which then will unveil the hero's battle with the fated, irreconcilable conditions of his world choices and his free choice and failure in the face of the impossible. Aristotle, unlike Plato prizes poetry, teaches that tragedy will engage our identification, fear, and pity for the good man who fails through fate and flaw. This is the very response that the villagers experience as Cesar and Ugolin swindle and destroy Jean. We can take pleasure and as Freud emphasized relief from anxiety in the face of the suffering and even the death of another. But where Agamemnon, Oedipus, Antigone, or even Creon were good people and as Jean certainly is, can we attribute sufficient goodness to Cesar or Ugolin to render them tragic?

Whereas Jean's failed struggle is tragic, plot development deepens our sympathy for without altering our disgust at the Soubeyrans' successful conspiracy. In fact, the elevation of each to a level of worthy identification heightens tensions that resolve into the resolution of poetic justice. Though each film stands alone as complete, the two together exemplify an instance of the poetry of justice actualized. The question at the finish of the combined work addresses the extent to which we can extract elements that can illuminate more general conditions for specifying poetic justice. The action takes place some ten years after the first film. Manon is one of many topics of village conversation, particularly those who do not farm but service the farmers. We learn that the hunchback's daughter is a goat herder, living in the hills with the Piedmontese widow, and has grown to be a radiant beauty. She has made her father's fantasized Eden her home. She looks like a gorgeous wild thing. But she reads and remembers what her father has taught.

We also quickly see that Ugolin's carnations have flourished. He is making money. But he is still living in squalor. He could be living in the farmhouse that he took over from Jean. (He had spontaneously, perhaps from guilt, and to Cesar's dismay offered the house to Jean's widow and Manon rent free forever. The offer was rejected with disdain.) Neither he nor Cesar experience any guilt with respect to Jean and the past. In short, with the exception of bountiful field of carnations that he lovingly tends, Ugolin is the same, so is Cesar who remains a figure of dignity and affluence if not trust in the village.

One day, Ugolin spots Manon in an idyllic setting. She is bathing naked in a naturally formed bath like a nymph, playing and dancing to a tune she learned from her father. He and we are entranced. He is stricken, pining for something beyond his carnations. He follows Manon and puts wild birds and rabbits he has captured into her snares and then watches forlornly, jealously, as Manon gives the rabbit to a new village teacher, Bernard, who had given her his knife.

Papet immediately discerns the Galinette is lovesick and checks out Manon's worth as the potential bearer of the Soubeyran line. He warns Ugolin that though beautiful, she will cheat on him when he is older. But by that time there should be many more Soubeyran children and he gives his approval. So armed and dressed in the fashion of a wealthy farmer and ludicrously out of character, Ugolin confronts a Manon who is repelled by him. He signifies his love, passion, devotion, and she is more repelled. His love unrequited, remains undiminished. He is perplexed about how to act. He is alive with jealousy about the way she looks at Bernard the teacher who seems to him indifferent to her. We who know what he has done to her father and family and know that she knows, nevertheless feel a sympathy for this lovesick Ugolin. In a particularly grotesque scene, we watch Ugolin find a piece of ribbon Manon has lost, and in physical pain sews the remnant onto his nipple.

Manon overhears two villagers who are out hunting and notice a bird in one of her snares. One says to the other that the catch from a person's snares is sacred. But beyond that these belong to the hunchback's daughter and the village has already caused her sufficient grief. Manon now knows that the villagers had knowledge of the crime against her father and family. She gets the opportunity for revenge when she follows a kid who has fallen down a crevice and strayed into an underground cave. She finds the kid drinking water in an underground pool. She blocks the pool a bit and runs to the village to check the water flow into its fountain at the receiving end of the village's water. Assured she has discovered the source of the valley's water supply she repeats the action of the Soubeyran's and effectively plugs the water flow. The villagers and farmers are in an uproar. Farmers are losing their squash, tomatoes, etc. We see the individual attachments to dying crops that matches Ugolin's hysterical despair about losing his beloved carnations. Though the threat is communal, we see the individual fear and rage at personal loss. The thematic clash identified between Cesar's peasant wisdom and Jean's commitment to science is revisited and broadened to include a tension between scientific modernity and old-time religion.

The mayor of the village, who says he is a mayor because he is the only villager with a telephone contacts the French authorities about the water disaster. This is the only contact with a state apparatus in the two films. The state water expert provides his various theories to the impatient gathering. His theories are complex and mystifying. The villagers press him to concede that no immediate help is on the way and that maybe the water will not return for a hundred years and that perhaps the farmers should leave the valley for better farming conditions. Cesar pronounces the theories bullshit which adequately expresses the villagers ire. The village insults the expert who , in turn, is enraged and comes close to being run out of town. He does promise that the state will truck sufficient water in everyday for basic existence needs, but this promise will hardly deal with crop needs. The village is in despair. Unsurprisingly, almost everyone but those called by the priest the "intellectuals" show up for Sunday mass. Cesar and Ugolin are there as well. So is Manon.

The priest has only been in the village a year but his sermon calls forth the story of Oedipus and the pollution that comes from individual crime. Christ will forgive the truly repentant he intones and more to that effect. The sermon is understood. Cesar and Ugolin are the criminals and therefore enemies of the people. Ugolin says to Cesar that the priest was talking to them. Perhaps he learned of the affair of Jean de Florette from someone's confession. Cesar wryly remarks that some confess to sins of their neighbors. We reach a climax.

Manon is importuned to lead a religious procession to bring water back to the valley. After all it was she who was transgressed and God will intervene because of her innocence. This sets Manon to accuse the village and particularly Cesar and Ugolin of their treachery. Cesar resists and fights back demanding a witness. Ugolin confesses and cries not only for forgiveness but pathetically for her hand in marriage. He will give her everything. He adores her. The peasant who had observed Cesar and Ugolin through his trespass vantage point responds that he can confirm Manon's accusation. Ugolin flees, with Cesar walking away with aggrieved dignity admitting nothing.

Two events alter the standoff. Bernard privately affirms his suspicion that Manon knows the cause of the water stoppage. He asks her what her father would do. He wanted to be friends with them. Her love for Bernard persuades Manon to show him where she has blocked the water. The two together free the flow. Cesar has called for some village leaders to come to Ugolin's where they find him hanging from a tree, a suicide. Cesar gets them to agree not to tell the priest or anyone the cause of death so Ugolin can be properly buried in the casket that Cesar has had made for himself in consecrated land. We watch Cesar, alone, cut Manon's ribbon from Galinette's nipple. The old man is still not defeated. He is still thinking. Ugolin leaves a will we hear Papet read where he gives his property to Manon and absolves Papet of any guilt. His end he writes was fated.

Manon does play her assigned part in the religious procession to the village well. The town's intellectuals mock the procession but when someone siphons the well the water does start to flow the villagers, Manon and Bernard excepted, fall to their knees.

The scene shifts. A bus arrives in town. Manon's mother and a companion get off along with a few other people. One of whom we later learn is Delphine,

Florette's confidant from her pre-marriage days and a lifelong friend. They arrive for Manon's wedding to Bernard. As the wedding party leaves the church and pictures are being taken, we see the old Cesar walking past them to Galinette's grave where he religiously places carnations. As Cesar trudges from the Church's cemetery, his footstep is recognized by the blind Delphine who is sitting by herself on a bench.

Tragedy unfolds in this penultimate scene. Delphine admonishes Cesar for his failure to respond to Florette when she needed him. When she sees that Cesar is in the dark about her reference, she tells him the truth, and we understand more about Cesar and the story's entirety. Cesar and Florette had been lovers immediately before he had to go off to war in North Africa. She became pregnant and wrote to him indicating that she would wait for him if he sent a letter that she could show to the village saying he would marry her. The letter never arrived. She tried to spontaneously abort, jumping from heights but to no avail. So Florette in shame left the village, met a blacksmith who, knowing about the pregnancy, nevertheless married her. Her child, Cesar's child was born a hunchback. Yves Montand, master actor that he was, allows the story and its tragic implications to sink into his being. Everything he wanted would have been his if only Florette's letter had arrived.

Cesar prepares himself to die. He is too ashamed to any longer face Manon or the villagers. Life now has no meaning. But he is warned against suicide. He says that will not be necessary. He will just lie down and die. Meanwhile at what seems an evening Christmas mass, the pregnant Manon has whispered to Bernard that she must leave to give birth.

Cesar has the last word, dead we hear his voice reading his will directed to Manon. He tells her the entire story, his anger at Florette and at her son, the fact of his discovery of his parentage, and that she is his granddaughter, that in heaven, Jean will not blame him but recognize him and that she should pray for Ugolin and himself.

We are left with both Ugolin and Cesar elevated by "fate" and character beyond their peasant greed. Ugolin, through love of Manon has attained a depth already signified as a possibility by his passion for the beauty of the flowers. He renounces his rage at Bernard because he would do nothing to further harm Manon. He blames no one for his love or despair. He kills himself not from guilt but from love sickness. Ugolin's suffering and suicide both assuage us and his despair at Manon's rejection and his self-inflicted punishment allows our sympathy. Cesar's end takes us to an even more tragic place. Cesar but for an undelivered letter could had the only true love of his life and the son to continue his line and a radiant granddaughter who looked just like her grandmother. Instead , Papet dies with a rosary in his hand and Florette's comb which he has secretly cherished with two fragmentary letters through his adult bachelor life. His son does not continue his name but is "de Florette" the son of his mother. Tragedy is not mere disastrous suffering by a good person through unavoidable flaw. Oedipus learns something about his genealogy and about the limits of human rationality. The movement of tragedy beyond pathos, fear, pity is the move from ignorance to a certain recognition. He had the love of his life, he had his son, he had the continuation of his line, in short he had everything he desired and he had no knowledge of any of it.

The poetic justice that these films depict is a justice that seems ontological, occurring without the intervention of a state and its apparatus of judgment. We have no policemen, no courts, no judgment but that yielded by the denouement of the narrative movement itself. Irony is certainly an element of the outcome. But the trope of irony in the reversals for Cesar and Ugolin is exceeded by the redemptive movement from vengeance to love that Manon experiences with Bernard. The villagers acknowledge their complicity, another factor that allows her a chance to forgive. Their need and acceptance of her fulfills her father's dream, a dream that she has made her own by staying on in the valley that caused her father's demise. The narrative movement is conditioned on the resonance with the Greek poetic, a pollution effected by transgression, a reversal of Oedipus where father unknowingly kills son. But justice which tragedy denies in the name of human freedom is ameliorated by recognition of transgression punishment, acceptance occasioned by love with material reward for the remaining victim, Manon who now has the entire inheritance. But is not this Christian tale of natural grace a fairy tale for we postmodernists? As the mayor says, is not the water flow a coincidence? We know it is not and the message is that it is not, but a fact of human agency. But that does not make it less a miracle. Human agency, the two films indicate, can, even given what Martha Nussbaum called "the fragility of goodness," be simultaneous with grace, God, and poetic justice , not from afar but from the playing out and contingency of the everyday. The water flow is not an either/or but an integration of aesthetic and ethical; the films are proof texts of the possibility, tragedy notwithstanding, of resolution, continuity, and harmony. The scales of an hypothesized weighing of justice cannot redeem the dead Jean, nor fulfill an Ugolin whose own father had committed suicide, nor give Manon's mother back her husband. If justice must establish a status quo ante, justice can never be even approached as possibility.

Jean de Florette and *Manon* together present certain conditions for what we are calling the poetry of justice. Can we extrapolate those conditions to future cases? This is a tricky project, one that calls forth a hundred years of jurisprudence in the United States.[12] Certainly few of us think that we can extract the essence of a complex and contradictory set of cases for the few rules that will guide a judgment in the next appropriate case—the Langdellian formal project. Nor do many of us think that the courts generally provide honest, cogent reasons, uninflected by ideological and power concerns the way the legal process people suggested. And yet the fact that many of us can look at art like that offered here and recognize a justice outcome provides a hope that is perhaps more significant than skeptical despair.

Notes

1. For a worthy recent contribution to the very extensive literature accounting for the relationship between philosophy and art, see Dennis J. Schmidt, *On Germans and Other Greeks, Tragedy and Ethical Life*, Bloomington: Indiana University Press, 2001.

2. Kathy Eden, *Poetic and Legal Fiction in the Aristotelian Tradition*, Princeton, NJ: Princeton University Press,1986.

3. See for Hegel=s project and thought on this subject, Shlomo Avineri, *Hegel=s Theory of the Modern State*, Cambridge: Cambridge University Press,1972.

4. See Hans W. Loewald, The Waning of the Oedipus Complex. In Loewald, *Papers on Psychoanalysis*, New Haven, CT: Yale University Press,1980. But concluding his essay, Loewald cautions that "We are reminded that the oedipal attachments, struggles, and conflicts must also be understood as new versions of the basic unionBindividuation dilemma.@ at 404.

5. For a recent and worthy continuation of the work of Robert Cover on the violence of the state and its law itself see Austin Sarat ed, Law, Violence, and the Possibility of Justice, Princeton: Princeton University Press, 2001. Legal analysis sometimes feels hermetically sealed. Cover=s notable essays, including Violence and the Word, Yale Law Journal95(1986) is indeed seminal for current legal academics. But Marx long before already more thoroughly indicted the liberal capitalist state as the committee for the bourgeoisie and the law as mere mystification of political and economic reality. Arguably, Covers cut is beyond Marxist polemic and goes to a claim that is rather Freudian, that law at its best remains violent beyond its normative right where the normative is defined in the terms of the system itself. For example, we are currently in the situation of yielding privacy in the name of national security for the purpose of preserving that very freedom of privacy, et al.

6. Sarat at7.

7. Ibid.

8. Id. at 8.

9. The Biblical proscription may be ethical as well but it remains ontological, fairness notwithstanding, the extent to which in the unfolding of reality the sins of prior generations do affect and determine the life (fate) of the children that follow. Can anyone deny that contemporary German life still is acted out with the experience of the Holocaust in its horizon?

10. These genre terms are on the back of the dvd package of *Manon of the Springs*.

11. George Steiner, *The Death of Tragedy*, New Haven, CT: Yale University Press,1980.

12. See for a quality version of this history, Neil Duxbury, *Patterns of American Jurisprudence*, New York: Oxford University Press,1997.

Contributors

Gabriel Ricci is associate professor of philosophy at Elizabethtown College.

Heribert Adam is professor emeritus and holder of the Simon Chair for the Graduate Liberal Studies Program at Simon Fraser University.

Jeffrey K. Olick is associate professor of sociology at Columbia University.

James Hatley is associate professor of philosophy at Salisbury University.

James E. Young is professor and chair in the Department of Judaic and Near Eastern Studies at the University of Massachusetts.

Tim Giago (Nanwica Kciji) is editor and publisher of *The Lakota Nation Journal* based in Rapid City, South Dakota.

Jordan B. Peterson is professor of psychology at the University of Toronto.

Maja Djikic is a Ph. D. candidate at the University of Toronto.

Derek Wilson is senior lecturer in the School of Policy Studies at the University of Ulster.

Leonard V. Kaplan is Mortimer L. Jackson Professor of Law at the University of Wisconsin.

Vincent R. Rinella is a lawyer in private practice in Philadelphia.

For Product Safety Concerns and Information please contact our EU
representative GPSR@taylorandfrancis.com
Taylor & Francis Verlag GmbH, Kaufingerstraße 24, 80331 München, Germany

* 9 7 8 0 7 6 5 8 0 9 9 9 5 *